£ 5.95

The revolution that never was

An assessment of Keynesian economics

Will Hutton

Longman

Longman Group Limited
Longman House, Burnt Mill, Harlow
Essex CM20 2JE, England
Associated companies throughout the world

Published in the United States of America
by Longman Inc., New York

First published 1986

British Library Cataloguing in Publication Data
Hutton, Will
   The revolution that never was: an assessment
   of Keynesian economics.
   1. Keynes, John Maynard   2. Keynesian economics
   I. Title
   330.15′6   HB99.7
ISBN 0-582-29603-X

Library of Congress Cataloging in Publication Data
Hutton, Will, 1950–
   The revolution that never was.

   Bibliography: p.
   Includes index.
   1. Keynesian economics.   II. Title.
HB99.7.H89   1986   330.15′6   85-16647
ISBN 0-582-29603-X

Set in 10/11pt Linotron 202 Plantin
Produced by Longman Group (FE) Limited
Printed in Hong Kong

Contents

Introduction and preface

Keynesian economics is on the defensive. Its public reputation is low: it has come to be synonymous with large budget deficits, unsuccessful attempts to contain inflation with income policies, and failing economic growth. Among economists its reputation is rather higher, but no longer are the basic precepts argued with any conviction. Here, too, there is the same sense that the theory, and the economic management it spawned, have been tried, and found wanting. The intellectual initiative has passed to those prepared to argue the merits and robustness of a more ancient tradition in economics; that of economic liberalism, and the capacity of the free-market model of the economy to resolve many, if not all, contemporary economic problems. Scepticism about the potential of the market and the limits of the price mechanism has ceded pride of place to an ardent belief in their power. In today's world, it seems, public action is 'out'; private action is 'in'.

The extent of the ascendancy of this new mood is revealed not only in the tenor of economic debate and the direction of policy, but also in the lack of effective opposition. Across the gamut of economic issues, 'classical' economic prognoses are advanced, with the old Keynesian retorts either mute or unconvincing. For example, unemployment is explained in terms of excessive real wages; inflation as an oversupply of money; low growth as the consequence of dynamising market forces being stifled. Even as recently as ten years ago Keynesians would have replied with references to aggregate demand, involuntary unemployment, and business expectations: today their argument seems tired and unpersuasive.

As in theory, so in policy. Exchange rates and interest rates have been left to find their 'market level'; attempts at their management are undertaken reluctantly, as an unwarranted obstruction of market processes, and therefore contrary to the new orthodoxy. In general the Government's responsibility is to limit its role and its claims: in the financial markets where it must borrow and intervene less, and in the product and factor markets where it must regulate and own less. The injunction is clear: because a market system has been shown to be the 'best' system, economic problems are only problems in so far as they are departures from a free-market model. The Government's task is to move the economy back to such a model.

Yet while the reorientation of policy, and the ideas behind it, are evident, there is a growing sense of unease. Rejuvenation of the economy remains as elusive as ever, and although there have been some benefits, the overall results are disappointing. Moreover the theory, confronted by today's economic realities, increasingly seems to fly in the face of common sense. The volatility of exchange rates and interest rates, for example, seems to belie the assertion that markets must always be 'right'. Similarly, pouring savings abroad at the same time as there is underinvestment at home, seems to suggest that either the price mechanism is perverse or that the long-term correction needed to change the relationship may be *too long term* for the current generation of unemployed. Again, public-sector investment projects are constrained because public debt is supposed to be inflationary, whereas private debt is not. Practical responses and public action are forbidden by a philosophy which seems to stand the world on its head.

For some, of course, this is only evidence that the policies have not been carried out with enough vigour and that substantial obstacles still stand in the way of the free and flexible operation of markets, without which satisfactory results cannot be expected. The 'vision' of the economy remains sound. The non-partisans, however, are becoming more and more dubious. They are suspicious of planning and economic blueprints, as these frequently involve an extension of centralised power and a loss of individual freedom, but they are also concerned about trends in the economy. If it *is* true that Keynesian economics no longer has anything to offer, and if the claims and policies of the free-market theorists *are* at the very least contestable, then what next?

This book was begun as an attempt to find some kind of answer to this conundrum, and it was with some surprise that the author discovered that the direction in which his own enquiries were leading largely paralleled those of J. M. Keynes – even if they were a great deal less exact and considerably more clumsy. But this was not the Keynesian theory described in the textbooks and used in popular debate, the reflex Keynesianism whose familiar nostrums have now correctly passed from fashion. Rather it was a theory that sought to revolutionise the terms in which economics was discussed and markets understood. Fifty years since its inception, the Keynesian critique presents just as much a challenge to established economic thinking since, in the act of translation and interpretation, the old economic orthodoxies have gradually reasserted themselves. In fact the integration of Keynesian economics back into the mainstream of economics has meant that the 'Keynesian revolution' has lost almost all its meaning. We are left with the slogans and empty theoretical categories; but the insights that filled them have been lost in the process of integration. The Keynesian economics that we are told has nothing to offer us today has little to do with the economics of Keynes.

The principal theme, then, of this book is that much of contemporary economic analysis, cast as it still is in the classical tradition of generalising the properties of single markets to that of *the market economy as a system*, is fundamentally flawed. There is considerable difficulty in moving from the classical construct of an exchange economy based around barter to one using money; and there is no less difficulty in moving from an economy where an initial stock of goods is assumed to be endowed, to one where goods are produced. In particular, there are the problems of expectations and time; problems that are introduced into the market economy by the existence of money and production. It is from this starting point, we shall argue, that Keynes constructed his theory, leading in turn to predictions concerning the limits to the power of the price mechanism, the quantity-adjusting tendencies of the market, the centrality of the financial markets and the portfolio preferences of financial institutions, and the inability of the market to co-ordinate the plans of savers and investors at a full employment equilibrium. These are the insights at the heart of the Keynesian critique: but without their comprehension Keynesianism is a 'Chesire Cat' theory, grinning at our problems without any prospect of helping in their resolution.

Writing this book, then, has been something of a personal rediscovery of a 'lost' theory. Although there has been a temptation to rewrite a number of passages as the manuscript has been revised, they have been left largely as they were first written, containing as they do all the surprise and freshness at communicating a view of economics that at the time was wholly new and unexpected. I hope the reader will agree with this judgement.

Chapter 1 sets out the main contours of the book, and tries to show the congruence between the key axioms of mainstream economics and classical liberalism. As Keynes's underlying philosophy is closer to the European 'social contract' tradition than that of English individualism, it is scarcely surprising that he should present such a challenge to economics and the British economic establishment. Chapters 2 and 3 are an account of the problems that bedevil both classical economics and its contemporary exposition by having to insist that individual exchange can only arrive at an equilibrium. Chapter 4 examines the theoretical difficulties in providing a theory of price and quantity determination that delivers a notional equilibrium in a market economy where goods are produced over time. Chapters 5 and 6 set out the main elements in Keynesian thought – how time, money, and expectations upset any market process towards an equilibrium – while Chapter 7 focuses on the financial markets and institutions and the key part ascribed to them in the Keynesian story. Chapter 8 sketches some outlines of policy, in particular the leverage that must be exerted over financial institutions, and the role of fiscal policy in both compensating for quantity adjustments and managing expectations; and discusses the structure of British Government in the Keynesian context of its obligation to play a more active role in economic management.

The book has a number of objectives. It is chiefly a critique of orthodox economics and an attempt to retrieve and restate Keynesian economics; but it may also be of interest to those engaged in formulating an intellectual basis for if not consensus, at least some continuum of views around which economics can recoalesce. I hope it will be useful not only to economics students but to all those concerned at the current stalemate in economic discussion.

In a project of this type an author has any number of individuals to whom he owes thanks. I owe a particular debt of gratitude to the two Longman readers who in their different ways allowed me greatly to improve on the final manuscript – also to Jonathan Storey, Nic Morris, Paul Ormerod, David Llewellyn, Tim Congdon, Meghnad Desai, and Roger Bootle, who all offered helpful and useful comment on earlier drafts. Erna Stuart-Bullock typed the first manuscript from beginning to end; Victoria Blunden and Clare Walker worked on later drafts and Anne Mills completed it. Sally Conover proof-read the manuscript and assembled her first index with remarkable skill. David Frost's cottage, and David Frost played no less a role. My thanks to them all. In addition, throughout the entire time of writing I am working for BBC Radio and Television Current Affairs Programmes and I must thank all my editors for their support: Vincent Duggleby, Alasdair Osborne,

Richard Tait, David Lloyd, and lastly to David Dickinson – who saw to it that the book was completed. Also thanks to the Wilson Center in Washington where this edition was finally despatched to the printers and a US edition begun.

But my final and most heartfelt thanks are to my wife, Jane. Without her understanding, tolerance, and sympathy I doubt the book would ever have been finished. It is, however, now done: and I remind the reader of the usual caution with more than customary fervour. Any mistakes that follow are mine, and mine alone.

November 1985

To Jane and Sarah

Acknowledgements

We are grateful to the following for permission to reproduce copyright material:

The Right Honourable Lord Kahn and Harcourt Brace Jovanovich Inc for extracts from *The General Theory of Employment, Interest and Money* by J M Keynes; John Wiley & Sons Inc for extracts from pp 213, 215–219 *Quarterly Journal of Economics* February 1937.

Chapter 1

The liberal tradition and the lost revolution

Summary

Three mutually reinforcing principles underpinned the philosophy of political economy; liberty, natural law and balance. These same principles are incorporated in contemporary economics, and the first section of this chapter, 'The liberal heritage', is an exposition of the outlines of classical political economy and an account of its origins. It will help illustrate both the congruency of ideas and the very particular philosophy they represent; namely, the capacity of individual interest to produce the public good. The second section 'Liberalism and economic theory', identifies five core concepts shared by the liberal tradition and by classical economics: rational economic man, exchange, equilibrium, diminishing returns, and competition. The renaissance of interest in the classical economic tradition, described in the third section, has seen a much bolder approach in the use of these concepts, not only to sharpen the conclusions of economic theory but also to redirect economic policy. There are, however, significant weaknesses in this body of theory and they are highlighted by a fresh appraisal of the Keynesian critique of the classical tradition, discussed in the fourth section. There are three key areas of dispute: the difficulty of using barter exchange as a model to describe a money exchange economy; the role of money, expectations, and the rate of interest; and the determination of prices. Taken together, the Keynesian argument is that the motion of the market economy is *not* towards the equilibrium that economics supposes, nor that the 'best' outcome inevitably results from free exchange between 'optimising economic agents'. A more promising perspective in which to analyse the market economy is to accept that it is quantity-adjusting (rather than adjusting to price) and is in a permanent process of uncertain experimentation; and that the key to its performance is the portfolio preferences of the financial system. In the fifth section the implications for policy are discussed. If the market does not spontaneously produce the right results then intervention by the state is imperative; in particular using the financial system as a major lever of economic management. However, this will require a different tradition in which to locate the state's responsibilities, perhaps even – given the weaknesses of the British government process – reformed state institutions.

The liberal heritage

In the 75 years between the publication in 1776 of Adam Smith's *Wealth of Nations* and the celebration of that wealth at the Great Exhibition, there developed in Britain a very particular system of ideas about economic and political organization that has come to be known as the 'liberal tradition'. Although it had grown out of Britain's unique history in the seventeenth and eighteenth centuries and had reached maturity during the special circumstances of the Industrial Revolution, its authors claimed for it the status of a universal truth. The objective was nothing less than to reveal the invisible and immutable laws that governed the harmonious organisation of human society, and in so doing to assert that the liberty of the individual was the absolute prerequisite for a just and prosperous political and economic order. The 'Science of Political Economy', the intellectual edifice fashioned by Smith, Ricardo, Mill, Bentham, *et al.*, was the demonstration that in liberty lay the key to individual and societal well-being.

The doctrine satisfied the needs of mid-Victorian England perfectly; for not only did it identify the laws that underlay an effectively functioning economy, it also suggested that those laws had reached their apogee in the England of 1850. The perspective was Newtonian, as befitted an age insistent that there existed laws governing human conduct paralleling the laws governing the behaviour of the physical world. In the same way that the laws of the universe produced the harmony of the Spheres, so the laws that governed human society would produce a harmonious society, as long as their operation was not obstructed. It was by respecting these laws that human societies were able to raise themselves up the ladder of progress, so that the higher a country had progressed, the more its institutions must comply with these hidden laws.

Balance, in this scheme of things, was seen as the stable state to which all natural forces tended: harmony in society, as harmony in Nature, required that elemental forces be balanced. The organising order in the physical world, gravity, rose from the mutual interaction of opposing forces: so order in the human world was provided by natural laws dependent on the interaction of opposing forces for their operation. The dynamic element in human society was clearly the action of the individual; so by according him his liberty the forces that would produce balance were set free. The task of economic and political institutions was to provide the forum in which individual actions, given their liberty, would be balanced.

In the political realm the object was to build a 'Balanced Constitution' which organised political activity into institutions that 'checked' and 'balanced' each other, so that one institution of government did not abuse another. The British parliamentary system, arising from the seventeenth-century compromise between King and Parliament, executive and legislature, seemed to meet this criterion admirably. The House of Commons, the legislature, consisted of a chamber of gentlemen elected by other gentlemen who freely deliberated on the laws that would or would not represent the public interest; while the Executive, in the person of the Queen and her ministers, could only survive as a government and enact legislation if it could muster a majority among these same gentlemen for the measures they proposed. If not, the Queen must appoint new ministers. A judiciary, appointed by the Queen, was independent of both Houses of Parliament, and interpreted the law free from political control: the rule of law thus stood as the guarantor of liberty. The Government was constrained to govern fairly and well, so that not only was the country protected from arbitrary and despotic rule, but the framework of law so established permitted the free pursuit of manufacture, trade, and commerce – and as political economy showed, this freedom was a vital prerequisite for their flourishing. The Constitution which conferred such benefits was clearly much to be commended, but then so were the principles by which the economy was organised.

Here again the object was to permit the expression of those forces whose interaction could be expected to produce a harmonious whole. Men spontaneously wish their self-betterment, and will deploy every means at their disposal in the attempt to achieve their aim. It is these elemental forces in the human world that represent the mainspring of economic activity, and their unification in a beneficent whole requires that each individual be permitted his economic liberty, that is, the freedom to sell his services and his goods to the highest bidder, and the freedom in turn to buy from the cheapest seller. If the two forces – those who buy and those who sell – freely meet, then the portfolio of goods that each individual trader has after exchange can only be exactly what each trader wants: otherwise he would have

3

continued trading until he reached that happy position. The single-minded pursuit of self-interest must bring a market economy to a point of balance: not only this, but it will assure prosperity.

This latter benefit is produced via the capacity of an exchange economy to encourage more and more specialisation. The famous Adam Smith dictum that 'it is not from the benevolence of the butcher, the brewer or the baker that we expect our dinner, but from their own regard to their own interest' (Skinner 1970; BK 1: 119) not only aimed to underline the importance of self-interest, but to dramatise the impact of specialisation: in this world every man was a merchant bringing the wares in whose production he specialised to market, be he 'butcher, brewer or baker'. Through buying at the cheapest price and selling at the dearest, the market would certainly arrive at a point of balance; but it also permitted each man to specialise, for he could exchange those goods he did not need for those he did – and specialisation lifted the productive power of the economy.

Specialisation, however, implied the organisation of production; and organising production requires capital. The great advantage of free exchange, argued Smith, was that by permitting each 'merchant' to make the highest profit he could, capital could be accumulated at the fastest rate: and as capital accumulated so there was more specialisation. Not only was the economy likely to achieve balance, it tended to progress and enrich itself, the only possible obstacle being obstruction to prices and profits as they worked their beneficent magic.

Economic and political organisation were thus linked. The State, according to this theory, had a responsibility *not* to intervene in the market process: in fact it must uphold and protect the market in its every facet. The free movement of prices and the free making of profits; private property and the rule of law; the unimpeded process of capital accumulation and specialisation; the ability to buy and sell goods in whatever market the price was highest or lowest: all these rights the State must strictly enforce however savage their consequences apparently might be. For although mid-Victorian England had its warts, the system's protagonists argued that no comparable society on earth had ever managed to harness Nature on such a scale. Its network of railways, its factories, and its trade were the envy of the world, and together with the economic and political freedoms enjoyed under the Constitution, seemed part of an indivisible process of advance and progression. Obeying the liberal injunctions was clearly the explanation of Britain's greatness. As the great apostle of free trade, Richard Cobden wrote (Weiner 1981: 28):

Not a bale of merchandise leaves our shores, but it bears the seeds of intelligence and fruitful thought to the members of some less enlightened community; not a merchant visits our seats of manufacturing industry, but he returns to his own country the missionary of freedom, peace and good government – while our steam boats, that now visit every port of Europe, and our miraculous railroads, that are the talk of all nations, are the advertisements and vouchers for the value of our enlightened institutions.

In this world liberalism was not merely a policy or a system of ideas: it had attained the status of a faith, a faith that had the advantage of being grounded in the scientific reality of a potential natural order in human affairs.

Adam Smith – the founding father of the liberal tradition in economics – provides no better example of the way the idea of a 'natural order' and the role of liberty intruded into the very essence of this nascent theory of the world. His *Wealth of Nations* was conceived as the second book in a series of three; the preceding volume, the *Theory of Moral Sentiments* (1759), was an exposition of the spontaneous, natural growth of civilisation, and the third and last, which Smith never lived to write, was to 'provide an account of the general laws of government'. The theme that united all three books was that there existed *natural laws* underlying the progress and governance of society, and that these laws were capable of being unveiled through observation and rational reflection. Moreover, these natural laws revolved around the degree to which human societies enjoyed liberty, for it was liberty that above all else permitted man to achieve harmony with himself and society.

It is difficult to grasp, some two hundred years later, the extraordinary grip the concept of liberty and its juxtaposition with natural order had upon the late eighteenth-century mind. It is said that in 1768 there was not a single door or shutter on any house along the roads between London and Winchester and London and Oxford that did not have 'No. 45' daubed on it,[1] '45' being the edition of the *North Briton*, the paper founded and edited by John Wilkes, which prompted George III to have Wilkes arrested for treason under a General Warrant. London's streets echoed to the cry 'Wilkes and liberty'. 'Weavers' wrote Walpole, 'took possession of Piccadilly . . . and would suffer nobody to pass without blue cockades' and distributed papers inscribed 'No 45, Wilkes & Liberty' (Kronenberger 1974: 94). The year that *Wealth of Nations* was published Richard Price's book *On Civil Liberty* sold 60,000 copies (Plumb 1979). Liberty had become a battle-cry; a summons to arms against a king attempting to reassert control over the Houses of Parliament and their hard-won right to be the locus of the nation's political authority; and a rallying point for the London merchants and Northern manufacturers who were finding the system of tariffs and imposts on foreign trade increasingly irksome. It united the mob, the merchant and manufacturing classes, and the Opposition into a formidable force; and one before which George III finally gave up his pretensions. The idea of liberty was in the air, and nothing could be more fitting than for Smith to argue that liberty in exchange provoked a natural order in the economy.

The task Smith set himself was not merely an intellectual exercise; it was a political and moral statement. In arguing that the invisible hand of the market is the secret of the 'wealth of nations' only as long as men are at *liberty* to buy at the cheapest and sell at the dearest price, Smith was providing further ammunition for the 'cause'. The public interest did not arrive from the actions of kings or self-interested legislatures, but as the unintended consequence of free and individual actions. Like the rest of his generation, Smith was infected by the enthusiasm for unfettered liberty.

The origins of classical economics thus lie in the spirited political and philosophical arguments of the 1760s and 1770s. In itself this proves absolutely nothing: many of the best ideas have a long pedigree, and the association of an idea with a particular time, place, or intellectual movement is no reason to devalue it. On the other hand, economics likes to regard itself as built on a series of *a priori* intuitive truths; and it is as well to recall that these 'truths' originated in the passionate conviction of eighteenth-century Englishmen that the most prized attribute of any society is the liberty it affords it members. They were not concerned to incorporate notions of equity, fraternity, the nature of the social contract or any of the other philosophical ideas of their age into their theory of the world. Their intention was to show how every aspect of the public interest followed in the train of the pursuit of liberty.

The founding fathers of classical liberalism were unashamedly ideological (Semmel 1970); and like all ideologies the importance of the theory is not so much the exactitude of its prognoses but the political work it has to do. Interpreting the processes at work in the economy and polity along classic liberal lines, therefore, holds great dangers because the suggestion that economic and political phenomena must always be explained as the outcome of individual interests and decisions can, under closer scrutiny, translate into a series of tautologous statements.

What is balance? It is the order that individuals will bring about if given the liberty to express their interests. Why is society not harmonious? Because the spontaneous action of individuals is frustrated by obstacles. How can order be regained? By removing the obstacles to the creation of balance and harmony. We are locked in a circular argument of assertion in which any obstruction to the expression of personal or individual interest is the cause of the system's difficulties, so lack of harmony in the real world proves nothing about the ultimate validity of the liberal order, only that it is obstructed in its working.

By locating the individual and liberty as the focus of the system, the classical theorist is forced into denying that the whole is more than the sum of its parts, and must insist that the public good is the sum of balanced private interests. It is profoundly unsatisfactory, however well it served the political and philosophical ambitions of its authors two hundred years ago; but this is the underlying philosophy of contemporary economics.

Liberalism and economic theory

How is the market to be understood? Economics within the classical tradition, as is already clear, makes a number of claims. An economy based on free exchange produces an economic order spontaneously. Moreover, the order so created must be the best for society as a whole because each individual has been allowed to come to his best judgement of how to meet his needs. And any interference with this process by an outside agency is likely to be counterproductive.

Herein lies the importance of the liberal tradition and the central roles played in it of the idea of liberty, of a natural order, of the drive to self-betterment and profit, of individual and free exchange as spontaneous economic combustion, and of the State as the guarantor and protector of the whole system. This tradition provides the question; and it provides the answer. The free market is the mechanism which allows these preconditions for a natural economic order to flourish – it is therefore the state of affairs most to be desired.

Now, economists like to think of their subject as the social science that has made the most substantive progress towards rigorously comprehending and interpreting its chosen area of enquiry. The textbooks and journals abound with algebraic and geometric expositions of economic phenomena; a scientific approach that the other social sciences can nowhere match. Yet the framework in which much of this analysis takes place is that of liberal/classical economics. It is not stretching a point to argue that the discourse of economics, its fundamental language and world-view, is that of the liberal tradition. There is equilibrium in the economy; it is achieved through the interaction of supply and demand; the price mechanism sends messages to producers and consumers about what to produce and what to buy, messages that they obey because they wish to maximise their advantage; and progress in the economy arises from constant experimentation and innovation under the spur of competition. These tenets run so deep that they are simply taken as read.

Part of the reason for this of course, is the intuitive logic of each proposition – confirmed by our own behaviour. We do respond to price signals in the way economic theory suggests, and in general we want more income and more profit if it can possibly be attained. Change does happen, and typically firms are anxious to install new machines and introduce new techniques because they will lower costs, improve profits, and so steal a march on their competitors. Equally, we can observe what happens in markets in general when prices rise or fall; if their is a shortage of oil, for example, the price rises and the quantity demanded falls – just as economic theory suggests.

Another contributory reason is the compelling liberal proof of the market's efficiency in achieving the optimum outcome in terms of the participants' welfare. The starting point is to define an optimal condition as one in which any individual can only make himself better off by making somebody else worse off; a Pareto optimum. The beauty of a system of voluntary exchange when it is at equilibrium is that it describes such an outcome.

For any individual economic agent to improve on his position must imply another agent willingly doing business with him. But 'equilibrium' is defined as a situation of 'rest', in which voluntary exchange has ceased. It therefore follows that 'equilibrium' in a system of voluntary exchange will only be reached when all economic agents, given their preferences and constraints, believe that their position can no longer be improved upon through exchange. In other words, 'equilibrium' is itself the Pareto optimum.

The apparent intuitive nature of the assumptions, the elegance with which an optimal outcome can be proved, and the ease with

8

which the characteristics of the market square with liberal values – liberty, freedom, the objection to centralised power – combine to make the envelopment of economic theory by liberal/classical economics near total. Not only this, we can actually observe prices leading to behaviour changes in markets along the lines that the theory suggests; and the fact that our economic institutions, created as they were in a liberal era, are embued with the same liberal values completes the cocoon. Values, theory, scientific objectivity, and experience mesh into a suffocating web; the truths of economics are liberal truths.

That identity of view between the discourse of economics, the liberal tradition, and classical economics is underlined by a closer examination of the basic postulates of the conventional theory. There are at least five congruent ideas.

1. The idea of rational economic man. Already the idea that man desires his self-betterment and that this impulse is a prime mover of the exchange economy has been observed as a central theme in classical economics. It is for this reason that voluntary exchange will lead to the most desirable outcome as traders jockey for advantage by exchanging goods they want least for goods they want more; if they did not wish to better their initial position there would be no motivation for trade. If we are to build a theory, however, we need a more rigorous construct than simply the desire for material self-improvement, and such a vehicle is provided by the concept of 'rational economic man'.

This creature's desire for self-betterment has been translated into the requirement that whatever end he (or she) has in sight, he will want to choose the optimal means of achieving that end. Rational economic man is an optimising agent who, as long as he can rank preferences systematically, can be relied upon to respond to stimuli in the manner predicted by market theorists.

There are two important claims that can be made for this definition. The first is that by Robbins (see Ch. 3), which is that it does away with the notion that economists insist that man is just a profit-maximising beast and nothing else. Man can have any end at all; all that economists require is that he chooses the optimal means of achieving it. The second is by Hayek (1948: Ch. 1), which is that the point of devolving decision-taking to individuals in a market-place is that they are the best judge of their circumstances, interests, and preferences. Economists in the market tradition do not want the objects of their enquiry to be profit-maximising; they want

9

them to be sensible enough to make decisions in their own best interests.

However, while it is apparent that rational economic man is a much more sophisticated construct than the man who inhabits the world of the *Wealth of Nations*, the stimuli to which he is required to respond are remarkably similar. Robbins wants them to be 'relative valuations', whereas Hayek openly advocates the market as the place where economic man will take his devolved decisions. Rational economic man is required to be rational in a market; and that will mean attempting to maximise his gain. It is only if he does so that the system has the potential to arrive at equilibrium.

2. *The idea of voluntary exchange*. The capacity to exchange an initial endowment of goods for a portfolio of goods that better reflects an individual's preferences is perhaps the most important attribute of an economic system if it is to conform to liberal precepts. It was exchange that Adam Smith saw as the key to the *Wealth of Nations*; it is exchange that permits a Pareto optimum to be achieved. Price and quantity determination in competitive markets results from traders exchanging goods and services; exchange is the trial-and-error process by which they attempt to improve their position, and it is exchange that allows the market to find a point of balance between their varying intentions and actions.

3. *The idea of equilibrium*. Although equilibrium in economic theory is presented as a strictly neutral concept, it is in fact redolent of liberal values. General equilibrium is Adam Smith's 'natural order' in contemporary guise. For Smith there could be no other result than a spontaneous natural order if the invisible hand of the market was allowed to work properly through complete freedom of exchange. In the same way, a general equilibrium will ineluctably emerge from the process of interlocking market relationships. There is even the same sense that the market as a system is incontestably the best means of organising an economy, and that this arises 'naturally', for there can be no equilibrium without the process that brought it about; in other words, an equilibrium presupposes a world of individuals freely exchanging goods and having a common interest in finding a point of balance (Sen 1983). Indeed, the fact of equilibrium validates the market; equilibrium can only arise from the circumstances of individuals exchanging goods and services. If it were created by any other mechanisms, it could not be an equilibrium because exchange is the only process by which a point of balance is achieved. Equilibrium can only happen in a world of

interacting and opposing forces. But if this is true, so is the converse: that if there are opposing forces voluntarily exchanging goods and services, then equilibrium must arise. The natural state, therefore, of a market economy is an equilibrium: prices and quantities are either in equilibrium, or in the process of finding another equilibrium. By this token, economic theory is able to protect itself from attack; disequilibrium is a departure from the norm, is to be expected, and in no way invalidates the central claim of economic theory, that free markets are the key to economic efficiency and progress.

4. The idea of diminishing returns. It is intuitively obvious that the more we have of any given commodity, so marginal additions to our total stock will yield less and less return. Equally, the more that is provided of any given commodity, all things being equal, the progressively more costly each marginal increment will become. Diminishing returns need not detain us at this point (see Ch. 4) but it is important to note that the existence of diminishing returns guarantees that the exchange economy will arrive at an equilibrium by ensuring that the plans of demand and supply will converge. Those who acquire a commodity require successively lower prices to persuade them to add to their stock: those who furnish the same commodity require increasingly higher prices to compensate them for the successive increases in cost. The interaction of the two elements is therefore certain to achieve a point of balance.

5. The idea of competition. Interaction between traders trying to improve their position is not just a means for the system to arrive at an equilibrium; it also dynamises the economy. Competition plays two functions. In the first place, it is the mechanism by which the economy finds its natural balance. Adam Smith looked to competition between traders to drive prices to their 'natural level'; in other words, there existed a natural profit that if exceeded would encourage capital to be attracted to that particular branch of manufacture. Contemporary theory uses competition in the same way: the perfectly competitive market is one with 'normal' profits, nobody can influence the price, and consumers' requirements are being perfectly satisfied by perfectly efficient producers. For such a condition to exist, there must be no barrier to the attraction of new firms into the industry so that profits can be bid competitively down to their normal level. Competition is the precondition of the 'best' prices and profits, that is, those that produce an economically efficient system, and markets should be judged by the degree to which they come near to this goal.

In the second place, competition causes capital to be accumulated at the fastest rate, and for Smith it was capital, through its ability to foster specialisation, that was the key to the wealth-creation process. So competition is now visualised as imparting a dynamic to the economy by acting as a spur to innovation and experimentation: if prices are given, then the profit-maximising firm must make sure its costs are as low as possible.

Competition for profits is thus pivotal, for it is this that makes the price mechanism work and persuades firms to be as technically and economically efficient as possible; and for Adam Smith, profit enriches not just the firm, but the system as a whole.

These key ideas define the scope of economic enquiry and allow it to project the benefits from an economy run along free-market lines: the most satisfactory matching of consumers' preferences with the ability of the economy to meet those preferences that could be conceived; the most efficient organisation of the resources of the economy into the chosen branches of production and distribution; and the tendency of the economy to find a point of equilibrium between expenditure and output while at the same time progressing and expanding at the pace and in exactly the directions that the members of the economy desire.

The renaissance of the classical tradition

Let us now jump from the world of theory to the world of practical problems. The economic performance of the UK is disappointing. There appears to be a chronic tendency to inflation and low growth. Inflation has persistently run at levels higher than that in comparable industrialised countries, and growth, on the same basis, has been persistently lower. Although it is true there has recently been a sharp reduction in inflation, it has been won at a heavy cost: high unemployment and an unprecedented loss of output, even larger than that of the 1930s. The prospect appears to be of a prolonged period in which economic activity is never likely to provide employment for anything like the full working population. What has economic theory to offer by way of explanation and possible solutions?

Presented with a problem of this type we should not be surprised, given the discourse of economic debate, that the conclusion of economics is that the UK's malaise arises because it does not correspond as closely as it could and should to the model of the free-market economy. The heart of the predicament is that the price mechanism is obstructed in too many areas of the economy for the market to function properly, if at all.

There has, for example, been a very substantial growth of a public sector whose output is not priced or marketed: the balance between this 'non-market sector' and the 'market sector' has become thoroughly lop-sided (Bacon and Eltis 1978) so that a growing proportion of national income is not subject to the constraints and dynamic of free exchange and the proportion that is, suffers a growing burden of financing the public sector. Then, again, of that part of national output that is marketed, a substantial element is in the hands of nationalised industries that enjoy a state-guaranteed monopoly and are effectively apart from the market process; a further nail in the coffin of the exchange economy.

In the labour market powerful trade unions obstruct the movement of wages to changes in market conditions: as a result real wages are too high, workers 'price themselves out of work' and unemployment results (Brittan 1981). And last but not least, the money markets are thrown into near-permanent disequilibrium by the financing of government deficits; money is printed rather than borrowed and the continual leakage of liquidity into the economy engenders inflation – too much government-printed paper chasing too few goods (Friedman 1977).

The diagnosis is familiar, as are the policies that flow from it: reducing the public sector, privatising nationalised industry, curbing the legal privileges of trade unions, containing the public-sector deficit and so ensuring that monetary growth is limited, and with it the potential for inflation. However, the economics profession is not united in either this analysis or in advocacy of this particular set of policies; protests have been mounted and alternatives offered – but there has been no real conviction in the response.

The reason is not hard to find. Economic theory's penetration by neo-classical economics is so total that the agenda for any discussion about the economy is already set. If the presumption is that a free-market economy will produce equilibrium and progress via the process of exchange, then the problem is pre-cast: it is *departure* from the liberal model that causes economic difficulties. The issue is not how a market economy functions, but what are the obstacles British institutions and practice put in the way of the operation of the economy as a market. Objections are pitched not at the basic validity of the agenda for discussion being cast in this way, but at the degree to which the real economy actually exhibits the characteristics necessary for it to function as a market economy could. For example, it is objected that prices tend to be relatively inflexible, not only in the labour market but in all the markets of the economy: in these circumstances pursuing a policy predicated on the assumption of price flexibility (or at least more flexibility than there actually is) is likely to be ineffective and costly.

This is a perfectly tenable intellectual position; but how should the economist respond if asked what his objection is to policy aimed at *making* prices more flexible? If his objection is simply empirical, but he accepts the basic logic of the classical position (as he may well since, as we have argued, it defines the discourse of economics) then he must, however reluctantly, concede the case. A policy designed to make the economy conform more to the constructs of economic theory can hardly be objected to: there can be arguments over the human cost, over implementation; but given the shared assumptions – on rationality, the ability of exchange to find equilibrium outcomes, the importance of competition, etc. – no central or serious critique can be mounted.

The truth of this is no more strongly felt than by today's more prominent advocates of the classical tradition. They feel themselves to be at the forefront of a renaissance in economic thought, spearheading a return to first principles. The economic crisis, not only in Britain, but in all Western societies, presents an unequalled opportunity to reaffirm economic and political truths, to reassert the liberal tradition and by doing so to find a way out of the crisis. What is required is not just a return to the principles that underlie the market, but for them to be extolled and extended. The exchange model can be used not only to explain how markets behave, but almost every facet of human behaviour (Lepage 1982). The same analytic devices – the individual desire for self-betterment, the ability through interaction and exchange to produce the result that individuals want, and so on – can be used to explain . . . even death.

. . . each individual inherits health capital at birth that depreciates over the years, at a rate that accelerates beginning in middle age. The individual can retard or accelerate this depreciation by conserving or depleting his own health capital. Death occurs when health capital falls below a certain physiological threshold. Since we choose the size of our investments to retard this depreciation, in effect we choose when to die, balancing our desire for immediate pleasures (which deprive us of resources to invest in health capital) with our desire for long life. (Grossman: 1972)

Impatient of the mainstream of economic theory's reluctance to pursue the logic of its position through to its conclusion, the classical 'counter-revolutionaries' are steadily transforming the economic debate. They are aided and abetted by the inability of mainstream economics to offer any solutions. Indeed, the willingness of mainstream economics to countenance forms of government management of the economy – the last nod in the direction of the Keynesian revolution – is seen as part of the problem.

The attraction of the ideas is widespread and has gathered momentum. In international forums such as the IMF and OECD, within an increasing number of Western finance ministries and on the world's financial markets, the doctrines (which were never far from the surface) are being reaffirmed with increased vigour. The marriage between interests and values that liberalism neatly underwrote in the nineteenth century with its simple but elegant view of the world, is in the process of being repeated – a process perhaps embraced with more fervour in Britain than anywhere else.

The rise in unemployment is excused as a failure of the labour market to produce real wage changes commensurate with changes in labour's real product; inflation is seen as a government failure to control an oversupply of money. The low growth in the economy is explained in terms of an overlarge public sector not being subject to the same dynamising elements as the private sector with its exposure to the market. Interest rates and exchange rates are allowed to find their 'market level'. Savings flow abroad, notwithstanding the desperate need for their use as investment at home, excused by the new orthodoxy as the inevitable flow of capital to wherever returns are highest. The philosophy is clear: because a market system has been shown to be the 'best' system, economic problems are only problems in so far as they are departures from a free-market model. For the time being, though, the results are at the very least contestable; in a 'liberalised' environment large parts of the economy still languish. Are we sure that the new economics, let alone the old economics, is right?

The Keynesian reassessment

The theme of this book is that, framed as it is in the classical tradition, much of today's debate in economics about the forces at work in *the market as a system* is miscast. The basic constructs are flawed; there is a very substantial difficulty in theory in moving from an exchange economy based on barter to one using money, and an equal difficulty in moving from an economy where goods are assumed to be 'endowed' to where they are produced. In particular, there is the problem of expectations and time. As a result, economics has not captured the essential motion of a market economy.

But, although this book challenges the classical interpretation of the exchange economy as a general system, it is none the less written from a perspective sympathetic to 'free enterprise'. It is common ground that the market economy affords possibilities of decentralised decision-making that alternative systems do not: the market economy affords its decentralised decision-makers the right to assess their interest in the light of circumstances in which they find themselves – circumstances and interests that no centralised system could hope to anticipate. It is also common ground that the price mechanism is an effective means of sending signals about the scarcity or abundance of commodities, and that self-interest and the profit motive will provoke economic actions that prove to have a rationality for the system as a whole, for example using scarce resources efficiently, experimenting with new production techniques, and so on. Indeed, the market economy has a value beyond any claims for economic efficiency: in its decentralisation of economic power and decision-making it is an important bulwark of political liberties.

The truth in these propositions should not inhibit us, however, from examining sceptically the central claim of economics that the motion of a system of free exchange is towards a point of balance that will be the 'best' outcome for the participants. As a result, the most appropriate policy is to let market forces 'go free'. The State is absolved from any action, indeed the State must stand back from the economic process because public good is being created by private interest. The public interest does not require to be asserted; it will be produced from within the economy.

The charge against this economic orthodoxy is that it has not surmounted the problem of time and money; indeed, that its attempts to incorporate these into the basic model are unsuccessful. This, we shall argue, is the essence of the Keynesian revolution – an essence that has been lost by the reinterpretation of Keynesianism into the mainstream of economic thinking. The object of the Keynes's *General Theory of Employment, Interest and Money* (1936) was to overturn the discourse of economics and to insist that the motion of the market system was *not* as the classical tradition claimed, a 'paradigm' shift. Fifty years later the Keynesian 'vision' has been lost, and once again the economics of the classicists organises our view of the market. So what is the essence of Keynesian economics? For this we have to turn to the fundamentals of economic thought. The outline that follows gives some idea of the principal themes in the chapters ahead.

Barter and money exchange

In a world where commodities are freely bartered, individuals are able to exchange goods they do not want for these they do want. They will exchange goods until they can no longer improve their position; the main problem is seen as being that of the 'double coincidence of wants' necessary to make barter work. Each individual must find another who both wants his goods and has the goods he wants. The importance of money from this perspective is that it makes the market more efficient: goods can be sold for money, and the money then spent on the goods the individual wants. The motion of the market is allegedly the same whether under barter or money regimes (Lucas, 1972).

Money, however, transparently does mark a departure from the world of barter. By exchanging goods for money and money for goods, the exchange model has to cope with time. Whereas before, each transaction was simultaneous – goods were either exchanged, or not – now there is an interval while the trader makes his purchase or sale. This interval introduces the problem of expectations.

The idea is easier to understand if we imagine each transactor in a market-place as having a balance sheet. Under a barter system the balance sheet is always squared; each acquisition of a good is exactly matched by a disposal. Under an exchange system using money this is no longer the case. A disposal of a good will mean an inflow of money; an acquisition an outflow. These receipts and expenditures will not, however, occur simultaneously. In other words, in an exchange economy using money, the individual economic agent is continually obliged to take a view on the future. If he is spending money he has to decide whether his future receipts will be sufficient to finance his current expenditure; and conversely if he is receiving money he has to decide whether his current receipts are going to be sufficient to finance his future expenditures.

The price mechanism by definition can only deal with the quantities that individuals are trading in the present, but those quantities are clearly going to be very substantially influenced by individuals' expectations of the future course of prices. A trader will bring forward or defer a disposal or an acquisition according to the view he takes of future prices – but the market-place has no means of knowing what the reasons are for any good being bought or sold. It simply deals with the goods that *are* traded for whatever reason.

17

In the classical interpretation a fall in the price of a commodity can be relied upon to increase the quantity demanded because prices are pre-assumed to contain all the information a rational economic agent needs to know. Everything, including uncertainly held expectations, is 'in the price' (the doctrine of 'rational expectations'). But in this latter interpretation no such result can be guaranteed. A fall in the price of a commodity may not encourage a transactor to buy more if he also anticipates that his future money receipts will fall: he may simply maintain his purchases at the existing level, or even reduce them. The key is his expectation as to his own future money receipts: an uncertainty which today, prices are *structurally* – incapable of relieving. They cannot foretell the future, thereby forcing an economic agent into a guess. Whereas in the classicist's exchange economy prices act to co-ordinate the volumes or quantities traded, in a money exchange economy prices have to deal not only with today's quantities but the quantities we anticipate trading in the future. Hopelessly overloaded, adjustment in the economy to expectations in the future takes place not through current prices but through current quantities. In other words, markets may not clear at the prices and quantities that are economically efficient, but at the prices and quantities that reflect tomorrow's fears.

This Keynesian perspective must await a fuller treatment in later pages (Chs 5 and 6) but already it suggests that the industrialised economy is quantity-adjusting rather than price-adjusting, and that price signals are limited in their capacity to drive the market economy consistently to an equilibrium in which planned intentions equal realised activity. But there is a more important conclusion still, which lies in the role of money.

Money and the rate of interest

In the classical conception money is strictly neutral, not affecting the underlying behaviour of the real economy which still conforms to the rules of barter (Barro R, 1977, 1980). Money is a commodity that has the special characteristic of being universally acceptable, but it is a commodity none the less and obeys the same rules. It is this perception, for example, that permits 'monetarism' to make the link between money and inflation. As money is just another good, if the supply of it increases while the supply of other goods is held constant, then the price of money must be devalued, that is, there is inflation. But money is anything but neutral; money embodies time and our future expectations – it transforms the operation of the economy.

The new role of money is dramatised if we take a closer look at those savings built by our future-guessing and uncertain market traders. At a classical equilibrium we know that Say's law must hold: the act of supplying goods will have brought forth a level of demand to warrant that supply, and prices will have acted across the markets in the economy to ensure that supply and demand were brought to equality in all the component markets. Now, if savings are being accumulated, that is a withdrawal from demand for today's goods and services; and if Say's law holds, demand must equal supply. In other words, the market must ensure that savings are translated into demand, and the means by which the classical model ensures that this takes place is by the rate of interest. A low rate of interest will persuade borrowers of savings to borrow more and by the same token to deter savings – and the converse will hold with a high rate of interest. As a result the savings market is always 'cleared', those who borrow savings (e.g. investors) translating the act of saving into demand, the rate of interest being the price which 'clears' the market.

Now, if we take the Keynesian position, there is a substantial difficulty with saving. It is not simply an abstention from present spending which can be brokered back into circulation by the rate of interest; it is the holding of potential spending power in a world that may change. And because the saver is uncertain about the future he will want his savings to be accessible; in other words it must be *liquid*. But those who borrow require just the opposite; the key attribute of investment is that it is *illiquid*. The only reason why those who invest require to borrow is because they cannot finance their expenditure from current receipts; they have to tie up money over time in order for the project to pay. Such activity is the key to the economy's ability to create wealth, but the requirement of investors to have illiquidity is apparently irreconcilable with the savers' need for liquidity. The rate of interest, if it is to bring savings and investment into identity, has to reconcile these two needs; and this, claim the Keynesians, is impossible for the rate of interest to achieve at the same time as ensuring that supply and demand across all the other markets in the economy are cleared at equilibrium.

The reason for this is quite simple. An investment will cost money, but it will also produce a return. The only means of arriving at a decision on whether to invest is by the use of the prevailing rate of interest. By capitalising the future expected stream of profit at this rate of interest the potential investor is able to compare a capital sum representing the anticipated return with the capital cost of the investment. Here is the conundrum. The decision to hold savings in varying degrees of liquidity is a trade-off between savers' ex-

19

pectations and the rate of interest. But the rate of interest also has to be that which persuades savers in aggregate to hold their savings in just the illiquid amounts that investors in aggregate choose to borrow. Moreover, investors can only assess how much they plan to borrow on the basis of the existing rate of interest. All these decisions need to be ones that drive the economy to its 'best' outcome.

But because the demand for funds is dependent on a rate of interest *already existing* (the decision to invest or not to invest requiring an existent rate of interest), it is impossible for the demand for funds to co-determine the rate of interest with the supply provided by savers. What is possible is that following a flow of saving and an interest rate so generated, a flow of investment then results. But this is not co-determination of the rate of interest; nor is the level of investment so produced certain to create a level of activity that will necessarily clear the other markets in the economy.

In the Keynesian world, savings only equal investment in the sense of being an accounting identity. The rate of interest cannot co-ordinate the different flows, and as a result the level of activity in the economy may settle at a whole range of points other than the equilibrium supposed by the classicists. Again, a more detailed exposition must await a later chapter, but the Keynesian 'vision' is apparent.

The determination of prices

In the barter model economic agents were assumed to have an initial endowment of goods. Armed with such a stock they foray into the market-place, exchanging the goods they do not want for the goods they do want. The exchange rates between goods will reflect how scarcely the goods were initially endowed and how intensely they are now desired. A market-place is where scarcity confronts tastes; and the terms of exchange between goods – their prices – reflect the results of that confrontation.

This is the heart of the classical notion of price determination, but again there are a number of problems to the overcome. In the first place there is the extent to which demand can be visualised as a set of preferences that are 'taken to market' and traded to co-produce a set of valuations. The process of price and quantity determination is supposed to be based on market experimentation with both buyers and sellers having plans of action that are independently formulated: a schedule of tastes interacting with a schedule of scarcity. It is this that allows the outcome to be described as optimal. However, the question arises: is it possible to conceive of the worth of a good without also knowing its price? In the same way that a demand for savings is only possible given a rate of interest upon which investment plans can be based (and thus a demand for savings), so it is only possible for a consumer to organise a preference ranking of goods if he or she knows their relative prices. This must follow since it is only by action in a market (in which there were already prices) that goods can be procured and their value assessed. In Chapter 4 more attention is focused on this issue and the unsuccessful efforts made to get round it, but if demand can not be envisaged theoretically as a phenomenon independent of price, then the fact that a market has cleared may not mean that the price and quantity at which clearing has taken place conform to an objective equilibrium.

In other words, the earlier example of savings and investment markets is not a special case. It is perfectly possible for markets to clear in the sense that the interacting schedules have arrived at accounting identities, but not in the sense of having produced the terms of exchange that would correspond to an optimal equilibrium. There may be unfulfilled intentions and plans that were unable to be tested within the scope of experimentation allowed by the particular shape of the demand curve, a shape that could not be a 'perfect' index of tastes because it had been influenced by some given set of prices in an earlier period of trading. This, it may be argued, does nothing to invalidate the notion of equilibrium because all that is required is another period of experimentation. Markets do not have to be constantly at equilibrium for a market system to be validated; they merely have to be shown to tend towards that point. The fact that the economy is constantly changing and adapting is proof of the improbability of a general equilibrium; and not even the most convinced market theorist would argue that the equilibria of the textbooks correspond to the reality of a market economy.

But this level of difficulty has arisen with exchange only having to deal with stocks of goods, not flows. Adding production into the system causes still more problems, for unless traders can find that range of prices and quantities that clears the market instantaneously, the fact that goods are being continually produced poses the market with an awkward dilemma. For after any period that the market has not cleared or has only cleared as an accounting identity, the next period must deal with both the goods that are produced in that period, and the carry-over of unfulfilled plans from the previous period. What quantity is then the 'right' quantity? And what price the 'right' price? The instant the market clears quantities that are 'false', receipts and expenditures then accrue which do not correspond to an equilibrium out-turn, and which therefore intensify the difficulty of driving the market into any kind of equilibrium.

Indeed, the problem of false quantities is endemic to the market, because market traders must adjust their expectations to accommodate a 'world' in which even they themselves do not expect market outcomes to be stable or in equilibrium. So if it happened that in one period the market was 'optimally' cleared, the markets would neither know it nor trust it; they would simply continue experimentation, and although receipts and expenditures would correspond to the optimal, their expectations would lead to them saving or overspending as they continued to experiment.

The way out of this dilemma is to hypothesise instantaneous clearing (the Walrasian notion of *tâtonnement* or auctioneering is the classic resolution), but markets in the real world, however flexible their pricing, do not operate on the basis of instantaneous price and quantity determination. The actual process is one of trial and error. Devising a theory by which experimentation alone will produce an equilibrium that represents complete fulfilment and co-ordination of all economic agents' plans is impossible; unless assumptions are made that are manifestly contrivances to produce a result that otherwise would not appear. The proof that markets will spontaneously find some general equilibrium is wanting.

Policy

This challenge to the classical system produces some interesting conclusions. If the economy tends to be quantity-adjusting around changes in expectations, then economic activity has the potential to settle at levels at which resources and labour go unemployed notwithstanding their readiness to work. For even if prices are flexible, the problem remains that the price mechanism alone cannot mediate between the present and the future: it cannot broker the irreconcilable liquidity needs between savers and investors that the fact of the future creates. It is because expectations dominate both sets of decisions that investment and saving are the volatile components of the economy, and that generally it is the level of economic activity that moves up and down to bring the two into an identity rather than variations in the rate of interest clearing the savings/investment market. This then poses the question: if the price mechanism is inadequate, how is it that the needs of savers for liquidity and of investors for illiquidity are reconciled? The financial markets and financial institutions begin to take on an importance that classical theory undervalues. The markets are not just mediating flows of savings and investment; they are reconciling different needs and in doing so are sharing the risk that expectations of the future by both investors and savers may prove wrong.

We are thus entitled to ask how well the risk-reconciling functions of the financier and financial markets are performed, because although these functions spring from the economy's intrinsic needs, there is no force that ensures that this financial role be played in a manner consonant with levels of economic activity that would produce full employment (see Chs 7 and 8). Yet it is the financial sector's balance sheet that is the pivot on which the economy turns. The financier's objective, necessarily, is to minimise his risk and maximise his return, and this can best be achieved by acting simply as a broker, matching liabilities with assets. But simple intermediation of this type does nothing to ameliorate the mismatch that exists between the liquidity wanted by savers (the liabilities of the financial sector) and the illiquidity wanted by investors (the assets of the financial sector). It is the balance struck by the financial sector between these two needs that is the key to the pace of capital accumulation and to the volatility of the business cycle.

This balance is represented therefore by the portfolio decisions of the financial institutions in their balance sheet; in particular, the terms and conditions on which long-term and illiquid debt is advanced to the business sector. The presumption of classical economics is that this will be an automatic function of the price mechanism; the Keynesian position is that the price mechanism cannot fulfil this role. A decline in business expectations, for example, will affect the banks as much as industry: yet this is just the moment when financial institutions need to counteract the decline in demand for their assets (in other words, their loans) by pricing them so that more, not less, are taken up. Market forces produce the contrary result; financial institutions become cautious and wary, and in the financial markets interest rates and yields rise as stocks and bonds are sold. Instead of acting as a contra-cyclical influence, the financial sector is actually reinforcing a downturn.

The financial institutions thus retain an immense influence over the economy. In Britain, for example, there is a marked unwillingness to go beyond a simple brokerage function; an unwillingness which limits the availability of external 'illiquid' finance and constrains the investment potential of the business sector. But if the economy is being enfeebled by the actions of the financial institutions and there is no spontaneous correction taking place as a result of market forces, then the question arises as to

23

whether the State should intervene. (If all banks took a different attitude to risk and lent more, investment levels would rise, and the macro-economic performance would be improved, thus reducing the risk of lending. But while this is true if all banks change their behaviour, it is not true for one bank; and this the price mechanism cannot solve.)

In the liberal tradition public good arises from private action, but if this demonstrably is not the case, does the State not have a role? In fact, given the characteristics of the market economy we are describing, the State has a number of potential roles. It must act to ensure that the problem of liquidity does not inhibit real investment, that is it must seek to resolve the problem of finance. Given the difficulties of the market in harmonising and integrating future expectations, the State must generate some credible idea of a 'better' future – it must manage and channel expectations. And as the market is quantity-adjusting, the State must act as a contra-cyclical economic agent: it must spend when the market is not producing enough spending, and reduce its spending when the converse is true. In other words, it must have an active fiscal policy. It must also act in the interest-rate and foreign-exchange markets to secure rates consonant with full-employment levels of economic activity – rates that the market cannot be relied upon to produce for itself.

But if the State is to act in this way it must possess a decision-making process that is rational and disinterested, and an executive machinery that is capable of coherent and well-organised action. On both counts the British State is weak. The constitutional format of 'Crown-in-Parliament' has created a political process that is especially vulnerable to vested interest groups – never a strong foundation upon which to build a political democracy – while the same constitutional form has sponsored an executive machinery of government that suffers from structural problems of co-ordination and an inability to act strategically.

The combination ensures that government in Britain tends to be clumsy, reactive, and unintelligent; the attempts of the British State to act as an economic agent have been singularly disappointing. Yet if our analysis of the market is correct, some economic initiative by the State is imperative. We are left with three possibilities: that we continue as we are; that the markets find some self-generated means of solving the problem of liquidity and uncertainty, in particular that the financial institutions substantially change their attitude towards risk; or that the institutions of the State are reformed so that strategic management of the economy is less inhibited by short-term considerations, vested interests, and poor coordination.

The wheel has now turned full circle. The British State has the form it has because it, too, is the result of the liberal tradition. That the State should stand aside from the economy, that its role is to enforce the rule of law and protect private property, that in the market the public good emerges from the interaction of interests, and that the job of Parliament is to be the forum where those interests interact: the institutions of the British State are built around these fundamental tenets, and it is this that makes attempts to use the State in a different way so ineffectual.

But the State structure in Britain is not the only means by which liberal values can be embodied; nor is the according of a unique status to liberty necessarily the best building block of a liberal society. The English liberal tradition is but one of many attempts in Western societies to work out the principles of a free economic and political system, and its evident failings demand more humility in our examination of other models. In particular, given that the State must necessarily have some role in the economy, the political and philosophical justification of the state as guardian of the 'social contract' seems worthy of more attention. The 'state tradition' (Dyson 1980) or the 'contract tradition' (Rawls 1980) stands in opposition to the English liberal idea: it is within these latter traditions that, for example, Keynes can properly be understood.

The perspective is that individuals sought to protect their liberty by an initial notional contract; that as everybody could not be winners in the about-to-be-created society and as nobody knew before society began who would be winners and losers, then the rational act before society begins is to enter a contract so that winners assure losers that they will be compensated for any loss they incur through joining the society. In this manner the gains from free association are assured at the same time as losers are compensated for any losses. Now the liberal attempt to show that such a contract is unnecessary is proved futile; free exchange does not mean there is no compensation required because no individual would allow himself to become disadvantaged. The system works in such a way – at least in an industrial economy in which there is time and money – that such a disadvantage can be confidently predicted. There will be losers through no fault of their own.

Liberty in association creates an obligation to the whole, an obligation that cannot be discharged through the simple prosecution of individual interest and exercise of choice. The State stands as guarantor that free association is beneficent; where it is not, the State must stand by the terms of the original contract and if the obligation is not being met, then the State itself must meet that obligation. In this world, intervention by the State is not only imperative, it is the mechanism by which the association ensures that its obligations to its members, especially to losing members, are performed. Liberty is a privilege, not a right, and the privilege can only be afforded if those who hold it admit the larger obligation to society and therefore the right of the State to act in its name.

British liberalism has arrived at a crossroads, and the values it embodied require to be reconstituted in a different system if they are to survive. In economics the effect has been to stifle understanding of the dynamic of the market economy. The Keynesian revolution has been imprisoned within the constructs of a theory whose objective is ideological, and which attempts to comprehend all economic phenomena within the boundaries of voluntary exchange. The weakness of the theory is reflected in the weakness of policy towards the economy, and paradoxically puts at risk the very values the whole enterprise is aimed at preserving. The liberal system needs to be rethought from its first foundations. This will not just entail the rethinking of economic policy, but questioning the principles upon which the City is organised – perhaps even the machinery of the British State. This is the measure of the Keynesian revolution; and it is small wonder that it has been smothered.

Note

1. Benjamin Franklin is quoted: 'I went last week to Winchester and observed that for fifteen miles out of town there was not a door or window shutter next the road unmarked [with No. 45]: and this continued here and there quite to Winchester, which is sixty-four miles.' Boswell noted the same thing visiting Dr Johnson in Oxford. Quoted in Kronenberger, L. (1974) p. 92.

References

Bacon, R. & Eltis, W. (1978) *Britain's Economic Problems: Too Few Producers*. Macmillan.

Barro, R. (1977) 'Unanticipated Money Growth and Unemployment in the United States', *Am. Econ. Review* March 1977.

Barro, R. & Rush, M. (1980) 'Unanticipated Money & Economic Activity" in Filscher, S. (Ed) *Rational Expectations and Economic Activity*. University of Chicago Press.

Brittan, S. (1981) *How to End the 'Monetarist' Controversy*. Hobart Paper 90.

Dyson, K. (1980) *The State Tradition in Western Europe*. Martin Robertson.

Friedman, M. (1977) *Inflation and Unemployment*. IEA Occasional Paper 51.

Grossman, M. (1972) *The Demand for Health: A Theoretical and Empirical Investigation*, Columbia U.P.: New York, for the National Bureau of Economic Research.

Hayek, F. A. (1948) 'Individualism: true and false', in *Individualism and Economic Order*. Gateway Editions Ltd.

Kronenberger, L. (1974) *The Extraordinary Mr Wilkes*. Doubleday: New York.

Lepage, H. (1982) *Tomorrow Capitalism*. Open Court Publishing Co.

Lucas, R. E. (1972) 'Expectations and the Neutrality of Money', J. of Econ. Theory (April).

Plumb, J. H. (1979) *England in the Eighteenth Century* (Pelican History of England). Penguin Books.

Rawls, J. (1980) *A Theory of Justice*. Oxford U.P.

Semmel, B. (1970) *The Rise of Free Trade Imperialism*. Cambridge U.P.

Sen, A. (1983) 'The profit motive', *Lloyds Bank Review*, Jan. 1983, No. 47.

Skinner, A. (ed.) (1970) *Wealth of Nations*, Adam Smith (1776). Pelican.

Wiener, M. J. (1981) *English Culture and the Decline of the Industrial Spirit*. Cambridge U.P.

Chapter 2

Exchange and equilibrium: the problem of the theory of value

Summary

The first and still most persuasive account of the ability of the market to produce the best out-turn was Adam Smith's *Wealth of Nations*. Indeed, it is the doctrines of Adam Smith that can be regarded as the fountainhead not just of classical economics, but of orthodox economics – and even of economic and political liberalism. It is the market that produces wealth; it is the market that produces harmony; it is the market that unites the apparently disparate interests of the individuals who comprise society into a functioning and beneficent whole.

But the interest in Adam Smith is not just that he was the first in a long line of economists to extol the virtues of the market as a system; rather that he was the first to wrestle with some of the problems detailed in Chapter 1. The issue was the move from exchange through barter to exchange through money. Goods were bought and sold for money; and the economy was required to be driven by such action to a point of balance. If there was no tendency to balance then the system ran the risk of breakdown, and this was unacceptable on two scores. Firstly, there could be no effective advocacy of economic liberty if a system based upon it demonstrably did not work; and secondly, the premise that the social world, like the natural world, always gravitated to a point of balance would be undermined. The question was, how could change lead to equilibrium?

The present chapter is an account of the controversy between the classical economists – chiefly Smith and Ricardo – about how the market system arrived at such a point of balance. The objective is to introduce the reader to the idea that the existence of equilibrium and the means by which it is achieved have been contentious from the beginning, and are not just Keynesian quirks. Moreover, a key element in upsetting the motion of the market is the existence of money. The chapter concludes with an assessment of the attack by Friedrich List on the classical system, which serves as an introduction to an intellectual tradition contrary to that of British liberalism – namely the European state tradition.

'Natural' prices and 'market' prices

'Labour', declared Adam Smith in *Wealth of Nations*, 'is the fund which supplies the nation with all the necessaries and conveniencies of life which it annually consumes'. (Skinner 1970: 104) It is the productive power of labour that yields the nation's wealth, and it is by the *division of labour* that its productive power has been raised the most. The division of labour permits concentration on fewer and fewer tasks; it is specialisation that has produced the great upsurge in the producing power of labour, and Smith details the now famous example of the pin factory, where by according every man a minute task which he endlessly repeats, each man's production of pins is raised from 'perhaps not one pin a day' to 'four thousand eight hundred . . . in consequence of a proper division and combination of their different operations' (Skinner, Bk 1: 110).

But the concentration of labour in the production of a single commodity necessitated the *exchange* of goods – for man could not live by one commodity alone. If the division of labour were to proceed, then it was vital that those who specialised felt confident that they could exchange their single product for the other necessities of life. Thus:

When the division of labour has been once thoroughly established, it is but a very small part of a man's wants which the produce of his own labour can supply. He supplies the far greater part of them by exchanging that surplus part of the produce of his own labour, which is over and above his own consumption, for such parts of the produce of other men's labour as he has occasion for. Every man thus lives by exchanging, or becomes in some measure a merchant, and the society itself grows to be what is properly a commercial society. (Skinner, Bk 1: 126)

Barter was all very well and good, but clearly it was a very limited process without money as an intermediary – so money was the instrument *par excellence* that permitted the extension and development of the division of labour.

Smith's view of the economy works thus: the wealth of nations originates in labour; the productive power of labour is raised by the division of labour; the division of labour demands a parallel system of exchange; that system is the market and markets in turn require money if they are to function well. Every man is 'in some measure a merchant', because of necessity every man is a buyer and a seller in the markets about him. The market is the key to all economic activity.

The conundrum was this. If labour was the source of all value, then could one be certain that the value of a good set in the market equalled the value of the labour expended in its production? In a barter economy the values of the commodities traded stood in a pro-rata relationship to the labour time invested in their production. But if money supersedes barter and becomes the medium in which goods are expressed, so the possibility arises of the exchange value of the commodity differing from the labour value. Instead of goods being valued directly by two owners of labour time bartering their labour time, the value is set in relation to money; money itself ebbs and flows in value, so no longer can the user of money be certain that labour values and exchange values are equal. But unless this identity of 'natural' values and exchange values is assured, then 'the natural price' cannot be 'the central price' to which the prices of all commodities are continually *gravitating* (note the Newtonian usage!) If this is the case, then will the market produce of itself a 'natural order' – an equilibrium?

Smith's solution to this problem is simple. He openly acknowledges that there are two different notions of price required to make the system come to a point of harmony. There is the value that embodies labour – the 'natural' price; and an exchange value – the 'nominal' or 'market' price. Any divergence between the two values, and the resultant competition, will drive them back to an identity as merchants bought what was 'cheap' and sold what was 'dear'. This begged the question of how merchants knew what the 'natural' price was. If the commodity was produced by the individual who sold it, then he would know how many labour hours were expended in its production; he, and the other producers, could adjust their buying and selling as 'market' prices departed from 'natural' prices and the system would find a point of balance. But as Smith knew, few commodities were produced in such a way that there was one owner of labour time, and one person who could know how much labour time had been expended in the commodity's production. Real life was more complicated.

The production of commodities was not performed by an individual labourer who then sold his commodity; it was performed by a group of labourers who received a wage in exchange for their labour, and the commodity they produced was then sold on the market. But it takes time to produce a commodity; labourers have to be kept alive and the materials have to be bought – all of which costs money. This fund, without which production could not be organised, Smith called 'stock' or 'capital'. Stock would only be attracted into a branch of manufacture or trade if there was a margin available for the provider of the stock, that is, profit. So the division of labour, implying as it did the organisation of labour, meant that the 'natural' price of a commodity comprised the wages that had been paid to labour, and the profits without which capital would not be forthcoming to organise labour. In addition, the act of production had to be situated somewhere, and the owner of the building or the land in turn required recompense, in other words, rent. A 'natural' price of a commodity contained a 'natural' wage, a 'natural' profit, and a 'natural' rent – the values of which all had to be determined, and then driven to an identity with their 'market' values so that the system would arrive at a point of balance.

So how are all these values arrived at in a world in which traders are no longer in effect bartering their own labour time? Smith began by looking at the entire price of a commodity, rather than its components. And the answer was simple: it was the competition for profit. If the 'market' value of a commodity exceeded the 'natural' value of a commodity then there were profits to be made in its manufacture; stock would be attracted into organising its production, and as the supply in the market went up, so the 'market' price would start to fall back to the 'natural' price – and the process would be reversed if the price relationship was the other way about. The 'market' price falling below the 'natural' price would imply the disappearance of profits and stock would be withdrawn from that line of production until the fall in the supply drove the 'market' price up to meet the 'natural' price. 'Masters', the furnishers of stock, were not following any charitable instinct or noble emotion, but the collective outcome of their decisions was a beneficial one; the invisible hand of the market was uniting buyers and sellers, producers and consumers in a self-regulating and efficient whole, with the 'market' value and 'natural' value of a commodity necessarily being driven to a harmonious identity.

That was reasonable enough as far as it went, but again, how were the furnishers of stock to know what was the 'natural' price of the commodity they were producing? Smith chose to get out of this conundrum by turning to the components of 'natural' price: wages, profits, and rents. If these could be shown to possess a 'natural' value, then the system could work.

Wages were the easiest. It was self-evident that the 'natural' wage was the wage that offered a labourer subsistence. This wage would rise as the general wealth of the country rose; the more abundant the general necessities of life then the more comfortable a subsistence wage would be – but it would none the less represent the 'natural' wage. The 'market' wage, though, was determined by the supply and demand for labour. Owners of stock would want to hire labour, and owners of labour would want to sell it. If the 'market' wage rose above the 'natural' wage, then the supply of labour would be increased. Labourers would be encouraged to have larger families because their real wage would be higher. The population would rise, and with it the supply of labour. But it was a cruel world – and the converse equally held. If the 'market' price of labour fell below the 'natural price', then the supply of labour would have to fall. 'Want, famine and mortality' (Skinner 1970, Bk 1: 175) will reduce the labouring population: 'the demand for men, like that of any other commodity, necessarily regulates the production of men; quickens when it goes on too slowly, and stops it when it advances too fast.' (Skinner 1970, Bk. 1: 183)

The pressure in the market for labour, then, was for an identity between the 'market' wage and the 'natural', or subsistence wage. The providers of capital try to keep the 'market' wage as near as possible to the 'natural' wage in order to keep their profits as high as possible. But it was right that they should do so. The higher the profits, the more rapid the growth of capital; and it is capital that raises the productive power of labour. And as that is raised, so is the nation's wealth; and in consequence the 'natural' wage rises. So the banning of combinations of workers, and the putting of capital in as strong a bargaining position in the labour market as possible was a key element in promoting the wealth of nations. But if the 'market' wage should ever sink below the 'natural' wage then the auguries for the labouring classes were not bright. They would starve: but only so as to reduce the supply of labour and raise the 'market' wage for the next generation.

If Smith can now deliver an explanation of the 'natural' profit, he is home. 'Natural' wage plus 'natural' profit equals 'natural' price (rent is explicable in terms of the general system, as we shall see); and this 'natural' price will be the value to which 'market' prices tend. But no theory of the 'natural' profit is available. The problem is that if profits are to act as signals that drive exchange wages and prices to an identity with 'natural' wages and prices, then there has to be some conception of what the 'natural' profit is beforehand. But how – and from where? The argument is dangerously near to becoming circular. As long as 'market' prices and 'natural' prices are in an identity, and as long as 'market' wages and 'natural' wages are in an identity, then the rate of profit is easy to calculate. It is the residual. But it cannot be the residual, because it was the means by which the other two values arrived at an identity. It is because merchants had an idea of what constituted profit they were able to drive the system to its point of balance. The other values cannot play a part in determining profit, because they themselves are determined by the prior existence of profit. Smith cannot use competition to produce a 'natural' rate of profit and is reduced to saying that a 'natural' rate of profit just 'is' 'though it may be impossible to determine, with any degree of precision, what are or were the average profits of stock, either in the present or in ancient times, some notion may be formed of them from the interest of money' (Skinner 1970, Bk 1: 191) and we are treated to a windy dissertation on interest rates through the ages. The great exponent of the market is foxed, although of two broad statements he appears convinced: that profits in the long run tend to fall, and that their determination has to be independent of the forces that determine wages.

The first idea depends on the rather apocalyptic thought that real wages will rise as the division of labour progresses and capital will inevitably accumulate; thus not only is the surplus available for profit likely to fall, but more capital will be competing for it. This process is inexorably brought about by the competition between merchants as their stock is increasingly turned into the same trades, the idea being that the pace of capital accumulation outruns the number of trades in which it can find employment. The second idea hangs on the notion of capital accumulation depending on frugality, parsimony, and thrift; it is an act of volition on the part of merchants and manufacturers, and if they will it and with-hold their capital, thus reducing the supply, the rate of profit will rise – and so will the 'natural' price –

Our merchants and master-manufacturers complain much of the bad effects of high wages in raising the price, and thereby lessening the sale of their goods both at home and abroad. They say nothing concerning the bad effects of high profits. They are silent with regard to the pernicious effects of their own gains. They complain only of those of other people. (Skinner 1970, Bk 1: 201)

The rate of profit is under the control of merchants who know what it is and can amend it as they will. There will, however, be a tendency for the profit rate to fall, but this is of no help in producing a tendency for the system to arrive at harmony. In fact it suggests that the end result may be rather undesirable. The ability of a market to equalise 'market' prices and 'natural' prices and come to an equilibrium hangs on merchants' assessment of the 'natural' profit – about which, necessarily, they will have different views. The market, as Ricardo argued, needs more robust foundations than these. But once a notion of profit is in place, the rest falls out relatively easily. Competition between merchants will produce a 'market' rate of profit, and as the merchants know what the 'natural' profit is, so they will be able to judge if profits are too low or too high. The system can find a point of balance.

Throughout Smith's account the accent is on competition, self-interest, and the inevitability of the laws at work. The natural tendency was for there to be a general level of wages, a general level of profits, and a conformity of 'market' prices to their 'natural' prices. This was all achieved by competition – between employers, between employers and employees, and between employees. The system was kept in momentum by the pursuit of self-interest and conformed to certain laws; profits tended to decline, wages tended to rise, and the wealth of nations increased as ever-increasing quantities of stock augmented the productive power of labour. In the background hovered land and rent, rising in value on the coat-tails of the mounting wealth of society as a whole.

This was the basic model. On it were hung various adornments; for example, it was important that stock employed only productive labour – by which Smith meant labour that produced a 'vendible commodity', and not something that perished in the instant of its performance. The balance between productive and unproductive labour was critical in determining just how fast the process of enrichment of a society would be: if the productive powers of the economy were encumbered by having to provide for too 'many servants of the public' or the livelihood of professions such as lawyers, physicians, musicians, opera singers, etc, then the pace of capital accumulation would inevitably be slowed down. The State's job was thus to reduce its charge on capital to the minimum, and to let a system of natural liberty prevail; only thus would prosperity be assured.

The best system is one in which all restraint and regulation of trade were removed and then:

Natural liberty establishes itself of its own accord. Every man, as long as he does not violate the laws of justice, is left perfectly free to pursue his own interest in his own way, and bring both his industry and capital into competition with those of any other man, or order of men. The Sovereign is completely discharged from a duty, in the attempting to perform which he must always be exposed to innumerable delusions, and for the proper performance of which no human wisdom or knowledge can ever be sufficient; the duty of superintending the industry of private people, and of directing it towards the employments most suitable to the interest of the people. (Smith 1977, Bk 4: 180)

The standard of value

Wealth production, growth, value, rent, wages, and profits are thus all seen as the outcome of market decisions, and which tend to the best outcome providing the market is free. The market economy is a series of interrelated markets all of which arrive at a point of natural balance through competition and the urge for self-betterment. But notice how Smith has solved the problem of exchange being a money transaction, not a barter transaction. The market participants are assumed to know what the barter value would be (the 'natural' price) despite the fact that exchange is taking place through the medium of money. Smith is able to make his markets not just clear, but tend towards balance because market traders are assumed to know 'natural' prices, and can take the appropriate action if 'natural' prices depart from 'market' prices. It was around this proposition that, in 1817, Ricardo launched his attack on Adam Smith: surely the most effective critique of an economic theory in terms of its logical foundations ever mounted.

Ricardo's criticism was that the system was circular and ambiguous: how did traders know what was cheap and dear if there were only the relative values thrown up by the process of exchange? Smith had only succeeded in getting over this point by merging what was supposed to be an absolute value ('the natural price') into an exchange value ('the market price'), and pretending that the merger had not taken place. 'Sometimes he speaks of corn, at other times of labour, as a standard measure . . . as if these were two equivalent expressions . . . but they are not equal; the first is under many circumstances an invariable standard, indicating the variations of other things; the latter is subject to as many fluctuations as the commodities compared with it.' (Ricardo 1978: 7)

The controversy over the theory of value is now regarded as of only historic interest: it is the view of today's economists that the problem has been solved. Costs and prices are brought into equivalence through traders calculating the marginal gain or loss from doing more or less trade: the distinction between natural and exchange prices, and what standard of value could be reckoned to exist to allow the distinction to be made, is thus unnecessary. Balance arrives through each market transactor balancing his balance sheet, his inflows and outflows: the market is the process by which costs and revenues interact, and the same competitive urge for profit ensures that, in a perfect market, the balance is so fine that only 'normal' profits are made, and wants could not be better satisfied. As we shall see, this solution suffers from exactly the same deficiencies as Ricardo found in Smith: it is circular in its reasoning and requires that a system of money exchange is analagous to barter exchange, that is, that the phenomenon of money can be understood within the same analytic constructs used to explain barter exchange. The starting point for a critique of classical economics is therefore Ricardo's attack on Smith.

The burden of his position is this. Consider the production of the commodity that above all others is vital for a labourer's subsistence – corn. What is the value of corn? Adam Smith argues that the value of corn is at one and the same time the amount of labour that has been expended in its production ('labour was the first price, – the original purchase money that was paid for all things' (Skinner 1970 Bk 1: 133)) and the value it has in exchange, and that the two values will tend to an identity (the 'market' and the 'natural' price). But if the first value is to have any meaning, argues Ricardo, then it effectively dispenses with the second.

To produce a quantity of corn necessitates the expenditure of labour – this is clear. Now, suppose that labour is paid not in money, but in corn – so that the corn that is produced is also the fund from which corn-wages will be paid. Corn is labour's fuel; some of the corn wages will be eaten, and some traded for the other goods labour requires to subsist. In other words, corn is 'producing' an input of labour. Over the season the corn fund is drawn down as corn wages are paid to the labourers employed in growing the next crop, and is replenished when the next crop is harvested. What determines the rate of profit and the rate of wages in such a case? The wages are the corn that labour requires to subsist; and the profit is the surplus, after those wages have been paid. The real wage is thus the cost in corn-wages of producing a given quantity of corn; and the profit is the balance after labour's requirements have been met – the surplus. If labour is really the source of value, as Smith claims, then these are the relations that determine value, not competition in the market.

Smith's claim is that a system of exchange will tend to harmony, because competition will drive 'market' prices to the 'natural' prices that are rooted in 'natural' labour values. Ricardo's criticism is simple. What does Smith mean by concepts like 'natural' price, wage, and profit? They are essential to his model, for without them there is no hypothetical equilibrium; but how can agents in the market-place have any idea what these 'natural' values are? Smith gives no clues but to suggest that they exist, and that they arrive from the mutual competition between the various participants in the market-place. How, for example, could a manufacturer in Smith's world tell if the 'natural' wage had changed?

Suppose that forty hours of a labourer's time bought more goods this year than last. This might suggest that the 'natural' wage had gone up. But could one be certain? There are two equally valid possibilities. The first is that the goods the labourer purchases have dropped in price – they require less labour time for their production – so that forty hours of labour time is worth more because the price of other goods has cheapened. The second is that the labourer's productive power has been enhanced so that his output is higher – the same labour time produces more goods – so while other goods have stayed at the same price, the value of the labourer's product has risen. Let Ricardo (1978: 11) himself take up the tale.

Suppose a labourer to be paid a bushel of corn for a week's work when the the price of corn is 80s. per quarter, and that he is paid a bushel and a quarter when the price falls to 40s. Suppose, too, that he consumes half a bushel of corn a week in his own family, and exchanges the remainder for other things, such as fuel, soap, candles, tea, sugar, salt, etc. etc.; if the three-fourths of a bushel which will remain to him, in one case, cannot procure him as much of the above commodities as half a bushel did in the other, which it will not, will labour have risen or fallen in value? Risen, Adam Smith must say, because his standard is corn, and the labourer receives more corn for a week's labour. Fallen, must the same Adam Smith say, 'because the value of a thing depends on the power of purchasing other goods which the possession of that object conveys,' and labour has a less power of purchasing such other goods.

Unless there is an absolute value by which the relative values in an economic system can be measured, then neither Smith nor his imaginary traders can have any idea about whether it is wages, profits, or the goods that are bought with wages (wage-goods) that have changed the relative values of commodities – and because they do not know that, they do not know what is cheap or dear. The whole Smithian system turns on the *a priori* existence of 'natural' levels of price, wages, and profits, because it is towards these levels that prices, wages, and profits 'naturally' tend. If these values have no independent existence, then to what is the system tending? Ricardo's answer is that they do have an independent existence: wages are the cost of 'producing' labour, and profits are the surplus after those labour needs have been met. Far from being two independent processes, as Smith suggested – wages a contract between master and worker, and profits an act of volition accumulated through parsimony – wages and profits are determined simultaneously through the same process. Once we know the level of corn-wages – or whatever other absolute standard one chooses to use – then we know all the other values in the economy. Value is not located in the market, but in the conditions of production.

But how are corn-wages determined, if not by supply and demand? If corn is the key staple commodity, then the labour time embodied in the production of corn is the core value in the commodity; but how can there be an absolute amount of labour contained in the production of corn? Ricardo's answer was in the labour cost of producing corn – at the margins of cultivable land. Food was absolutely necessary, so cultivation had to be continued to the margins of cultivation so that the community's food requirements could be met. As the land grew less fertile, so more labour time had to be invested in cultivating the land; in other words, more corn had to be expended to 'produce' the labour that produced the corn.

As the level of real corn-wages rose in the key industry – agriculture – so real wages rose throughout the economy, and profits lowered. In the manufacturing sector employers found that they must pay a higher subsistence wage as the real price of corn rose (more labour time had to be expended to produce a unit of corn), and their profits fell. The process of competition equalises the rate of profit across employments, because if profit rates stay high, then more capital will be attracted to those branches of trade until the rate of profit is equal. Here Ricardo's analysis returns to Smith's, but the market's role is much diminished. It equalises the values that have resulted from the real forces at work within the conditions of production.

But it is not only the level of wages and profits that are determined by the conditions of production at the margin of agricultural cultivation, but also the level of rent. As less and less fertile land is brought into cultivation, so existing land becomes more and more valuable; comparatively less labour is required to grow the same amount of produce. The differences between the labour required to work the various classes of land is the premium, or rent, that landowners can levy on the farmers who work the richer land. The exchange value of corn is set by the labour cost of producing corn on marginal land; thus corn produced on more fertile land and sold for the same value yields a higher return. However, profits have to be the same on poor land as on rich land, or else it would not be cultivated. That higher return goes to the landlord as rent – and the more fertile the land, the higher the rent.

Thus Ricardo was able to show how values were determined independently of market relations. For Ricardo markets were simply transmission mechanisms – the most effective transmission mechanisms – for the sending of signals about wages, profits, and rents, but whose 'natural' values were located in the actual productive conditions of the economy. Any balance or equilibrium achieved by the market must reflect the conditions of production, because it was only here that absolute values could be created. There had to be a yardstick by which commodities could be judged cheap or dear so that the market could gravitate towards its hypothetical balance. If 'market' and 'natural' prices were determined wholly by competition and exchanges, then 'market' and 'natural' prices could mean almost anything, because no market or natural value had any absolute criteria by which it could be measured.

But Ricardo, having demonstrated that the distinction between 'natural' values and 'market' values was bogus, and having shown how a market system could only find a point of balance if there was an absolute standard of value – and having even got as far as suggesting what the standard of value might be – ended up, like Smith, with a problem. Which was that the standard of value itself might change in value! Its conditions of production could change. Gold, which served as a proxy for a standard of value, could change in value to the extent that the conditions of its own production changed or to the extent that the conditions of production of the commodities it bought changed. Had gold become more valuable because it was in short supply, or because the commodities it bought were in oversupply? What were the 'natural' prices to which all market values were tending? Without an absolute standard – and Ricardo recognised that corn and gold were both only proxies, because they too could change in value as the circumstance of their production changed – the market economy had no hope of stability. Smith's system of 'natural' prices and 'market' prices guided by the 'invisible hand' to a 'natural' point of balance was a logical impossibility. But then so was an immutable standard of value. It was a conundrum that Ricardo was never able to solve.

Equilibrium and the transformation problem

The importance of the Ricardian argument today is that it underlines the need for certainty in describing the motion of a market system. Smith needed his market agents to know what the 'natural' value of goods were in order to suppose that they would drive the market to a point of balance. Ricardo showed that they could not know what this value would be unless there was some standard of value by which all goods could be priced, and that Smith, in effect, was facing in two directions at once. He made his system of exchange work by having a notional system of 'natural' values co-existing alongside it, a labour standard of value.

Contemporary market theorists are able to make their price system work by simply arguing that price is the result of the interaction of relative scarcities and preferences. Once the market is cleared, then scarcities and preferences can be described as balanced and the market has done its work. For Smith the solution is not enough, for the market exchange relationship so produced must correspond with the 'natural' exchange relationship that would have prevailed had the transaction been barter and the relative values those that incorporated some measure of labour time expended. A market clearing, producing an identity in money terms of both supply and demand around a particular money price, does not mean necessarily that real or 'natural' values are also in equilibrium. This is not a problem in market theory now because the values that result from exchange are hypothesised to do no more than reflect a rate of exchange between intensity of preference and availability of supply. Market transactors do not have to drive prices to some objective value; prices have to reflect their subjective valuations given the terms on which goods can be procured. But there is a problem here, too. Market transactors can know their preferences in the present, and they can come to an assessment of scarcity in the present. But what about the future? In other words, the problem that appears for

Smith as one of 'natural' values and 'market' values, and for Ricardo as how to compute an absolute standard of value, appears in today's theory as one of expectations. And expectations enter the lists with the introduction of *money* exchange.

If this is a problem for market theorists, it is no less a problem for Marxist economists. What appears in market theory as a problem of equilibrium appears in Marxist theory as a problem of 'transformation'. Marx took up where Ricardo left off. The fact that value lay in the conditions of production was developed into a theory of labour exploitation. But Marx, like Ricardo, had a difficulty with deciding on how an absolute standard of value could be created – doubly important for Marx, because without this there is no index of exploitation nor any clue to the trends in the rate of profit. While value had to lie in the conditions of production, there was undoubtedly a transformation in value when goods were sold in the market. The rate of profit could therefore depart from the rate set in the conditions of production; and relative prices need not reflect rates of profit.

However technically brilliant the formulation, and Sraffa (1977) has now developed a system of equations which allows relative values and profit to be determined wholly by the conditions of production, in the process creating a standard commodity which can act as the Ricardian standard of value, the Marxist tradition must needs confront the reality of an exchange economy. Goods *are* sold at money prices, and money prices *do* depart from any real values deducible from the 'conditions of production'. What then is the dynamic of a market economy?

The national system of political economy

The other approach to the market is to make no attempt to make it yield laws; just to use it as a system of incentives, a means of producing and distributing goods, making no attempt to claim that it is 'good' or 'bad'. It just *is*, and can be used as long as it is managed. The most interesting nineteenth-century proponent of this view was Friedrich List (1789–1846). Economics as an attempt to produce laws governing the behaviour of markets was seen by him as a sham. It was no more than any other system of thought, intimately bound up with ideology, political power, and objectives. And the objectives of the British school of political economy were clear. 'The monopolising islanders', he wrote in 1841, had made the 'Germans humble themselves to the position of hewers of wood and drawers of water for the Britains'. (List 1977: 388) The argument mounted by the British, that free trade was a universal good, was little more than hypocrisy:

Any nation which by means of protective duties and restrictions on navigation has raised her manufacturing power and her navigation to such a degree of development that no other nation can sustain free competition with her, can do nothing wiser than to throw away these ladders of her greatness, to preach to other nations the benefits of free trade, and to declare in penitent tones that she has hitherto wandered in the paths of error, and has now for the first time succeeded in discovering the truth. (List 1977: 368)

The distinction between Ricardo – who argued that the market could not find an equilibrium without an absolute standard of value, and who advocated cheap agricultural imports to keep down real wages – and Smith, the protagonist of the view that the division of labour, capital accumulation, and the extent of the market were the three elements that gave the capitalist economy its dynamism, and who advocated free trade as an essential adjunct of capital accumulation, was lost on List. To him they were all the 'school', who however they expressed it were simply dressing up a system of British supremacy as an economic theory.

Of course List was right. Even Smith gave qualified approval to the Navigation Acts – and Ricardo was no less hard-headed. The debate that masqueraded under the sobriquet 'political economy' was in fact a debate over the best strategy Britain could pursue to maintain her leading position. Ricardo's theory, for all its theoretical complexity, translated into a policy of cheap food imports to depress real wages and increase profits. He was a vigorous protagonist of the view that Britain should industrialise at all costs, and landowners, with their concern to keep the price of corn as high as possible, were obstacles to that process. He was even moved to argue that the proof of a country's prosperity was the extent to which it imported food (Semmel 1970). Britain had outgrown her protective mantle, and must shed it.

But if List was to attack the English, then he had to attack the theory of political economy they used to justify their policy, and substitute another for it. That was his aim in *The National System of Political Economy* and if English economists have tended to neglect his work, his reception in Germany has been warmer. His was the intellectual rationale behind the German *Zollverein* (customs union) and to the extent that Bismarck built on that foundation, List could be regarded as one of the prime figures in German industrialisation in the nineteenth century. He scorned Ricardo for defining economics as determining the laws by which the produce of the soil ought to be shared between the landowner, the farmer, and the labourer; and Smith for his confusion – as List characterised it – between the values of the market-place and the value of production. Invoking Burke and his declaration that 'a nation must not be governed by cosmo-political systems, but according to knowledge of their special natural interests acquired by deep research' (List 1977: 397–8) he insisted that political economy was the science of production; that the job of the political economist was to uncover those rules that governed the 'power of producing wealth'.

List's importance is not just that he was the first to argue that 'political economy' had a very partial view of the world, but in singling out what he saw as the principal weakness to call for determined and purposive action by the State. His starting point was that: 'the power of producing wealth is infinitely more important than wealth itself; it ensures not only the possession and the increase of what has been gained, but also the replacement of what has been lost'. (List 1977: 133) The productive power of a community was best enhanced by manufacturing, but the process Smith identified as at the root of wealth creation seemed to List to be hopelessly awry and ahistorical. Every community that had raised its commerce and industry had done so under the sponsorship of the State – whether it was the Hanseatic League, the Dutch, the Venetians, the Portuguese, the Spanish, and now the English. Denying that the state played a role in the 'wealth of nations' was flying in the face of the evidence.

The world was not a republic of merchants, as posited by Smith, but a network of nation states struggling to raise their productive power; the State had to be part of the process because productive power did not happen spontaneously. Wealth creation was not simply a 'natural' process having its roots in individual enterprise. The division of labour that Smith identified as the cause of economic progress happened in a social and political context, and could not be understood in abstract terms like 'capital' and 'competition'. They disguised the importance of the *sectors* in which an economy specialised and the degree to which they were integrated into a whole.

Attacking Smith's famous example of the pin factory, List argues that while individual workmen may be specialising in different facets of pin production, the important fact is that they are united in a union of production; that while there is 'a division of different commercial operations between different individuals', there is at the same time 'a confederation or union of various energies, intelligence,

43

and powers on behalf of a common operation' (List 1977: 150) List insists that whereas it is perfectly reasonable to argue that specialisation has important benefits at the level of an individual enterprise, it is impossible to broaden the principle to the whole economy without taking into account the context and environment in which each enterprise is functioning.

A pin factory needs to be certain that mines and metalworks actually exist to supply it with the material necessary for production; needs to be certain that the supply network will not be interrupted; needs the transport network to distribute its products; and needs a supply of skilled labourers and inventive minds to operate and create pin-making machines. These necessities for pin manufacture are independent of the division of labour as described by Smith, which is more or less a system of simple technical specialisation permitted by the extent of the market. To argue that the requirements for manufacture are 'naturally endowed' is clearly specious; the preconditions for manufacture cannot be called spontaneously into existence by market forces – they have to be nurtured and the only public agency that can perform this role is the State.

The heart of List's case is that capital is a much more complex notion than Smith's concept of accumulated saving. Smith, accuses List, has taken 'the word capital in that sense in which it is necessarily taken by rentiers and merchants in their book-keeping and balance-sheets, namely as the grand total of their values of exchange'. (List 1977: 226) But capital embodies mental as well as material attributes – science and technology are embodied in machines – and to argue as Smith does that the accumulation of capital is solely a process deriving from the market-place is to ignore this fundamental and qualitative difference of manufacturing from other forms of economic activity.

Once this point is accepted the rest follows relatively easily. Smith's dictum that 'What is prudence in the conduct of a very private family can scarcely be folly in that of a great kingdom' is attacked as an abdication of the responsibility of the State to act in the general interest. In the same way that List criticises Smith's conception of the division of labour as suggesting that specialisation is a spontaneous process and that manufacturing 'capital' has no special characteristics, so he criticises the idea that the State has to conduct itself by the same rules that govern private interest. What the State has to do, he argues,

It merely says, 'It is to the advantage of our nation that we manufacture these or the other goods ourselves; but as by free competition with foreign countries we can never obtain possession of this advantage, we have imposed restrictions on that competition, so far as in our opinion is necessary, to give those among us who invest their capital in these new branches of industry, and those who devote their bodily and mental powers to them, the requisite guarantees that they shall not lose their capital and shall not miss their vocation in life; and further to stimulate foreigners to come over to our side with their productive powers. In this manner, it does not in the least degree restrain private industry; on the contrary, it secures to the personal, natural, and moneyed powers of the nation a greater and wider field of activity. It does not thereby do something which its individual citizens could understand better and do better than it; on the contrary, it does something which the individuals, even if they understood it, would not be able to do for themselves.' (List 1977: 167)

The most important role for the State is thus to pursue a commercial policy that is conducive to the growth of manufacture. Although List includes many facets of State behaviour as important in raising the productive power of a nation – a system of freehold land tenure, liberty of the Press, and public control of State administration – one policy stands out: a trade policy that favours domestic manufacture. The most important weapon of trade policy in his view is the setting of tariffs; tariff policy accorded to a set of fairly simple principles. No tariff should be levied on any export of any manufacture, nor on any import that contributed to the manufacturing process – so that food and raw materials should be tariff-free, as should any item of machinery that promised to raise the productive power of the nation. As for manufactured imports there was a case for complete prohibition, especially of items of general consumption; this class of manufacture brought into motion 'large masses of natural, mental and personal productive powers, and gives – by the fact that it requires large capital – inducements for considerable savings of capital, and for bringing over to its aid foreign capital and power of all kinds' (List 1977: 311) and was thus a special target for limitation.

List argued that the right level of tariff at first was around 60% and it should be progressively lowered as the industry grew stronger, but if at a level of around 30% the industry remained uncompetitive then 'the fundamental conditions of manufacture power are lacking'. He was against subsidising exports, arguing that the money could be better spent in developing new enterprises rather than attacking markets in which a competitor had a proven advantage. His approach was to establish the conditions for manufacture and then allow the enterprise to do the rest – despite his advocacy of State power he was no central planner. It was simply because manufacturing enterprise demanded nurturing that the State was compelled to take this kind of action – and whatever the British political economists said in the 1830s about free trade, a brief survey of British economic history was enough to prove his point. (List 1977: 366–8)[1]

This then was the burden of the case against Smith. His political economy was individualistic and ignored the necessity of State action to create the special circumstances in which manufacturing could prosper. It was concerned solely with an analysis of market relations and not in exploring what caused the productive powers of a nation to be increased, arguing that these were the 'natural' outcome of market forces; and it denied the reality of the world as it was and supposed it to be a 'republic of merchants' rather than an imperfect world of struggling nations and states. Worse still, it was a system of ideas that the English were now using to further their commercial interest – and List suspected that the British Government's motives in paying newspaper editors and opinion leaders throughout Europe to spread the gospel of free trade were not entirely honest.

Conclusion

Friedrich List represents an alternative intellectual tradition to that of British liberalism. He has no truck with individualism as the basis of social scientific enquiry or political action. Individual liberty and free exchange are plainly not the sole recipes for industrial and commercial success; nor do they provide an adequate framework in which to understand the dynamics of a market economy. A market system does not spontaneously gravitate towards a point of balance any more than it spontaneously produces wealth. This is obvious in theory, but even more obvious in fact. The proponents of this view are deluding themselves and others; the most sympathetic interpretation is that the exercise is ideological, aimed at buttressing an existing distribution of wealth and productive power. And in the nineteenth century this meant Britain's.

The economy is a collective enterprise and as such it requires management by the collective institution above all others: the State. The State is not the enemy of the individual; it is the embodiment of the contract of association by which individuals live in communities. The policy that List advocates the State should pursue – protectionism – is less important than the recognition that the State must have a purposive and interventionist role if the economy is to prosper.

But although List pulls down the classical model, he offers very little in its place. A policy of protection may be very effective as a means of rapid industrialisation, but what happens afterwards? How can we expect a market to behave if it does not inexorably tend towards some equilibrium? List offers a form in which policy might be cast – namely national action – but the only content is protection. To ground national action in a wider range of policies, we must have some idea of the market's motion; and for clues of this we must look elsewhere.

The tradition, though, of the classical economists is unpromising; and not only because of the strictures of List. It is apparent that the demonstration of the market's motion is inadequate. Smith requires 'natural' values to exist before exchange values can function, and has tremendous problems providing some explanation of whence those 'natural' values came. The Ricardian answer – that natural value does arise from the conditions of production, and that this provides the values to which exchange values tend – gets into tremendous difficulties over what an actual standard of value based on the conditions of production would be. But even if this was soluble, the thesis comes four-square against the reality of the money exchange economy. There *are* money prices, and economic agents respond to them, not the values set by the conditions in production. The job is to explain the price system as it is – not as it could be. And this is where our enquiries will hopefully lead.

Note

1. 'Let us now state summarily the maxims of State policy by means of which England has attained her present greatness. They may be briefly stated thus:

   "Always to favour the importation of productive power, in preference to the importation of goods.

   "Carefully to cherish and to protect the development of the productive power.

   "To import only raw materials and agricultural products, and to export nothing but manufactured goods.

   "To direct any surplus of productive power to colonisation, and to the subjection of barbarous nations.

   "To reserve exclusively to the mother country the supply of the

colonies and subject countries with manufactured goods, but in
return to receive on preferential terms their raw materials and
especially their colonial produce.

"To devote especial care to the coast navigation; to the trade
between the mother country and the colonies; to encourage
sea-fisheries by means of bounties; and to take as active a part
as possible in international navigation.

"By these means to found a naval supremacy, and by means of
it to extend foreign commerce, and continually to increase her
colonial possessions.

"To grant freedom in trade with the colonies and in navigation
only so far as she can gain more by it than she loses.

"To grant reciprocal navigation privileges only if the advantage
is on the side of England, or if foreign nations can by that
means be restrained from introducing restrictions on
navigation in their own favour.

"To grant concessions to foreign independent nations in
respect of the import of agricultural products, only in case
concessions in respect of her own manufactured products can
be gained thereby.

"In cases where such concessions cannot be obtained by treaty,
to attain the object of them by means of contraband trade.

"To make wars and to contract alliances with exclusive regard
to her manufacturing, commercial, maritime, and colonial
interests. To gain by these alike from friends and foes: from the
latter by interrupting their commerce at sea; from the former by
ruining their manufactures through subsidies which
are paid in the shape of English manufactured goods."

'These maxims were in former times plainly professed by all English
ministers and parliamentary speakers. The ministers of George I in
1721 openly declared, on the occasion of the prohibition of the importation of the manufacturers of India, that is was clear that a nation
could only become wealthy and powerful if she imported raw materials
and exported manufactured goods. Even in the times of Lords
Chatham and North, they did not hesitate to declare in open
Parliament that it ought not to be permitted that even a single
horse-shoe nail should be manufactured in North America. In Adam
Smith's time, a new maxim was for the first time added to those which
we have above stated, namely, to conceal the true policy of England
under the cosmopolitical expressions and arguments which Adam
Smith had discovered, in order to induce foreign nations not to imitate
that policy.'

References

List, Friedrich (1977) *The National System of Political Economy* (1841). Kelly: Fairfield N.J.

Ricardo, David (1978) *Principles of Political Economy and Taxation* (1817) (Everyman edn). Dent.

Semmel, B. (1970) *The Rise of Free Trade Imperialism*. Cambridge U.P.

Skinner, Andrew (ed.) (1970) *Wealth of Nations*, Adam Smith. Pelican.

Smith, Adam, (1977) *Wealth of Nations* (1977 Everyman). Dent.

Sraffa, P. (1977) *Production of Commodities by Means of Commodities*. Cambridge U.P.

Chapter 3

The rationality of individual action

Summary

In Chapter 1 it was noted that although economic man was asked to be rational only in the choices he made, those choices always ended up being about buying and selling in markets. This chapter is a closer examination of the attempts by economics to develop a notion of rational economic man that is not as overtly materialistic as Adam Smith's conception of every man 'being in some measure a merchant', motivated by the desire for 'self-betterment', but at the same time is sufficiently robust to produce an equilibrium in a system of voluntary exchange.

The opening passage follows on from Chapter 2. The early classical economists recognised the degree to which spontaneous market processes might require, if not the intervention advocated by List, at least enabling action by the State. Individual rationality might not lead to collective rationality – and both Ricardo and Malthus advocated State action to help the market help itself. Notwithstanding this, the basic 'vision' of contemporary economics remains to identify individual rationality with collective rationality. The mechanism is voluntary exchange, and the main body of the chapter is given over to an assessment of the assumptions that are made to define individual rationality, and the processes by which a collectively rational outcome is produced.

The pivotal idea is the separation of preferences from valuations. Valuations are the means by which differing individual preferences are mediated into a collective distribution of 'preferred' goods. It may be impossible, however, for economic agents to separate preferences from valuations in practice; and valuations may be inadequate as a means of representing preferences if there is uncertainty. As a result, an equilibrium outcome is only conceivable if a particular definition of economic rationality is accepted.

Economic rationality

The early debate in economics revolved around Smith's judgement that the market – if left to its own devices – will spontaneously produce the best out-turn. Political economy did not doubt that individuals pursued their self-interest nor that the best world was one in which the greatest number were permitted the freedom to pursue their interest; but where it had strong doubts was in Smith's claim that the 'invisible hand' of the market was all that was required to produce harmony and prosperity. Ricardo's and List's criticisms have already been chronicled; Ricardo argued that exchange as a system could not logically produce a natural order unless the values corresponding to that order were already known, and List, that exchange as a system did not produce spontaneously the preconditions for industrialisation.

The argument centred on the degree to which the development of the economy could be left to individual action and the market. Although Ricardo, like Smith, rejected the idea that the State itself should become an economic agent, he disputed that the market could of itself produce the values necessary for economic progress; the market had to be enabled to work through the creation of circumstances that favoured certain conditions of production over others; in other words, low real wages. As this enabling function could not be reliably produced from within the market, the State must supplement its actions. List, of course, took the argument a great deal further. Enabling action by the State included tariff setting and a whole panoply of commercial policies aimed at fostering capital accumulation not simply as money profit but as machines.

The objection to Smith is clear in that other great founding father of political economy – Malthus. His name is now associated with Cassandra-like fears over population growth, but that was only a small part of his contribution. Economic development needed to be balanced between the agricultural and industrial sectors. Lop-sided development – overindustrialisation – not only created moral and political problems, but risked being stifled by its own success; there had to be demand for the commodities which industry produced. The market would not spontaneously correct the trends, therefore once again the State had to act.

The ruthless pursuit of interest and the accumulation of capital was unbalancing the British economy, argued Malthus, the agricultural sector was being neglected in the headlong process of industrialisation and the bias towards manufacture threatened to produce a surplus of commodities with no potential demand. Not only would there be a crisis of overproduction and profitability, but the run-down agricultural sector would be unable to produce the food for an overexpanded urban population. No rescue was available from overseas because the same processes were at work there, and food imports would become progressively more expensive. The problem was not just one of lop-sided economic development, but of the whole relation between accumulation and demand. Accumulation implied saving, and saving by definition implied non-consumption; that there should be enough consumption to warrant the level of manufacture was a matter of luck, and competition in the market leading to more and more accumulation was actually driving the economy away from a point of potential balance – a point that was to be emphasised later by Keynes. Rational action on the part of the individual held no promise of rational behaviour by the system.

These early doubts about squaring the pursuit of individual interest with the general interest have now been quelled. Indeed, there has been a subtle rewriting of the history of economic thought; classical economics is seen as a largely homogenous tradition stretching back through Marshall to Ricardo and Malthus and so to Smith. Yet building a theoretical system around individual action in a market so that the whole represents simply the sum of individual decisions demands the same sleights of hand and circularity of argument that so troubled Smith's critics. Keynes, and paradoxically the Austrians,[1] are arguably the latter-day versions of Ricardo, List, and Malthus, objecting to the idea that the market can be comprehended in terms of individual actions and demanding that it should be understood first and foremost as a system with characteristics that go beyond the rules of individual behaviour. The mainstream of economics remains untouched by all the clamour about its inconsistencies: it remains the disciple of Adam Smith, determined to begin with a definition of individual interest, to generalise that interest into the collective interest through the medium of the market and to insist that the result cannot be improved upon. It has fallen to the Marxists to interpret the market economy as a system of behaviour which transcends the notion of individual interest, and in the absence of any other alternative it is their analysis which alone challenges the classical hegemony.

Yet Marx was only developing the insights of Ricardo and Malthus – the 'golden age of political economy' as he called it – and by adding a little millenarian yeast was able to insist that capitalism would collapse under its own contradictions. Malthus's concern that the system was locked into overaccumulation and Ricardo's worry that the rising price of wage-goods would cause a calamitous fall in profits are the stuff of Marxist economics – yet neither Ricardo or Malthus felt the need for a Socialist revolution. As long as political economy warned of the dangers the market system was running, State action could be taken to avert collapse – but this required that the individual be moved from centre stage and the system understood as a system. The insistence of contemporary economics that economic rationality can only be defined in terms of individual interest and that a theory of a rational economic system begins with an assessment of what is rational *individual* action, means that only Marxist analysis makes any attempt to approach the problem from the other side – as a *system* of relations which defines individual action.

But if Smith was wrong and there is no 'natural harmony' produced by the invisible hand of the market, and if there is a germ of truth in the criticisms of Ricardo, List, and Malthus, then economics is embracing a philosophy and interpretation that both confounds the truth and leaves the only attempt at uncovering the dynamic of the market economy to its enemies. As we shall argue in this book, it is this dangerous position that economics now inhabits, and the starting point is economic's first building block: economic man and rational action.

If the market is to succeed in uniting the interests of all, so that not only the most technically efficient production methods but also the most socially preferred mix of production and consumption are to result from free exchange, then it must be axiomatic that individuals will buy commodities for the cheapest price and sell them for the dearest. In other words, price signals actually have to be effective; there has to be a predictable and systematic response to 'high' and 'low' prices.

It is in order to prove that this felicitous behaviour can be relied upon that economics turns its attention to what motivates economic man, and all kinds of intellectual gymnastics have been performed to demonstrate that economic man is solely responsive to price. In essence, the task is to provide a more solid theoretical definition of Adam Smith's aphorism that man has a universal wish for 'self-betterment' or Edgeworth's claim that 'the first principle of economics is that every agent is actualised only by self interest' (Edgeworth 1881). If man can be assumed to want to maximise his money advantage then he will want to buy cheap and sell dear, and the first prerequisite for a functioning market is in place.

The difficulty is that the twentieth century has brought with it a host of other explanations of individual conduct, in particular those advanced by sociology and psychology – few of which correspond to the economists' requirement that motivation should be reducible to self-interest. Gratification may be achieved by action that is 'other' oriented; social mores that stress loyalty and solidarity in behaviour can completely overturn self-interest as a basis for individual action. For example, a high-cost producer may be kept in business because consumers continue to buy from him out of loyalty; class solidarity may enable groups of workers to achieve higher real wages than their 'productivity' warrants; and a high social estimation of habit and custom in relationships may lead to consumers and producers ignoring price signals and sticking to existing and apparently non-economic trading patterns.

The fact that these kinds of motivation for human conduct exist is beyond doubt; it is how to accommodate them into a schema of rational economic action that concerns the contemporary economist. Marrying the ideas that conduct is based around the maximisation of individual interest and that conduct is also influenced by a range of motivation, none of which is reducible to straight economic interest, might appear to be a hopeless task, but one should never underestimate the ability of economists to find means of justifying their ends. The object is to prove that the market economy is the best of all possible worlds and tiresome obstacles in the way of that proof can expect short shrift. The ingenious route out of this particular dilemma is a trick that will become familiar as our analysis progresses. The field of economic enquiry is narrowed to exclude all those phenomena that might be subject to 'irrational' motivation, namely those that cannot be reducible to an expression of self-interest, so that only economic man is left to inhabit the world that economics has defined as its territory. Economics can then make the claim that it does not purport to provide a theory of motivation, but that it merely explores those areas where motivation can be expected to be 'economic'.

The master of this Houdini-like escape is Lionel Robbins, and his *Essay on the Nature and Significance of Economic Science* is compulsory reading for all those who wish to witness master-conjury at work. Economics, declaims Professor Robbins (1979: 39), is the science in which 'we examine the implication of the existence of scarce means with alternative uses'. It is not *ends* that concern the economist, but the *means* that are adopted to achieve those ends, and because those means are by definition scarce, and because there are many alternatives between which those means could be deployed, the economic agent is required to make a choice. All that economics has to assume is not that the end is rational, but that the *choice* of means to that end is rational. The economic agent is assumed to be purposive, to want to bring about the end he desires. The rationality lies not in the desirability of the end, but in the means by which that end is achieved. If individuals arrange their preferences in a consistent order, and then can be relied upon to choose the best means of achieving their end, then economics can take over and examine the consequences. In Lionel Robbins's words (1979: 43–4)

> The fundamental concept of economic analysis is the idea of relative valuations . . . we do not regard it as part of our problem to explain why these particular valuations exist. We take them as data. So far as we are concerned, our economic subjects can be pure egoists, pure altruists, pure ascetics, pure sensualists or – what is more likely – mixed bundles of all these impulses. The scales of relative valuation are merely a convenient formal way of exhibiting certain permanent characteristics of man as he actually is.

The audacity of the claim is breathtaking, but something similar is in the front of every economics textbook (Samuelson 1980; Lipsey 1980). Notice the steps in the argument. Firstly, the narrowing of economics to the simple study of scarce means to achieve a multiplicity of potential ends. Secondly, the disavowing of the importance of ends, and the stress on choice and means. Thirdly, the requirement that economic agents want to achieve their ends, and thus choose the means to those ends rationally – whether they are 'pure egoists, pure altruists, pure ascetics, pure sensualists'. And finally, relative valuations are the result of these choices, 'a convenient formal way of exhibiting certain permanent characteristics of man as he actually is'.

As a result Professor Robbins is able to prove that the idea of economics assuming a world of economic man concerned only with money-making and self-interest is 'foolish and exasperating'. On the contrary, the 'fundamental position of economic analysis are the propositions of the general theory of value' (Robbins 1979: 37); i.e. the explanation of why valuations are as they are. And if the reader has not already guessed, valuations are as they are because buyers, with certain preference orderings, confront sellers, who have only limited supplies of scarce goods, and through their interaction in a market produce the valuations that are the raw data of economic science. Economic man, says Robbins, is purely an expository device by which 'valuations' is explored, and those who claim that the whole of economics is built on a psychological assumption about economic behaviour, namely that at all times it is self-interested, are talking absurd falsehoods.

55

The key step in the Robbins argument is the leap from the world of individuals making choices about scarce means to achieve many ends (no matter what ends) to the world of relative valuations which reflect those choices. The unwritten assumption is that the choices are exercised in a market-place in which goods are exchanged, so that the choice of means is actually a choice about what is cheap and what is dear. In other words, the rational choice of means is in fact a choice about how to maximise advantage in a *market-place*. Man is economic in so far as he creates relative valuations; and relative valuations can only be created by economic man. It is a neat turn which amounts to no more than the idea that the market is predicated on our self-interest but that our self-interest, in turn, is defined by the market. With one stroke the market is justified as the rational means of expressing economic activity, and economic activity is defined to the extent it creates a relative valuation, that is, it takes place in a market. Moreover, the mainspring of the market is individual choice. All that remains is to show that the market result is the best or 'optimum' result and the job is done.

The beauty of this position is that it means that the question of rationality never has to be answered. Individuals are clearly purposive and want to act according to their preferences; and can also be assumed to want to maximise their advantage. A system that permits this cannot be any less rational than its participants – and as the system is defined as only permitting this type of action, it can only be rational. The process is clear: assume a rational individual concerned to make choices; let him trade with other rational individuals in the rational system of free exchange; and the outcome will be both rational and optimal, because rational beings can be relied upon not to take irrational decisions that are against their interest.

What are the *exact* characteristics that such an individual must possess if the market is to work properly? Robbins required that individuals must be able 'to arrange their preferences in an order' but the definition needs to be tighter than that. Rational economic action has come to be defined as having three requirements: 'completeness', 'reflexivity', and 'transitivity' (Hahn & Hollis 1979). If an individual action conforms to these standards, then a trading system can be relied upon to produce an optimum equilibrium; anything less and weaknesses begin to appear. These are the qualifying elements for rational action.

The requirement of 'completeness' means that economic agents are assumed to trade on the basis of a complete and exhaustive examination of all their preferences. Every preference is thus somewhere on the individual's preference ranking, and for any choice of action one course is always preferable to another – if no preference is expressed the agent is assumed to be indifferent to the outcome.

'Reflexivity' guarantees that choices are actually expressed solely in terms of each other, so that no extraneous factors intrude into the decision-making process. Choices are thus made entirely by reference to the preference ranking, and the possibility is ruled out that traders could take decisions in the light of data other than those comprised in the choice. It is not possible, for example, if action is 'reflexive', for the basis of decisions to vary; exactly the same criteria are applied to all choices.

The last requirement of 'transitivity' ensures that the preference ranking is consistent and possesses an internal logic. By insisting that pairs of preferences link up in a transitive chain, so that, for example, if I prefer tea to coffee and coffee to cocoa, I prefer tea to cocoa, action is made predictable and consistent.

Now, with these close definitions of what constitutes rational economic man, what happens if trade commences? Rational man can be expected to exhaust all his preferences; to make no mistakes about what he needs to do to meet his preferences; and his decision on one bargain will be logically related to his other decisions. Each agent is assumed to have an initial stock of goods. Individual traders will have different preference rankings, and will surrender those goods that least meet their preferences for those that do; trading can be expected to continue until every agent finds that no option is open to him that can improve his position, and that the portfolio acquired through trade is the one that best reflects his preferences given the alternatives before him. Nothing interferes in the process of trading, so no trader can claim that he was not at liberty to express his preferences – and the final prices represent perfectly the balance of preferences between the various traders. Once trading has stopped, the fact that nobody has any potential for improving his position, given their preferences, defines the result as the 'best' outcome for the participants in the trading process. The pursuit of self-interest has lead to the general good.

This conclusion is of course contained in the assumptions. Firstly, we said that there were no preferences that the traders were allowed to omit (completeness), so that we know that at the end of trading they must have experimented with all the various preference combinations they hold. Secondly, we know that *all* the goods must have been included in traders' calculations because all the goods relate to each other (reflexivity). And thirdly, we forced the traders to behave logically by requiring that judgements between pairs of goods carried over to other pairs of goods (transitivity). Above all we insisted that the traders were capable of ranking their preferences.

Once trade ceased we could be certain that nothing could happen to disturb the equilibrium; nobody could try and upset it by stumbling on some preferences that had not been experimented with – that is ruled out by definition (completeness). Equally, no goods could suddenly be released on to the market, because all combinations had been tried (transitivity); and no one could claim that they wanted to change a decision on the basis that they had acted mistakenly (reflexivity). In short, the circumstances have been created for a competitive equilibrium in which the best interests of each individual have been served within the finite set of possibilities that are open to him; and because the final resting point is unimprovable for any individual trader it is unimprovable for the system. Rational individual action produces a rational system, and the general and the private interest are married. Happiness and rationality reign.

It is worth making a few observations on this result. Robbins took the view that economics was about choice and relative valuation, and that nothing more rational was assumed for economic man than that he should rank his preferences in an orderly fashion and react to relative valuation. But in fact, as soon as traders start to bargain with each other the overwhelming injunction is to cast individual preferences in terms of market valuations, so that economic rationality is transformed from the exercise of innocent choice to the calculation of profit and loss. To make the point better, suppose the traders are in fact entrepreneurs, consumers, and workers. What kind of decision is each category being obliged to make?

The choice confronting the entrepreneurs is twofold: choosing a practicable programme of activity that allows a profit to be made, and then choosing the particular programme that maximises advantage – at least in the eyes of the entrepreneur – from that activity. The relative valuations among which the entrepreneur chooses are not 'means' to an end, they are the end itself. The entrepreneur does not have an ordering of preferences; he has but one preference, for the attainment of the maximum profit. It may be true that the entrepreneur confronts choices: over what to buy, and what to sell; over how to transform inputs into final outputs; but about the end he has no choice at all. The market and its valuations only function to the extent that entrepreneurs respond to profit signals, for it is via profits that the message is passed from buyer to seller over what and how much to produce. Profit may be a *means* for the system, but it is an *end* for the entrepreneur. His rational action is rational only in so far as it achieves the object of maximising advantage in the market; and to define it in terms of *response* to market valuations, as Robbins must, is clearly misleading.

For the worker there is an equally subtle implication about what constitutes rational behaviour. It might appear that the worker has simply to identify the means by which his preferences can best be attained, namely selling his labour to the bidder that best meets his preference ranking for wages, security, holidays, working conditions, and so on. But again the market imposes its own categorisation of 'rational' behaviour. The rational worker is one that having made his labour contract then understands that his interest has become the interest of the enterprise, because his prosperity will flower with that of his firm. Rational workers are those who put the interest of the enterprise before their own requirement, and thus do not obstruct the process of management of the firm through insistence, say, on certain manning levels, pay rates, etc. 'The rationality so defined is thus a *complementary, derivative* and *dependent rationality*, which the worker needs to possess in order that the capitalist's rationality may be fully effective'. (Godelier 1972) Once again the logic of the market and relative valuation is to impose a particular type of rationality upon the economic agent – on this occasion the worker. Whence the idea of choice between scarce means?

For the consumer there is a parallel obligation, because the consumer has the responsibility for the expression of the preferences that valuations must ultimately reflect. But here there is a conundrum. If consumers are to determine valuations, their choices must be independent of the valuations they are determining. They cannot at the same time determine valuations and be determined by them. Hence consumers too must define their rational conduct in a particular way; they must formulate their preferences by a scale of measurement that is independent of market valuation. The rational consumer is the consumer that can express value in terms of 'utility' or indifference – thereby permitting preferences to be ranked independently of market valuations. Only in this way can choice be exercised free from the logical impossibility of simultaneously determining and being determined by relative valuations.

The view that rationality is simply about the choice between means, so that ends are achieved in the most effective manner, is thus demonstrably bogus. The rational entrepreneur must maximise his profit; the rational worker must stick to his labour contract; and the rational consumer must have a ranking of preference that is independent of market valuations. There are no 'means' here, only 'ends'. But this economics cannot, indeed must not, concede. On the one hand there must be market transactors with sets of preferences; and on the other hand there must be valuations. The interaction of the two must change the valuations, not the preferences; nor can the preferences be formulated by any circumstances or foreknowledge of the valuations. If the means – namely choices and preferences – are entangled with the ends – valuations – then exchange may not necessarily end up at equilibrium. If there is a world of rational men making rational choices according to their preferences, then there is the system of valuations which are derived from those choices. Only thus can exchange work as in the model, for if valuations start changing the rank order of preferences there is no fixed potential set of choices between individuals that might reflect equilibrium. Everything would be in a permanent state of flux.

For the Keynesians, of course, this is just the point. Everything *is* in a permanent state of flux, and at the foundations of the argument is a challenge to the received view of rationality. It is impossible to conceive of an actual market system in which the behaviour of the participants can be boxed into the exclusive categories of preferences and valuations, and in which the interaction of the two produces an equilibrium. Valuations do not contain all the information agents need to know; nor are all preferences exhausted by experimentation with current market prices. What about time and uncertainty? How are *they* to be incorporated into the system? The Keynesian clash with the classical tradition is at heart over the limits of rationality in a market-place.

The problem is that preferences are not atemporal; of necessity they contain judgements about the future. The transactor is not just involved in assessing his own future desires, he is involved in coming to an assessment of future probabilities between which he must choose. But there only exist today's valuations. If equilibrium is to be attainable, today's prices must be able to accommodate an expectation of tomorrow's preferences and valuations. The Keynesian contention is that they cannot.

This fundamental division is best illustrated by the debate over involuntary unemployment – a debate that we will be exploring more fully in a later chapter. For the economists in the classical tradition the fact that men may be unemployed despite their willingness to work does not deny the validity of their view of rationality: for the Keynesians it is an essential element in the challenge to that view of rationality. The market system cannot accommodate preferences in its current valuations, otherwise there could not be involuntary unemployment. For the classicist the very notion of involuntary unemployment is an *a priori* impossibility; unemployment must be *preferred within the context of a set of valuations*.

The workers can be conceptualised as having preferences for work and leisure; and these preferences then interact with a series of valuations for the same commodities. There is a reward in working; but there is a cost in foregoing leisure. There is also the cost, if a worker starts without a job, of finding work. Given these valuations, unemployment is the preferred response. The price mechanism cannot be said to be at fault in the Keynesian sense of an inherent failure to co-ordinate the preferences of economic agents; it is simply being made to produce valuations that workers respond to rationally by opting for unemployment. The valuation of leisure may be too high, for example, because the Government provides too generous a level of welfare payments in relation to available wages; or alternatively wages may be set in the context of the preferences of job-holders, not job-seekers – trade unions prevent wages from falling to the level that would allow job-seekers to price themselves into work. The conclusion to draw from unemployment is that markets are being prevented from working as they should, and not that they cannot and do not work at all. The Keynesian explanation for involuntary unemployment is not just wrong; it is inadmissible because it denies the very foundations of economic rationality.

Economics, in effect, is setting up an assumption of rationality as a means of preserving its view of how markets will produce equilibria. Everything an economic agent needs to know must be contained in current prices; and nothing in the formulation of his preferences must be allowed to upset the exclusivity of current prices in determining his actions. An important reason why Keynesians argue for the existence of involuntary unemployment is that the price of labour cannot contain all the information which parties to the wage bargain need to know. What will the level of demand be in the future? How can the unemployed induce the labour market to express the fact that they themselves embody potential unsatisfied demand, and that potential demand will translate into actual demand once they are hired? Expectations of the future must enter the labour-hirer's preference set, since current prices cannot tell him all he needs to know about the justifiability of hiring labour. It is because his expectations may be depressed (unwarrantedly) that he may be unwilling to hire labour; nor will lower money wages necessarily change his mind. In short, workers and hirers of labour may be behaving perfectly rationally but the market for labour may not be able to clear because it cannot contain all the information needed to allow it to do so.

At this stage the reader is not invited to make a judgement about the rights and wrongs of the argument over involuntary unemployment. The important point to make is the differing conceptions of rationality that are at issue. On the one hand the idea of rational man as sketched by Robbins; on the other the idea of time and uncertainty crowding in on the organisation of preferences and the setting of prices, so that the neoclassical conception of preference rankings encountering valuations becomes harder and harder to sustain.

The Robbins approach to rationality is much more comfortable for economics because, as outlined above, it can be so easily used to yield an equilibrium. If economic agents can be assumed to know their preferences, and current prices can be assumed to contain all the information they need to know, then the price mechanism *can* co-ordinate all their various actions. The Keynesian accusation is that time and uncertainty cannot be incorporated into the basic model without so changing its workings that equilibria cannot automatically be assumed to be produced.

Herein lies the importance of the doctrine of 'rational expectations' – a contemporary extension of the Robbins argument. The hypothesis is that whatever the range of future expectations of economic valuations, the valuations that result prove to be the same, on average, as the original expectations. Economic agents may be uncertain about what will happen, but the future none the less turns out to be the same as they (uncertainly) thought it would be. However uncertain we are, we have to take actions; and on average the results of those actions turn out to be what we initially expected (Sheffrin 1983).[2]

This reassuring view of the world restores at one stroke the whole shaking edifice of economic rationality. Uncertainty ceases to be a problem since, on average, economic agents are always proven right – their judgements about the future are subject to no more uncertainty than judgements in the present. It is therefore still possible to maintain the model of agents making preferences in the face of valuations because all preferences are held with the same degree of conviction, expectations on average are likely to be fulfilled, and current valuations thus contain all the information economic agents need to know. The future exists, but individuals integrate it into their current preferences and choices so that all –

even those that rely on expectations – are held with equal certainty. As long as this happens, equilibria can unfold in the time-honoured fashion. As for involuntary unemployment, that, as before, must be a problem of the valuations in the market causing workers to respond by 'preferring' unemployment. The problem of uncertainty has been withdrawn by definition (Lucas 1970, 1972).

Uncertainty, however, cannot be abstracted out of agents' calculations. The quality of an expectation is that it is uncertain. Agents know that their expectations are as likely to be proved wrong as right. And because valuations do not turn out to be as expected, agents know that current valuations do not contain all the information they need to know. Preferences are held conditionally: they are volatile, and are dependent on the unfolding of valuations. In other words as the rational-expectations hypothesis maintains, the question, of whether the range of individually held expectations is likely to correspond to some objective range of actual results, is irrelevant in terms of understanding the motion of the system. Preferences are conditional upon actual valuations because individual preferences cannot be certain; thus predicating the ability of the market to arrive at equilibrium on the separateness of preferences and valuations is impossible. Transactors arrived at an equilibrium because their ranking of preferences was complete, reflexive, and transitive; but as soon as there is uncertainty, preferences cannot be complete – those preferences which relate to future events must be uncertainly held *by the individual*, so rankings must be conditional on what actually happens, that is, on the level of valuations. But these, allegedly, are arbitrating between preferences, not playing a role in determining them. Equilibrium becomes elusive.

The aim of economics is to locate rationality at the level of individual decision-making and to organise a hypothetical system of exchange which allows the individuals through trading to arrive at the best collective outcome. Preference rankings are reflected in valuations, and the system is driven to a point of balance with the final spread of valuations corresponding to the distribution of preferences. Preferences are analytically distinct from valuations; but it is the Keynesian contention that as soon as uncertainty enters the equation, the distinction is muddied and the potential for equilibrium dramatically weakened. The only way to get round this, and to retain rational individual decision-taking as the driving force of the system and the reason for its ability to produce rational collective outcomes, is to ascribe a certainty to the behaviour of economic man in theory that has no parallel in practice. But we are stepping ahead of ourselves; the separation of valuations from preferences is problematic even when there is no uncertainty – and this is where the next chapter begins.

Notes

1. The Austrian school of economists, notably F. A. Hayek, view the market as a *process* rather than tending to any equilibrium of individual intentions and actions. As a process, however, they heartily endorse it.
2. Sheffrin argues (p. 11) that: 'The most general statement of the rational expectations hypothesis (is): The subjective probability distribution of economic actors equal the objective probability distributions in the system.'

References

Edgeworth, F. Y. (1881) *Mathematical Psychics* (London).

Godelier, Maurice (1972) *Rationality and Irrationality in Economics*. Monthly Review Press: New York, London.

Hahn, F., & Hollis, M. (eds) (1979) *Philosophy and Economic Theory*. Oxford U.P.

Lipsey, R. G. (1980) *An Introduction to Positive Economics* (5th edn). Weidenfild and Nicholson.

Lucas, R. E. and Rapping, L. A. (1970) Real Wages, Employment and Inflation, in Phelps, E. S. (ed) *Microeconomics Foundations of Employment and Inflation Theory*. Norton.

Lucas, R. E. (1972) 'Expectations and the Neutrality of Money', *Journal of Economic Theory*, April 1972.

Robbins, L. (1979) 'The nature of economic generalisation', in F. Hahn and M. Hollis (eds) *Philosophy and Economic Theory*. Oxford U.P.

Samuelson, P. (1980) *Economics* (11th edn). McGraw-Hill/Macmillan.

Sheffrin, S. M. (1983) *Rational Expectations*. Cambridge U.P.

Chapter 4

Demand and supply

Summary

The demonstration that voluntary exchange between rational economic agents must inevitably produce some equilibrium relies on a number of key assumptions. In particular the plans of demand and supply must be independently formulated and convergent in response to price changes so that trial-and-error experimentation alone can produce the required equilibrium.

The simplest model in which to posit these relationships is a 'Robinson Crusoe' economy, where there is no specialisation, money, or production. Every agent tries to assuage all his needs in some notional confrontation with Nature: there is an opportunity to barter any endowment of goods so as to improve his position, but exchange is effected through barter not money; and production is the acquisition of Nature's bounty – there is no systematic and continual organisation of production.

In these circumstances each agent can be supposed to bring a set of preferences to the market which have been formulated independently of exchange values through the agents' attempts to assuage his preferences in his confrontation with Nature. Diminishing returns will make the plans of demand and supply converge, and the nonexistence of money prevents the problem of 'false quantities' being traded as a result of the failure by market participants to identify the true equilibrium.

These assumptions cannot easily be transferred to a money economy with continual production. There is the problem of the formulation of preferences: economic agents confront not Nature but a system of money prices, and it is impossible for them to evaluate the relative worth of goods without also knowing their prices – a problem paralleled with utility and which G. E. Moore identified in the 'naturalistic fallacy'. The naturalistic fallacy of economics is repeated in the doctrine of revealed preference which seeks to explain behaviour through behaviour. It is, however, market behaviour that needs to have an independent basis of action if equilibrium is to be proven to be the inevitable tendency of a market economy.

The common feature over much of output in a production economy is one of increasing returns, but if the plan of supply is to converge with demand, diminishing returns have to be inserted into the system. This can only be done by freezing the production possibilities of a firm, so that within a given factor endowment there must definitionally be some threshold of production beyond which diminishing returns are experienced. This freezing can be done in three ways: defining it as one of the characteristics of firms in a given market structure (perfect competition); assuming it through taking an instantaneous 'snapshot' of a firm's cost structure; or hypothesising some phenomenon that will automatically produce it, for example managerial failure to control costs above certain levels of production. In all cases, however, the notional freezing of production possibilities demands a compatible notional process of price and quantity determination; that is, there has to be instantaneous adjustment.

In fact, systems of price and quantity determination make just this overt assumption – that time has to be suspended. In the *tâtonnement* process outlined by Walras, the fact that goods are produced, not endowed, has to be ignored if equilibrium is to be attained.

The achievement of equilibrium thus requires the theorist to adopt increasingly unreal assumptions that have little correspondence to potential actual market systems. The role of time, and the certainty and stability with which preferences are assumed to be held, are major weaknesses in applying the axioms of the 'Robinson Crusoe' economy to the money, production economy. Equilibrium with markets clearing may not be the inevitable tendencies of the market economy. This is the Keynesian view, and it is upon time, money, and preference formulation that the Keynesian critique is constructed.

The world-view of economics

Before we can begin any detailed assessment of Keynesian economics, there needs to be a rather fuller account of the economic view of the world that it challenges. Rational economic men ranking their preferences and trading in a system of voluntary exchange are the core conception of the classical tradition: but how is it organised into an economic theory that describes the market economy? And how satisfactory is it even within its own terms?

The departure point is that at any moment there is some hypothetical distribution of goods and services in the economy that would 'best' conform to the balance of preferences as they are actually distributed and to productive potential as it actually exists. This is the objective equilibrium at which the plans of economic agents, although constrained by scarcities, are fulfilled to the highest degree possible, and beyond which any further trading on their part can only reduce the level of utility achieved: it is the point where the subjective assessment of their own position as being beyond further improvement squares with the objective reality. In short, it is a stable point of balance.

Free exchange between rational economic agents has to be shown to be able to arrive at this point spontaneously and without any external interference. The only signals that exist, therefore, are relative valuations, and it is the response of economic agents to those valuations that must produce the desired result.

The two great categories into which the preferences of economic agents are organised and by which equilibrium is achieved are demand and supply. Preferences in the sense of desires, wants, and tastes are grouped into the category of demand; and preferences in the sense of plans to requite demand by organising scarce productive resources are grouped into the category of supply. It is through their interaction and experimentation that the price and quantity conforming to equilibrium are found. Demand and supply, to echo Alfred Marshall, can be thought of as blades of a pair of scissors, independently interacting to co-determine the prices and quantities of good and services throughout the economy. Vilfredo Pareto, the great Italian economist, conceived the process as 'tastes' confronting 'scarcities', and it was Pareto who delivered the proof that the ineluctable result of exchange was to arrive at an 'unimprovable' point of balance (the Pareto optimum, see Ch. 1). If exchange is voluntary, if economic agents are left wholly free to experiment with any set of choices they want, and if their preferences are 'rationally' organised, then trade will only stop when all agents are happy with their position. Demand and supply will be balanced and an objective equilibrium will have been attained.

The demonstration that a system of voluntary exchange must tend to an equilibrium and that equilibrium is a 'Pareto optimum' is central to the classical thesis. For without this tendency the system is open to the criticism that its motion may take it anywhere, in particular delivering results that individual economic agents would regard as irrational. The question would then be whether some collective action should be taken to assert a public interest that the markets themselves could not spontaneously attain. So it is that the motion of the free market must be proven to be towards an equilibrium, and that this equilibrium must be proven to be the 'best' result, by being both identical with the public interest and the most efficient way of achieving that interest. Without this proof the market system cannot be claimed to have both beneficial and self-regulating properties.

For such an equilibrium to be achieved spontaneously, the plans of demand and supply must have a different response to price: indeed, because the only co-ordinating signal *is* price their plans must be convergent as prices change. In other words, a change in price must produce a diametrically opposed reaction: lower prices meaning more demanded and less supplied, and higher prices the opposite. Quantities traded are thus guaranteed to progress, via trial and error, to an identity.

Schedules of demand and supply drawn in the textbooks conform to this requirement, with a schedule of demand tracing successively higher quantities of goods demanded, the lower the price; and a schedule of supply tracing a relationship in which *less* is supplied, the lower the price. But to get this result a very important and contentious assumption has to be made; namely, the law of diminishing returns.

Baldly stated, the notion of diminishing returns rests on the intuitive truths that there are satiation and scarcity. Thus it can be supposed that the more is acquired of a commodity, the more satiated the buyer becomes, and so each additional purchase is progressively less valuable. That is, the plan of demand is to pay less per unit, the more that is bought. And equally it can be supposed that because of scarcity, the more that is supplied of any commodity, the more expensive each additional unit will become. That is, the plan of supply is to charge more, the greater the amount that is supplied. Thus the two schedules are mirror images of each other, and experimentation with varying prices and quantities will lead to converging plans and ultimately to equilibrium.

Here, however, there is an awkward problem: in a production economy the characteristic feature of supply is not diminishing returns but increasing returns; that is, the higher the output, the more costs *fall*. There may be no guarantee, therefore, that the plan of supply will necessarily converge with that of demand. This, as we shall argue later in the chapter, has important consequences for the theory of price determination because it opens up the whole issue of time and the logical impossibility of prices containing *all* the information that economic agents need to know.

In addition, the categories of demand and supply must be independent. There must be 'two blades to the scissors'; preferences must not be influenced by valuations; tastes have to confront scarcities. The independent formulation of preferences is the only guarantee that the equilibrium will be recognised in the subjective behaviour of an economic agent once the values corresponding to equilibrium have been reached. In other words, the agent has to be visualised as 'taking a set of preference rankings to market' and it is these which will be the subjective standard allowing him to judge when the market options open to him represent his 'best' choice.

This becomes easier to understand if we ask how an individual agent is to judge whether at any time the market has cleared in the sense of having reached the equilibrium out-turn. At all moments in the trading process, demand and supply must equal each other as *ex post* accounting identities; what the trader has to assess is whether there is still any point in price and quantity experimentation, and this he can only do by reference to his original preference ranking. However, if his preference ranking is *not* independently formulated, but influenced by relative valuations and changing market conditions, then there can be no hypothetical point where his own assessment of his position will square with the 'objective' equilibrium. The independence of preference formulation is thus critical to the whole process of equilibrium determination.

The question then becomes: is it possible to construct an array of preferences that are independently formulated from the pre-existing structure of prices? After all, the value of any commodity can only be known through its possession, and in a market economy possession implies an act of purchase. And once an economic agent knows the price of the goods whose preference ranking he is organising, how is he supposed to disentangle the knowledge of their price and how he would have judged their innate qualities had he not known their relative prices? The search for an independent source of preference formulation is one of the most ancient in economics, and one whose theoretical resolution is the least satisfactory. But it is a crucial plank in neoclassical economic theory.

Independent preference formulation and diminishing returns are, however, least difficult to hypothesise in a barter economy where agents do not specialise and goods are 'endowed'. It is hardly surprising, then, that the 'Robinson Crusoe' economy is one of economics' most familiar heuristic devices, and one of which the student should be especially aware. Classical economics is introduced, via this means, by the backdoor; and very quickly it becomes a habitual mode of thought from which escape, as Keynes insisted, can be a very long struggle indeed.

Robinson Crusoe and economics

Consider the primitive barter economy. Let us suppose that all goods are non-produced; they are endowed by Nature, and the only cost in their provision is the cost of their collection – hunting, foraging and fishing. Economic agents do not specialise in the collection of any one commodity but aim to meet all their needs through their own efforts. If it happens that there are surpluses or shortfalls in an agent's collection efforts, these can be resolved through barter in a market-place, exchanging those goods that the individual has in surfeit for those which he needs.

Now, in this model, voluntary exchange can be shown to produce the optimal result for all economic agents. Individual preferences will be formulated in the light of individual endowments of goods and the extent to which they can requite the individual's tastes and needs: in other words, given an endowment of goods and a structure of preferences the individual will 'take those preferences to market' and barter goods to try and meet the preferences. An overendowment of meat, say, as the result of a particularly successful hunting expedition may be bartered for some amount of fish in the light of the individual's preference for fish over meat. The terms of exchange of fish and meat will reflect the overall availability of the two commodities, and the preferences for fish and meat that are held by economic agents while they barter. And because exchange is a direct swop of commodity for commodity within a finite stock of commodities (it is assumed that all commodities are 'perishable' so that all stocks have to be sold at the end of the market period) there can be no doubt when the market has cleared. Goods can either be held or bartered: and experimentation will continue until there are no more goods to be bartered at a given rate of exchange. The final distribution of goods will reflect the objective equilibrium; that 'best' balance between agents' preferences and scarcities of goods will have been achieved.

In this world, preferences can be regarded as independently formulated because their construction will have evolved from the endowment of goods that the agent actually possesses and that endowment he would plan to have. Each economic agent will have attempted to assuage all his preferences by an individual confrontation with 'Nature', and his relative success or failure will leave him with a particular endowment of goods, whose ability to assuage his preferences he will have been able to decide upon *before going into the market*. Moreover, he can be supposed to have worked out beforehand what trade-offs – *solely in terms of his preferences* – he would be prepared to make in order to improve his portfolio of goods through barter. And because each market 'day' will have to deal with the finite quantity of goods that the agents have collected and want to trade, there can be no problem of 'false quantities' (see p. 76, 'Production and diminishing returns' and Ch. 1) as more produced goods come on the market. When the market has cleared, not only will an independently formulated set of preferences have been satisfied to the highest degree attainable, but the individuals can be in no doubt that their position is now unimprovable.

Experimentation in such a world can also be shown to produce convergent behaviour between traders because of the simple operation of the law of diminishing returns. The case of demand is relatively simple: progressive additions of the same commodity can be assumed to be less valuable to a buyer, so that in order to persuade him to buy more, prices have to fall. The demand curve can be said to slope downwards from left to right. With supply, however, the law of diminishing returns can be understood in two ways: but both serve to make the supply curve slope upwards from left to right, the opposite way to the demand curve.

In the first place it is probable that the stock of Nature's food is limited, at least geographically if not literally, so that after a certain time it will become harder to catch the same number of animals, fish, or whatever. Either the hunter will have to go further afield to find his prey, or to spend more time in the same vicinity to hunt the same number of animals; as their numbers fall, so they become progressively more difficult to find. In short, the more the amount of food that has to be gathered, the more than proportional amount of time that has to be spent in getting that food; there are diminishing returns.

Even if the stock of food were unlimited, diminishing returns could still be hypothesised – at least from the point of view of the hunter. Although the physical yield would in this case be constant, a larger amount of food would none the less require more labour time spent on its collection; time the hunter would be progressively less willing to give up. He would have to be paid 'bonus rates' to stay out in the wild, so that even while he returned with a 'catch' exactly proportional to the labour time he had expended, he would demand a higher price to compensate for his own diminishing returns.

In these conditions the supply curve for the commodity slopes upwards, because the greater the quantity supplied, the more it has cost to produce; either because the physical yield of nature falls more than proportionally as more food is collected, or because the hunter has to be compensated for spending more and more time hunting, or a combination of both.

So, if preferences are grouped into demand and supply the plans behind each category are demonstrably convergent in relation to price and the market will be driven to a point at which it must clear. For not only is supply an 'upward-sloping' schedule, but the circumstances which lie behind its slope are completely different from those which lie behind the demand curve. Supply represents Nature's bounty and the effort to get it: demand represents economic agents' tastes and needs. The two schedules are independent indices of scarcity and tastes; their interaction will spontaneously produce an equilibrium and the only imaginable interaction which will bring that equilibrium is experimental and voluntary exchange in a market.

This is the core of the theory, and its extension from this point is relatively easy. Suppose, for example, after one market period the price of (say) fruit was higher and that of meat lower than in an earlier period. This would be a signal to increase the 'production' of fruit by encouraging foragers to switch from meat-hunting expeditions to the search for fruit, and to the extent they were successful there would be more fruit available for trade in the next market period, and less meat. Find more fruit, hunt less meat, is the injunction from the market-place; and economic agents respond, all trying to improve their trading position by holding goods that the market values more highly than others. So it is that self-interest produces economic good.

This, then, is the basic Robinson Crusoe model. The question is: does it work other than in a world of barter exchange, with economic agents in the mould of Robinson Crusoe directly confronting Nature?

Demand in a money exchange economy

The first difficulty is to draw the parallel between the preference formation of an economic agent confronting Nature and the preference formation of an economic agent who has and will only confront a system of market prices. This is no longer even acknowledged as a problem in contemporary economic discussion, with the question of preference formulation seen as being resolved in the doctrine of 'revealed preference', but the founding fathers of political economy properly understood it to be of central concern. Marshall, Pareto, and later Hicks, all attempted to construct some index of consumer satisfaction that could be seen as the source of stable, independent, and objective preference rankings that could be 'brought to market'. For Keynes the classical notion that preferred price/quantity relationships were taken to market in some kind of objective preference set was one of his key areas of attack; in his judgement it was because preferences were always being revised in the light of changing prices and expectations that full employment equilibria were impossible to achieve (see Chs 5 and 6). The origins of the schedule of demand, and the nature of its relationship with price signals, are thus among the principal issues on which the debate turns.

Marshall's resolution of the problem lay in the idea of utility, a concept he borrowed from the English utilitarian philosopher, Jeremy Bentham. Goods, he argued, have a use-value which could be measured notionally in terms of the 'utils' they possess; the more useful they were, the more 'utils' they would have. All that consumers needed to do was to assign a good the number of 'utils' that in their judgement they considered it to have; and a rank order of goods could be created according to their different number of 'utils'. The law of diminishing returns was transmuted into the law of diminishing marginal utility, so that for each additional good that was bought the number of 'utils' that would be assigned to it would fall. When consumers began trading, they did so with some *a priori* notion of the varying trade-offs in terms of additional utility that each transaction would mean: so behind the demand curve lay utility, an independent and objective index of consumer satisfaction.

Utility, however, was a concept that quickly began to attract criticism: not from economists, but philosophers – and the reasons for that criticism bear on later efforts by economists to escape from the conundrum posed by utility. The question raised was: is it possible to define utility independently of the objects which are said to have utility? If not, clearly the role assigned to it by philosophy, not to mention economics, becomes impossible to fulfil. Now, if utility is to be an independent standard of measurement it cannot be an object or a good: it must be non-natural. The difficulty is that in reality we cannot distinguish the idea of utility from the object which is supposed to possess it.

This is what G. E. Moore called the 'naturalistic fallacy', and one of Moore's most devoted followers in the Cambridge of the early twentieth century was J. M. Keynes. Moore's philosophic point could not have been lost on him, nor its implications for economists.

Utility is a non-natural quality whose attributes are defined by our knowledge of natural objects. We can only come to know of the utility of an egg (say) through a knowledge of eggs and 'eggness'. In other words, to define utility independently of the objects in which it is contained is impossible, because we can only come to know how much utility a natural object has through the very fact of its naturalness.

The philosophic dilemma is exactly paralleled by an economic dilemma. Utility is not an *a priori* value: it is indissolubly linked to goods and their market prices. We can only know how much utility an object has in relation to other objects by having purchased it, in which case its notional utility is bound up with its relative market price; but that is precisely the relationship we wish to avoid. The entire exercise is to provide a basis for the determination of relative market prices that is independent of them; it is the index of consumer satisfaction behind the demand curve that has to be hypothesised as co-determining prices – not prices as playing a role in determining the index of consumer satisfaction. Unless the economic agent can be provided with some basis for his preference ranking that is independent of market prices, then equilibrium cannot be guaranteed; yet how are goods to be procured and valued in a money exchange economy without the agent having to buy them, and thus knowing their price?

The doctrine of 'revealed preference', the current theory behind the demand curve, overcomes this problem in apparently a very neat way. Instead of struggling to find some objective mechanism through which consumers could be said to bring their preferences to market, 'revealed preference' makes the claim that market behaviour is *itself* objective. 'The individual guinea-pig', wrote Samuelson (1948), 'by his market behaviour, reveals a preference pattern – if there is such a consistent pattern.' All economics has to suppose is that observation of a choice in a market reveals a preference. From the point of view of the economic agent the process is preference leading to choice: but for the economist the process is objective choice leading to revelation of preference. A way is opened to the construction of an independently formulated demand curve based on preference, but without the economist having to go through all the hoops of constructing some index to measure consumer satisfaction. Behaviour contains its own rationality and preference ranking; therefore behaviour needs to be explained 'without reference to anything other than behaviour.' (Little 1949: 97)

But although the construct seems watertight, there are a number of difficulties. In the first place, need choices be rational? It is perfectly possible to conceive of behaviour that produces unintended consequences and thus gives no clues whatsoever as to the preferences of the economic agent. Sen (1973) uses the 'prisoner's dilemma' to show that choice may not always indicate rational preference. This famous paradox from games theory is about the choice that two prisoners, who cannot communicate with each other, should make as to whether or not to confess to a crime. The best result is if neither confess, but the risk is that if the other prisoner does confess, non-confession will bring the heaviest possible sentence. Both run the risk of this sentence if the other confesses and they do not; but confession only brings an intermediate sentence. The best guess is that the other prisoner will confess, in which case the best option is to confess as well. Both confess: both get the intermediate sentence. But had neither confessed, both would have gone free. Choice on this basis would 'reveal' a preference for an intermediate sentence over freedom – which intuitively is nonsense.

In fact, argues Sen, it is only because we ascribe some standard like utility to the exercise of choice that we are so ready to suppose that choice would be rational. An outcome such as that of the prisoners' dilemma is not the result we intuitively believe would be revealed by choice, precisely because our belief is that choice is grounded in some objective index of relative value such as utility. So we go along with 'revealed preference' even though its empirical validation is impossible. To discover the revealed preference, even for two goods, would require the economist to observe an economic agent making an infinite number of choices at different prices and with different incomes; and the observation would have to be executed simultaneously to avoid the danger that the choices might be non-comparable if they took place sequentially. The agent and the goods would age. 'Faith in the axioms of revealed preference arises, therefore, not from empirical verification, but from the intuitive reasonableness of these axioms interpreted precisely in terms of preference . . . the whole framework is steeped with implicit ideas about preference and psychology'. (Sen 1973)

Since empirical validation is clearly absurd we are willing to go along with the notion that behaviour reveals preferences only because we suppose that behaviour has been based on a standard of rationality like utility; that choices reveal a sensible structure of preferences and that behind that structure lies some objective standard allowing preferences to be ranked. But this brings us back to the naturalistic fallacy of the impossibility of judging a good's qualities apart from the good. Mr Samuelson's economic agents 'revealing' their preferences are buying and selling goods in a market, but the rationale for their decision-making needs to be such that the system automatically tends to equilibrium: in other words, their rationale needs to be independent of market valuations – but this is a role that revealed preference does not perform.

Although 'revealed preference' has been shown to have grave weaknesses as a theory of demand, very few contemporary economists would concede them: indeed to do so is to make a major concession in the case against mainstream economic theory. Yet this is one of the principal obstacles to an understanding of the Keynesian argument. Later, in Chapters 5 and 6, in the discussion on liquidity preference we will be arguing that wealth-holders do not bring preference rankings for liquidity 'to the market for money', so that it is impossible to posit a stable relationship between money holdings and given rates of interest; rather there can be almost any level of money holding against any rate of interest depending on expectations, on an idea of a normal rate of interest, on the degree of uncertainty, on the intensity of the desire to hold liquid assets, and so on. At this stage the detail is not so important as the main point. In the Keynesian conception the demand for money is not a plottable schedule whose origins lie in some objective preference ranking and whose preferences can be 'revealed' by behaviour; it is a volatile and ever-changing function whose shape is dependent on expectations and perceptions of market conditions which therefore disallows its inclusion in any hypothetical equilibrium. It is a perspective that the Robinson Crusoe-bound world of economics has never been able to accept.

Production and diminishing returns

The supply curve in a primitive economy can reasonably be supposed to embody the notion of diminishing returns, so that as the quantities supplied are increased so the cost per unit rises. The problem in a production economy set up to produce a continual stream of goods over time is that returns tend not to diminish, but to increase as production increases. As a minimum there is the theorem of the experience curve (Boston Consultancy Group 1974)[1] which postulates that as the experience of production is accumulated, so costs fall. No qualitative improvement in skills, capital, or technology is required, just the simple accumulation of production; and costs per unit will fall as the economic organisation 'learns' to produce more and more effectively.

This presents economics with a difficulty. Trial-and-error experimentation can only automatically produce an equilibrium if the plans of demand and supply can be hypothesised as having convergent responses to price changes. If a producer's cost curve is structured so that the more that is produced the lower the cost per unit, and if producers know that accumulated production will *merely of its own* lower their unit costs, then the prospect opens up of a schedule of supply whose planned responses to price changes may not be convergent with those of demand. The existence of innovation, technological improvement, and the economics of large-scale production only underline the point: in a production economy, as repeated empirical studies demonstrate (Pratten 1971; Wiles 1956; Review of Monopolies and Mergers Policy 1978)[2] returns *increase* as quantities supplied rise.

Clearly diminishing returns has to be reintroduced by some means for the model to be made to function, and the mechanism is to focus attention not on supply or industry as generic categories, but on the firms that comprise any notional aggregate or industry supply curve. At any moment, whatever the market structure, firms will have chosen some combination of economic factors (land, labour, capital) through which production is organised and which, definitionally, cannot *instantly* be changed. Thus, their plan of supply at one moment is likely to exhibit diminishing returns because beyond some limit of output their factor endowment will be unable to deliver increasing production without rising costs. The factor combination must possess a threshold beyond which it becomes increasingly overloaded, bottlenecks of production occur, and unit costs start to rise. A 'snapshot' of the cost structure of any firm, given a fixed factor endowment, must therefore exhibit diminishing returns over increasing levels of output.

The success of this approach is that it allows diminishing returns into the cost structures of firms in whatever market context they operate. For firms in a perfectly competitive environment the issue is not a problem in any case, because a perfectly competitive market is defined as one in which there are many small firms operating plants whose factor endowment is pre-assumed to produce diminishing returns at higher levels of output.

However, few, if any, actual market structures conform to the perfect competition model; typical market structures exhibit varying degrees of monopolistic control by the firm of the prices and quantities at which it chooses to sell. And if it can fix the price and quantity at which it sells, it can choose whatever combination of factors it wants and can continually revise that decision in the light of a falling cost pattern. In short, the firm in an imperfectly competitive market is not locked into a plant structure with a 'U'-shaped cost curve; it can continually take advantage of increasing returns by increasing its plant size. The constraint is not the cost curve, but the potential demand for the product.

This weakness in the theory of the supply curve in imperfectly competitive markets is not a new discovery. Sraffa (1926: 536) said that in terms of economic theory it was 'the one dark spot which disturbs the harmony of the whole'. If an industry enjoyed increasing returns, then how could those returns be denied to the individual firms that comprised the industry? Businessmen were not constrained by the prospect of rising cost curves as they produced more, indeed they would find 'absurd the assertion that the limit of their production is to be found in the internal conditions of production in their firm . . . the chief obstacle against which they have to contend . . . does not lie in the cost of production . . . but in the difficulty of selling the greater quantity of goods without reducing the price'. (Sraffa 1926:543) Sraffa's charge against the idea of diminishing returns at the level of the firm was plain: the division of labour brought increasing returns, and the distinction between firm and industry was a 'modification' forced upon economics in order to deny increasing returns to the firm and thus produce the symmetry between the opposing forces of supply and demand upon which the theory of value was built. But as a device it had no relation to how firms and industries really organised themselves – if returns rose for the industry, then they rose for the firm. If the industry cost curve fell, then so did the firm's.

This meant, Sraffa went on to argue, that the idea of equilibrium was now a hit-and-miss affair, because costs could fall faster than prices, and profits could carry on rising and the firms could continue to expand without any limit. Equilibrium could only be expected in the long run once firms had settled into a pattern of pricing and costs that produced profit stability; but such a pattern might be a long time coming. For one thing, it required that returns should start to level off, otherwise the possibilities of expansion without equilibrium were infinite. Because such developments could not be guaranteed, wrote Sraffa, the prospect of equilibrium in a world of monopolistic firms is 'indeterminate'.

Hicks, in 1939, also acknowledged the threat that falling costs pose to economic theory, and declared: 'Marginal costs must rise as the firm expands, in order to ensure that its expansion stops somewhere'. (Hicks 1978:83) The project was to save something 'from the wreck of economic theory' and the key was 'to assume that the markets confronting most of the firms do not differ very greatly from perfectly competitive markets'. (Hicks 1978:84) In order to do this, however, it must be assumed that: 'Marginal costs do generally increase with output at the point of equilibrium (diminishing marginal costs being rare), then the laws of an economic system working under perfect competition will not be appreciably varied in a system which contains widespread elements of monopoly. At least, this get-away seems well worth tyring.' (Hicks 1978: 84)

Hicks admits that his assumption is a 'get-away' and in other passages that it is a 'dangerous step', but he knows that no other option is open to him as a theorist trying to preserve 'the greater part of equilibrium theory'. If firms have both increasing returns and, in an imperfectly competitive market, a measure of control over their own demand curve, then Sraffa is right to say that equilibrium becomes indeterminate. The difficulty is in how to reincorporate diminishing returns into the model and so make the cost curve rise to produce the determinate outcome that economic theory requires.

The constraint is that once it is accepted that there is no logical means of insulating firms from the benefits of returns that rise in an industry, then the only avenue left (if costs are to be made to rise) is to find some phenomenon shared by all firms internally that is separate from the external circumstances in which the firm is operating. Hicks was forced back on a postulate which he himself considered weak: 'The only reason why marginal costs should increase is the increasing difficulty of controlling an enterprise as its scale of production grows'. (1978: 83) So, what makes costs rise and equilibrium possible is the hypothesis that at some level of output there is a collective loss of managerial ability to control costs. It was – and is – a thin reed upon which to build general equilibrium theory.

Time and equilibrium determination

To recap, diminishing returns can be contrived into the production economy by freezing the production plan of the firm: either by definition (perfect competition), by assumption (the 'snapshot' of the cost structure of the firm in an imperfectly competitive market), or by hypothesis (loss of managerial control). These are theoretical contrivances to achieve a specific objective – not only of the notion of equilibrium, but also the automaticity of its arrival through trial-and-error experimentation in a market. The plan of supply will converge with a plan of demand.

The important aspect of this from a Keynesian perspective is the role played by time. Diminishing returns have been reintroduced, by whatever means, through a *freezing in time of the production possibilities of the firm.* But if the production plan of the firm is suspended in time, then the only theoretically compatible process of quantity and price determination is not trial-and-error experimentation, but *instantaneous adjustment*. What is the process by which the market can be supposed to clear?

Market experimentation, even with demand and supply curves sloping in the right way and with no requirement for adjustment to be instantaneous, is a hazardous theory of price and quantity determination. The problem is to explain how traders react when they make a mistake, because although the economist can see that they are not at the correct equilibrium, the traders themselves are not in so privileged a position. Each error in experimentation will lead to some traders having more goods than they should, and others less – 'false quantities' in the sense of falsely corresponding to the objective and final equilibrium. These false quantities will make traders revise their plans, so that even if there is no production and the market is one of simple exchange of pre-existing goods, the distribution effects will throw the price-determination process out of kilter. Traders who have unexpected windfalls of goods will spend more, those who have suffered unexpected losses will withdraw: as a result the well-endowed traders will be able to impose their preference ranking on the market prices, and the system will pull away from the 'objective' equilibrium.

The first recognition of the weakness of trial-and-error experimentation as a means of equilibrium determination was by Leon Walras (1900). His solution is the now famous concept of *tâtonnement*: groping through a system of auctioneering towards the prices and quantities that will produce equilibrium, given that consumer preferences, the distribution of wealth, the level of technology, and total resources are held constant.[3] Although these are fairly breathtaking assumptions, Walras's aim was not to exactly replicate true market conditions but to demonstrate that if the dynamics of a competitive market trying to reach equilibrium are abstracted, then the underlying processes are identical to the mathematical processes required to solve a system of simultaneous equations in which the unknowns are the economic variables – price and quantity – associated with equilibrium. Walras was not trying to say how the market works; he was saying that if it is to produce equilibrium it must work according to the principles of tâtonnement, and that 'groping' is the same mechanism as solving simultaneous equations. He was not trying to model reality, but to create some explanatory insights. To borrow Friedman's (1979) analogy, the same way that the billiard player has no idea how to calculate the angles when he plays a shot, so a market does not consciously solve simultaneous equations in its day-to-day business – but whether billiard player or market know it, the results of their endeavours correspond to angles being calculated or equations solved: and the task of the theoretician is to uncover the laws that govern either the calculation of angles or the solving of equations. And if restrictive assumptions help, so be it. The fact that tâtonnement may be a little abstract or the assumptions very tight is thus of no interest.

To avoid 'false quantities' Walras hypothesised a notional market process in which an auctioneer 'cries' a certain set of prices at random and traders submit 'tickets' ('bons') informing the auctioneer of the quantity of goods and services they would be willing to buy and sell if those random prices were the ruling prices. Now, the auctioneer's job is to assess not only when the demand and supply in one market are equal, but in all markets; in mathematical terms this occurs when the sum of the excess demands in the various markets that comprise the system is zero. The auctioneer carries on with his 'cries', moving some prices up and some down until the tickets submitted by the traders suggest that their intended actions at the cried prices will produce an equilibrium of quantities traded. The auction is declared over; trade takes place at the agreed price and there is equilibrium. Because no trade can take place until the prices are agreed, there can be no false trading and no prospect of the market spiralling off into a disequilibrium.

Now, consider how the 'cried' prices would work if goods were being *produced* all the time the 'crying' is under way. If one cry of random prices does not clear the market, then when the firm submits its next ticket it must take account not only of how much it intends to produce in the next period, but also of the backlog of unsold goods from the last round of price-crying.

In addition to this problem, the firm is posed with a dilemma over the cried price. Suppose it is higher than the firm needs to make a profit; should the firm inform the auctioneer that it will increase its intended production, reckoning that the price in the next period will be the same, or should it stick with its current level of production – always taking into account that it is already landed with a whole lot of unsold stock from the last period? Superimposed on every *flow* to be sold is an accumulating *stock* of unsold goods, and this further complicates the firm's decision on how to respond to each price cry – should it raise production, or take the view that the accumulated stock is quite sufficient to meet any quantity commitments it makes. As Walras himself admitted (1954: 242), the process of groping (tâtonnement) in production entails a complication which was not present in the case of exchange . . . In production, productive services are transformed into products. After certain prices for services have been cried and certain quantities of products have been manufactured ('certain prix de services étant criés, et certaines quantités de produits étant fabriquées'), if these prices and quantities are not equilibrium prices and quantities it will be necessary not only to try new prices but also to manufacture revised quantities of products.

So what is the answer? If no production takes place until the system is in equilibrium, or conversely if production adjustment can be made instantaneous, then the problem of 'false trading' can be averted; in other words, we wish away the problem of time. As Walras (1954: 242) concedes,

there is still another complication . . . production . . . requires a certain lapse of time. We shall resolve the second difficulty purely and simply by *ignoring* the time element at this point.

It was a problem to which he did not return.

Price and quantity determination in a production economy thus pose some awkward, if insufficiently explored, theoretical dilemmas. It is not enough to freeze the production plan of the firm so as to tease into being a hypothetical upward-sloping supply curve: to avert the problem of false quantities, even in a perfectly competitive market, production itself has to be suspended, or conversely the 'auctioneer' has to be able to assign prices and quantities instantaneously. In an imperfectly competitive market, experimentation has an even stronger risk of being locked into a circle of false quantities because the monopolistic firm has not only to decide on what level of production, but what combination of factors of production it will choose to produce that level of production, thus superimposing on any false quantities a whole new cost and supply structure. In these circumstances equilibrium may be very elusive indeed, so that the freezing of the monopolistic firm's production plans becomes a precondition not only of securing an upward-sloping supply curve but also a means of making even a hypothetical tâtonnement process theoretically feasible.

Suspending production; instantaneous adjustment; *deus ex machina* in the form of auctioneers; freezing production plans – economics has to equip itself with some constructs on the way to proving a spontaneous proclivity of the market system to equilibrium that seem increasingly tortured. Moreover, they correspond less and less to the institutions and behaviour of market systems as we know them. Maybe the Robinson Crusoe view of the world cannot be made to work in a production, money exchange economy; maybe the market system has no propensity to equilibrium at all, but is in a continual process of experimentation and permanent disequilibrium. What do time and money do to the market system when it has to create and distribute flows of continual production? Enter Mr Keynes.

Notes

1. The Boston Consultancy Group in their document *Perspectives. The Experience Curve Reviewed. 1. The Concept* (Bruce Henderson, 1974) make the following assessment:

   Costs of value added decline approximately 20 to 30 per cent in real terms each time accumulated experience is doubled. The above relationship plotted on ratio paper (i.e. logarithmic co-ordinates) appears as follows:

   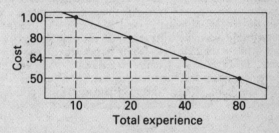

   If the growth rate is constant, then annual physical volume grows at the same time as total experience. The approximate ratios are shown below.

Annual growth rate (%)	Approximate annual cost decline (%)	Years to double experience
19	$5-7\frac{1}{2}$	4
12	$3\frac{1}{2}-5$	6
6	$1\frac{2}{3}-2\frac{1}{2}$	12
2	$\frac{1}{2}-\frac{2}{3}$	36

   Such cost declines are after removing inflation.
   They continue indefinitely as long as the growth rate continues.
      If the growth stops, costs continue to decline, but the rate of decline is cut in half each time the accumulated experience doubles.

   The report closes on the note 'The experience curve cost effects are an observable fact. They can be confirmed by observation' and provides a graph of the price experience curve of the Model T Ford.

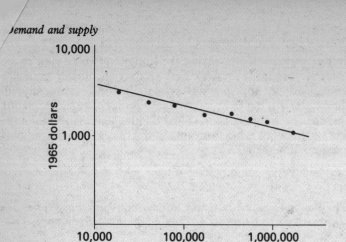

2. Wiles is quoted (Sawyer 1981), after summarising 44 sets of data on cost-output relationships, 'that sharply increasing costs with size are practically unknown, and even slight increases are rare'.

   The Review of Monopolies and Merger Policy (1978) said that manufacturing assembly costs fell by 25 per cent for every doubling of output, while machining costs fell by 14 per cent for the same increase. Pratten (1971) makes a similar assessment, while for the Boston Consultancy Group and their conclusions, see note 1.

3. See William Jaffe, 'Walras' theory of tâtonnement: a critique of recent interpretations', *Journal of Political Economy*, Vol. 75, No. 1, 4.

References

Friedman, M. (1979) 'The methodology of positive economics', in *Philosophy and Economic Theory*, F. Hahn and M. Hollis (eds). Oxford U.P.

Hicks, J. R. (1978) *Value and Capital*. Clarendon Press; Oxford.

Little, I. D. (1949) 'A reformulation of the theory of consumer's behaviour', *Oxford Economic Papers*, Vol. 1.

Pratten, C. R. (1971) *Economics of Scale in Manufacturing Industry*. Cambridge U.P.

Sawyer, M. C. (1981) *The Economics of Industries and Firms*. Croom Helm.

Review of Monopolies and Mergers Policy (1978). A Consultative Document, Cmnd 7198. HMSO.

Samuelson, P. A. (1948) 'Consumption theory in terms of revealed preference,' *Economica*, vol. 15.

Sen, A. (1973) 'Behaviour and the concept of preference,' *Economica* (new series), vol. XL, no. 159.

Sraffa, P. (1926) 'Laws of returns under competitive conditions', *The Economic Journal* (Dec.).

Walras, L. (1954) *Éléments d'Économie Politique Pure*, trans. William Jaffé. Allen and Unwin: London. Irwin: Homewood, Illinois.

Wiles, P. J. B. (1956) *Cost and Output*. Blackwell.

Chapter 5

Enter Mr Keynes

Summary

This chapter is an attempt to give an account of the distinction between a Keynesian and the classical/orthodox view of the market economy. It is argued that the model of a barter economy is not transferable to a money exchange economy because of the role of expectations and uncertainty. As a result the price mechanism alone is unable to co-ordinate the actions and plans of different agents in different parts of the economy; adjustment may be through quantities traded, rather than price.

The chapter opens with a description of the classical view of money, and a survey of how Walras was able to explain the generation of money from within a trading system. Money, in this view of the world, is the counterpart of the potential of the market to arrive at a competitive equilibrium. A barter economy and a money exchange economy, however, *are* different because of the role of expectations and uncertainty; which leads to the 'dual-decision hypothesis'. Economic agents are visualised as having 'balance sheets' through which buying and selling decisions may or may not be matched. Every purchase implies a financing plan involving the anticipated receipts which will be used to finance expenditure. The chapter ends with the Keynesian adjustment story told through the model of a four-market economy – for labour, commodities, bonds, and money – and highlights the degree to which Keynesian theory challenges the three basic postulates of classical economics. The author freely acknowledges his debt to R. Clower and A. Leijonhufvud, and the chapter closely follows their reappraisal of Keynesian economics.

The classical view of money

What is money? Why is money required? And how does the move from barter to money exchange affect the functioning of the market economy? For a study of the market an answer is imperative; and for the economist in the classical tradition any account of money's origins must be consistent with the wider claims for price and quantity determination. In other words, money must not upset the account of competitive equilibrium; its formation and valuation must be the result of the same processes that throw up values in the rest of the economy.

Strangely, theories of money formation are not easy to be had, and by far the most exhaustive within the classical tradition is that by Leon Walras (1954). He provides not only a theory of markets and equilibrium determination, but a theory of the money that markets use. The explicitness of his assumptions and the rigour of his system are the clearest in classical economics. Walras seeks to demonstrate how money is nothing more than another commodity, and to show that the rules of a barter economy hold in an exchange economy using money.

The starting point is the definition of economic rationality. Transactors in a system of exchange are assumed to want to maximise their own advantage, and that they do so by buying at the cheapest price and selling at the dearest price. The demon of self-interest demands that they experiment with every option open to them, so as to best meet their preferences; as a result the market has the constitutional property that every commodity necessarily has a price that can and must be adjusted to traders' preferences for it. After trading, whatever the traders' preferences, the process they have been obliged to undergo will guarantee that each market will clear at some price and quantity. The question is, how is the unit of measurement to be created so that trade can begin?

The key to unravelling this conundrum is the assumption that once the numeraire has been created the system of exchange will carry on the bartering of every trader's preference/goods until it has 'cleared'. The market is constitutionally obligated to clear because not only must every trader experiment with every single good in an attempt to best meet his preferences, but he must do so solely in the light of current prices. He may have no expectation of future prices, nor may he speculate about them: the process of price adjustment cannot afford time to disrupt its workings, so either the process is assumed to be instantaneous, or alternatively it is assumed to happen without time affecting graders' calculations or expectations. In this world there is no future, only an extrapolation of the present.

If this is given, then the Walrasian solution is astoundingly simple. For any number of goods traded there will always be one less price;

for example, if there are two goods traded, then there will be one price; if there are three goods traded then there will be two prices traded; so that for n goods traded there will be $n - 1$ prices. There is always a good left over whose price remains undetermined, but whose value like the rest of the goods lies in its 'rareté' (scarcity) as revealed by exchange. All markets must clear by definition, so the market for this last good must clear as well; once its price is known it becomes the numeraire in which that of all other goods is expressed.

The process Walras provides is via our familiar friend tâtonnement. Instead of crying out the prices of every commodity in the market, the auctioneer now cries out the price of all the commodities except the one he chooses arbitrarily to be the standard commodity, or numeraire: the $(n - 1)$th commodity for the n commodities being traded. Finally the auctioneer arrives at a price range which clears the markets for the n commodities, leaving him to find a price for the standard commodity. He continues with his cries until a price is found that will clear the residual demand and supply for this, the numeraire. Because all traders must express their preferences, this, the last market, must clear as well; and when it does so not only is there an equilibrium, there is also a numeraire, the standard commodity which can be used as money. In algebraic terms there are $n - 1$ independent equations to determine the $n - 1$ prices of the non-standard commodities, and the nth equation must solve because its values are given by the residuals. If one market can clear, all markets can clear.

This is only another way of expressing the old truth about a perfectly competitive market; that because any good can be sold immediately for cash in such a market and because no sale can influence the price, then effectively any good can serve as money because all goods are perfectly liquid. All that money has to be is universally acceptable, convenient, and durable; it could just as easily be gold or iron nails. In a Walrasian system the same is true; the standard commodity can be any commodity the auctioneer chooses because its price is determined in exactly the same way.

Of course money can only be regarded in this light if the conditions for perfect competition or a Walrasian equilibrium actually hold. Economic rationality, tâtonnement and the creation of a numeraire are all part of a whole – a whole which Walras himself was inspired to create because he wanted to show that the celestial 'harmony of the spheres' could be emulated on earth in the world of exchange;[1] but if we suspect any part of the system for possessing earthly flaws, then the whole comes tumbling down. In its own terms, of course, it solves many problems, not least of which is the paradox presented by Arrow in the impossibility theorem.[2] As long as the trading system can be assumed to use the good offices of a *deus ex machina* in the form of an auctioneer then the system can arrive at a rational result and can create the numeraire to do so. Arrow disallowed this possibility explicitly by insisting that the process of decision making had to be created by the traders or voters themselves, but this seems an unduly harsh restriction. It would be perfectly possible for the traders to hire an auctioneer and charge it to the market; in fact the example of the London Gold Ring or the London Stock Market would suggest that this is exactly how traders might behave in real life.

The weak link in the Walrasian system is its treatment of time, as argued in the previous chapter; any process of price determination is time-consuming and in a producing economy time implies the accumulation of increasing stocks as the tâtonnement process wears on, so that any final vector of prices must clear not only current consumption and production needs but also a backlog of accumulated stocks. To avoid the problem of false quantities Walras assumed that time would not affect the final result – an assumption which is clearly unrealistic. If classical theory is to explain money, it must protect the notion of competitive equilibrium; if it is to do that it must find a means of determining prices that does not suffer the weaknesses of Walras's system. Can we look to the traders themselves to find prices and quantities and do without some *deus ex machina*? This brings us to the concept of the 'search'.

Yes, admit the latter-day Walrasians, it is true that the process of finding an equilibrium set of prices is time-consuming, but why not let the traders themselves do the work of finding out the information and abandon the role of the auctioneer? Let the traders themselves shop around to see what prices and quantities are available and thus what potential pattern of expenditure and receipts are open to them. Whether buyer or seller they 'have to check the market', to search for information, and inevitably the process of finding that 'vector' of prices that allows them to trade according to their best interest is time-consuming. But this can be regarded as simply *a charge* on the market, so that the equilibrium price contains a premium for the fact that information is expensive to obtain.

The idea is that each trader puts a reserve price on his goods while he sets about finding out whether he could deal on better terms. The reserve prices will conform to some rational ordering of preferences, but will not necessarily correspond to the best potential deal; for that the trader commences his search. Searching naturally yields diminishing returns – as more market information is gathered, each additional piece of information becomes progressively less useful. Meanwhile the costs of searching rise, in that there is a cost of not trading and holding stock if one is a manufacturer, a cost of abstaining from consumption if one is a consumer, or a cost in not working if one is selling one's labour. The search will continue until the marginal cost of the search is equal to the marginal gain from dealing on improved price information, the additional cost of the process being charged to the market. The market price includes search costs, and these will be driven to a 'normal' level by the same ineluctable process that drives profits to a normal level – competition. An abnormally long period of searching will be penalised by not being able to fully charge it to the market, so inefficient 'searchers' are lost in the competition.[3]

Instead of having to assume away time, the market can now handle it explicitly: time is charged to the market, and any equilibrium price contains a premium for the fact that setting it required time. Rather than time being telescoped into an instantaneous adjustment process, it is now telescoped into the price. Price can co-ordinate the plans of all the traders in the market, can provide all the information that they need in order to decide on their actions, can induce them to structure their actions according to their preferences, and can be the mechanism for arriving at an equilibrium in a market. Search activity has therefore a key role to play in the revival of neo-classical economic theory because it puts the price mechanism back on the map; the problems of time and false trading are overcome, and a world of equilibrium and optimal outcomes can be reintroduced – always of course if we can assume that the other elements of the system, economic rationality and the pre-defined constitutional properties of the market, remain inviolate (Lucas & Prescott, 1974: Hellwig, 1976).

If we leave aside the question of whether the search corresponds to how traders actually behave in markets (as we shall see it is neither empirically nor theoretically proven that unemployed workers, for example, attempt to price themselves into work through tramping round the country's factories and offices offering their labour at ever lower wages), is it *a priori* possible that the processes of price experimentation and searching by individual traders are exactly equivalent? The defining characteristic of a competitive equilibrium is that no one trader has more influence on the price than another, but the search mechanism for determining prices is open to the charge that some traders are more 'equal' in the price determination process than others (Hart, 1983).

Consider a firm that is 'searching' for the price structure that allows it to maximise its profits, and the unemployed worker who is 'searching' for the best wage offer. Is the process identical? In the case of the firm its search must take the form of varying the price of its product and seeing how sales respond; in other words, during the period of the 'search' the role of the firm is analagous to the role of a 'price-maker', offering varying prices and quantities to the market; a job that perversely it will abandon as soon as the market clears. A seller of labour services – or in plain language, someone looking for a job – is in the business of assembling as many offers as possible and picking the best one. There has to be a job before there can be a wage associated with it, and overlaid on that is the fact that the searching labourer is essentially in a passive position; he is one of many, and takes price and quantity offers that others are making. In one case it is a question of sellers quoting a price and seeing how the market responds; in the other it is up to the seller to choose between the quoted prices he has collected – his wage offers – and accept the best one. Market power lies in the more concentrated side of the market, and any 'co-determination' of prices will be skewed in that direction.

All this effort to establish a price-determination process that gives equal weight to supply and demand is not just an intellectual game – it is deadly serious. If markets are skewed in favour of one side or the other then traders may find themselves trading 'falsely' at quantities or prices at which they would not want to trade if they had perfect information, or if the price-making process were different. The system of exchange will still guarantee that all goods are traded and all markets clear, but the final prices and quantities will not correspond to the perfect equilibrium, the equilibrium that perfectly reflects consumer preferences and producers' costs. The reality of market power means that despite the markets clearing the final result is not 'optimal'.

The search does not rescue competitive equilibrium completely, but it has a pretty good try. It only works in the manner it does, however, because the market behaves according to strict rules. All goods are traded one for another so a price must be arrived at which conforms to the traders' collective preferences; the search always leads to a bargain being struck, because the traders have no other option open to them given the rules under which they are assumed to operate and the behavioural characteristics attributed to them.

The rules are essentially those of a barter economy; all commodities are not only tradeable, but they *will* be traded if so doing improves the owners' economic advantage (Diamond, 1982). The traders are not allowed to withhold their goods from the market because rational action is pre-defined as forbidding such behaviour;

traders can only trade on the basis of knowable information, that is, information whose existence cannot be refuted. This disallows any speculation about the future and what changes to prices and quantities that might bring, because such information cannot be knowable; traders are thus obligated to try and maximise their advantage uniquely on the basis of the prices and quantities available in the market in the present.

Side by side with this view is a perspective about the role of money: it cannot be allowed to upset the barter world. Money's job is to facilitate barter and exchange; to do nothing more than oil the wheels of the exchange economy. Instead of each trader having to go through the irksome business of finding someone who wants to trade the goods he wants with the particular goods in his possession, he can sell his goods for money and spend them on the goods he requires. So it is that the textbooks (Lipsey 1980) typically define the role of money in three ways: as a medium of exchange, so that all traders have a common medium in which they can exchange goods; as a unit of account, so that traders can have a common index in which to express their preferences; and as a store of value, so that in between buying and selling the money will hold its value in terms of the commodities which are either bought or sold and thereby not inhibit the process of exchange. Money is just another commodity that makes exchange a great deal easier. As long as we can assume a market economy tending to equilibrium and a process that will yield the prices and quantities corresponding to that equilibrium, then money's role as the numeraire of the system can be fulfilled by any commodity. Money is a neutral veil.

However vigorous our assaults on this world view, the classical tradition always seems able to produce a fresh assumption that can protect a seemingly indefensible position. To succeed we have to challenge not just the major categories and constructs of classical economic theory but also its fundamental view of how decentralised decision-making in a market economy can be conceptualised. The critique of time, for example, in the tâtonnement process has been met by the idea of the search, but are we happy with the idea that time can be telescoped into the market price and that traders are assumed to only trade in the context of current market prices? Equally, are we happy with the idea that the introduction of money into a system of exchange does nothing fundamentally to amend the processes at work in the barter exchange economy? Can the idea that traders are certain about the consequences of their actions (the doctrine of rational expectations, see Ch. 3) and even, hypothetically, have perfect knowledge, be acceptable to any economist trying to grasp the dynamic of the market economy?

The Keynesian schism – the barter economy and the money exchange economy

In the last resort the litmus test of any economic theory is its success in providing a 'vision' of how the economy might be expected to work. Although it is true that classical theory makes any number of convolutions and incredible assumptions (like those over time), the criticism is not so much that it is theoretically implausible (which it certainly is) but that even as a model it has little to tell us about how the market as a decentralised process of collective decision-making actually functions. None of the central assumptions bear any relation to the actual behaviour of market transactors; nor does its chief objective, to prove that a market system will tend to an equilibrium, bear any resemblance to what actually happens in a market economy. Perhaps we should not be surprised given analytically that the main elements in the analysis, supply and demand, are so interdependent. Thus their supposed interaction to determine prices and quantities is necessarily going to be difficult, if not impossible to prove; but in the course of critically examining such phenomena, logic can only take us so far. The acceptance, for example, that the supply curve slopes downwards and not upwards, owes as much to our grasp of empirical evidence and intuitive reasoning as to a demonstration in logic that the means by which classical theory makes it slope upwards can only be true under the restrictive assumptions imposed by classical theory itself.

It was this point that Keynes laboured in the opening chapters of the *General Theory*; that whatever classical theory seeks to tell us about the market economy it happens not to conform with the behaviour of the 'economic society in which we actually live, with the result that its teaching is misleading and disastrous if we attempt to apply it to the facts of experience.' (Keynes 1978: 3). It was a point that economics has chosen to ignore; today's economics textbooks might just have well been written as though Keynes had never lived. Economics continues with its central assumptions intact: that rational economic man need not regard the future with any less equanimity than the present, and concentrates all his efforts to maximising his advantage in the present; that rational man is able to calculate exactly the consequences of his action and thus to be always capable of knowing when he has made a mistake; and that money does not alter the principles of exchange as hypothesised in a barter economy.

The reality is that time, uncertainty, and money pervade the market economy and transform its functioning – but this the classical theory wishes away in a cloud of extraordinary assumptions; and all to prove what we never seem to find in the real market, that there is an equilibrium, that supply always equals demand or will tend to, that there can be no such thing as involuntary unemployment because labour must always price itself into work, and so on. 'The classical economists', wrote Keynes,

resemble Euclidian geometers in a non-Euclidian world, who, discovering that in experience straight lines apparently parallel often meet, rebuke the lines for not keeping straight – as the only remedy for the unfortunate collisions which are occurring. Yet in truth there is no remedy except to throw out the axiom of parallels and to work out a non-Euclidian geometry. (Keynes 1978: 16).

Suppose then we do just this. If traders were not compelled to trade by the constitution of the system, if they withheld goods from the market in the expectations of a better price in the future, what would happen to the neatly functioning Walrasian world? We introduce time into the system by allowing traders to worry about what will happen to prices in the future; we introduce uncertainty by not allowing traders to know for certain what those future prices will be; and we allow traders the option of not being obliged to trade if they choose – they can hold money instead. In Walras's world all goods are traded necessarily, so even 'false quantities' are cleared; a disequilibrium has the limited meaning of an equilibrium of false quantities. But in a world of time, uncertainty, and money goods may not be traded; uncertain expectations may be translated into inaction, inaction into idle resources.

The harmonious economy of Walras and the classical school is shattered into a thousand fragments. No more can price alone unite the actions of all the transactors in the market-place because some may choose not to trade if they are uncertain about the course of future prices; no longer can prices exactly reflect today's preferences because nobody can be certain to what extent prices have been influenced by transactors' views of how they believe prices will move in the future. The present and the future are no longer bound together in a unanimous price judgement, but divided by the fact that traders cannot know the future and that in money they possess the means to translate that uncertainty into action or inaction as the case may be. For Keynes the key to unravelling the dynamic of the market was the fact of the future.

I accuse the classical economic theory of being itself one of those pretty, polite techniques which tries to deal with the present by abstracting from the fact that we know very little about the future. (Keynes 1937: 215)

With one jump we are free and in a world peopled by individuals whose actions we can recognise and in an economy whose behaviour even at this early stage can be seen to correspond to our own. Instead of our expectations and tastes being reduced to a rank order of preferences that are 'complete, reflexive, and transitive', our expectations are plagued by doubts, lack of information, and uncertainty. Uncertainty is not part of a continuum with certainty at the other end, as the devices of preference and probability theory attempt to suggest, but a qualitatively different phenomenon. Uncertainty *cannot* be reduced to the same calculable status as certainty itself. Keynes again:

We have, as a rule, only the vaguest idea of any but the most direct consequences of our acts . . . our knowledge of the future is fluctuating, vague and uncertain . . . the sense in which I am using the term (uncertain) is that in which the prospect of a European war is uncertain, or the price of copper and the rate of interest twenty years hence, or the obsolescence of a new invention, or the position of private wealth-owners in the social system in 1970. About these matters there is no scientific basis on which to form any calculable probability whatever. We simply do not know. Nevertheless, the necessity for action and for decision compels us as practical men to do our best to overlook this awkward fact and to behave exactly as we should if we had behind us a good Benthamite calculation of a series of prospective advantages and disadvantages, each multiplied by its appropriate probability, waiting to be summed. (Keynes 1937: 213)

The future is incalculable; we simply do not know what the future holds. This is not to say that we make no attempt to make a judgement about the future; indeed the paraphernalia of probability theory are just about such an attempt. But the probability that an event may happen is qualitatively different from *knowing* that it will, and it is upon this qualitative difference that Keynes develops his alternative view of how a market economy can be expected to behave.

In a barter economy goods are exchanged directly one for another and there is either exchange, or not. In other words, the terms of exchange are the terms under which traders are willing to exchange goods, and as each transaction is a swop of one good for another, at the end of trading each trader holds a portfolio of goods that corresponds to what he was willing to trade. Moreover, no goods are wasted, because either a good was exchanged, or it remained in the hands of the trader. There is an equilibrium: all goods are in circulation, none are wasted, and after trading, each trader has that portfolio of goods that best meets his own preferences.

Now, introduce money. Money changes the links in the trading game. Instead of a commodity being traded for a commodity, a commodity is traded for money and then back into a commodity. This may appear to be a change of only modest significance – indeed in the classical model of no significance – but it transforms the exchange economy. Whereas before, each transaction was a swop carrying with it the certainty of realisation, now each transaction is a swop of money for goods or vice versa. Each transaction in itself is certain, but what has become *uncertain* is whether the two transactions, commodity for money/money for commodity, will roll into one as before. 'The dark forces of time and ignorance' are unloosed into the neatly functioning world of the barter economy.

The dual-decision hypothesis

The root, therefore, of Keynes' dispute with classical economics is that in a market economy money separates buying and selling decisions. This has also been called the 'dual-decision hypothesis' (Clower 1965: 118). If we can assume with Clower (1965: 116) that 'no transactor consciously plans to purchase units of any commodity without at the same time planning to finance the purchase either from profit receipts or from the sale of units of some other commodity', then spending decisions in the market-place are continually being financially constrained by actual realised receipts or expectations of receipts. In other words, whatever a transactor's preferences and initial stock of goods, his ability to transform those preferences into his desired portfolio of goods depends not only on his expectation of receipts, but on whether those expectations are actually met. In a world of uncertainty about the future this 'dual' nature of every market transaction limits the ability of price to co-ordinate the actions of the economy and to drive it to equilibrium.

The best analogy is the balance sheet. Each agent engaged in a transaction can be thought of as running a notional balance sheet of inflows and outflows. When a good is sold that will be a money inflow; when a good is bought, that is a money outflow. Now in the barter economy goods are swopped, so inflows always match outflows, even if there is time and uncertainty. As a result the transactor's balance sheet is always squared. In a money exchange economy where the transactions are separated from each other by the necessity of being bought and sold for money, this squaring of each transactor's balance sheet is less likely to happen. Indeed, because of the time factor it is almost certain not to happen.

The money receipts from the sale of a good are therefore likely to occur at a different time to the time when the agent wants to spend those receipts. Every participant in a money exchange economy is faced with having to juggle a flow of income with a flow of expenditure, and the two flows cannot be expected to coincide. Moreover, because the mismatch is over time each agent cannot be certain that his income will be as he expects it to be, nor his planned expenditure. All of a sudden he is at risk, and this fundamentally changes his behaviour if for any reason something happens to upset his expectations.

This is the kernel of the Keynesian challenge to the received orthodoxy. Each transactor in a market economy based on money exchange is confronted by uncertainty as in the very nature of things. The key to the behaviour of the market is the extent to which transactors will allow their balance sheets to become 'stretched' in the face of uncertainty over the future. The liability side of the balance sheet is represented by money claims on the transactor; the asset side by the transactor's money claims on others. If for any reason the inflows through the balance sheet exceed the outflows then the agent will find himself building up his assets; if outflows exceed inflows then the agent's liabilities will rise as he finances his outflows by accepting increasing claims on himself. How transactors distribute their assets and the extent to which they accept increasing liabilities depends completely on their expectations of the future; and on their decisions in aggregate depend the overall level of economic activity.

This view of the market requires a redefinition of the idea of equilibrium. In this context equilibrium is not where all the markets have been cleared; it is where all the markets have been cleared so that not only have transactors' actual receipts equalled planned receipts, but actual expenditure has equalled planned expenditure. Before any trading can take place transactors must have both a notional idea of how much they plan to spend and how they will finance it, and the market can only be said to be in equilibrium if both plans and what actually happens are fulfilled. If an equilibrium is produced where plans to buy and sell are not fulfilled, then clearly somewhere in the system there is unsatisfied notional demand and supply, an amount of economic activity that was planned to take place but did not. The question is, can the price mechanism act to flush out this unsatisfied expression of traders' preferences, or do time and uncertainty so transform the model of the exchange economy that some other adjustment process comes into play?

Let us suppose there is a change of expectations and a group of traders revise downwards their estimate of planned receipts. This revision immediately confronts them with a financing problem, because if they are to maintain their level of planned expenditure then, given their expectation of receipts, they must either accept an increase in their borrowing and a deterioration in their balance sheet or cut their planned expenditure. What will provide the basis for their judgement? There is no means at this stage for a price signal in the market to do anything to influence them, for they have yet to show their hand. Suppose that they have a preferred balance-sheet structure and they do not wish to accept any further increase in their liabilities. As a result they must lower their planned expenditure; the downward revision of their *expectations* is of its own accord enough to cause a cut in their spending. What happens next?

In other markets, traders have not changed their expectations of purchases or receipts but to their surprise they find that realised sales are not as high as they expected; the drop in the first group of traders' spending rebounds on the second group as an unexpected fall in receipts. Even if the second group lower their prices in an attempt to coax the first group back into the market, they are unlikely to be very successful unless they cut prices by enough to more than compensate for the first group's reduced expectations. In any case, while they are waiting to see how their price cuts affect the quantity sold, they too have to make a judgement about how high they are prepared to see their liabilities go. Depending on their expectations and willingness to run the risk of building up liabilities they will cut spending in turn. This lowers current receipts for yet another group of traders, so the same process is set in train again and expectations of future receipts begin to fall alongside the fall in current receipts. There is a general pulling in of horns around the market. Effective demand falls throughout the system because although groups of traders have notional demands higher than those they actually plan, the financing constraint, given the lower expectation of receipts, prevents them from translating the notional demand into effective demand. Demand falls; quantities sold fall;

prices chase quantities downwards; and the level of economic activity is reduced. Instead of prices taking the burden of adjustment, the level of economic activity falls.

Interestingly this effect still happens if the second group of traders succeed with their first round of price cuts and persuade the first group of traders to maintain their level of purchases. For although the same quantity will have been sold, the fact that it has only been achieved at a lower price means that their total receipts are lower. In other words, the second group will still find that their actual receipts differ from their planned receipts, and as a result the decision remains as to whether they will maintain the level of expenditure (and run up their liabilities) or cut it, with all the third- and fourth-round effects described above.

This danger, called 'income effects' in the literature, has long been recognised as a potential problem for the price and quantity/classical school. Hicks (1978): 129) as usual is candid about the probable outcome: 'If very extensive transactions take place at prices very different from equilibrium prices, *the disturbance will be serious*. But I think we may reasonably suppose that the transactions which take place at 'very false' prices are limited in volume.' However, in the classical system these income effects are limited by assumed price adjustment in other markets. In this case, the fact that the first group of traders have managed to finance the same·quantity of purchases at a lower price means that they can build up their cash balances, and these balances can be lent in turn to other traders who want to increase their money liabilities and so increase their spending. These other traders might take the view that the lower prices available on the first group of commodities represents a bargain, and use the borrowed money to finance expenditure of those same commodities, thus bidding up the price and limiting effects on the second group of traders.

In this view of the world any excess supply or demand in one market must simply carry over to another so that the sum of excess demand and supply in the system must always equal zero (Say's law). Instead of traders having a notional demand which cannot be translated into effective demand because of a financing constraint, prices react across the system to ensure that any displacement of effective demand in one market is mediated into an increase in effective demand in another market. The increases and decreases knock on across the system until the equilibrium position has been reached with all resources fully employed.

In terms of our example, the fall in the first group of traders' expectations may produce a fall in planned spending and thus a fall in the second group's actual receipts, but because prices are assumed to be flexible the fall in expenditure is not translated into a fall in quantity sold. Total receipts may be lower but that is matched by a compensating increase in money balances among the first group and that increase is mediated through the system until it is translated into effective demand. The process of exchange in a money economy: commodity–money–commodity does not matter; nor does the resulting problem of the 'dual decision' over spending and financing. Prices in the classical model still act to unite the system into a harmonious whole – yet this can only happen if the same rules hold for the money economy as for the barter economy, i.e. that all traders must trade and all transactions must ultimately match. But traders are uncertain; they do take a view of the future; and money does stand between the exact matching of transactions. The classical school can only deny the Keynesian view of the market process as essentially quantity-adjusting by insisting that the old maxims hold; that time, uncertainty, and money change nothing. But those are the very issues at dispute.

Keynesian price and quantity adjustment in a four-market economy

To make the issue clearer consider the process of adjustment in an economy of four interrelated markets: a labour market, a commodity market, a securities market, and a money market. In the labour market entrepreneurs hire labour to contribute towards the production of commodities and borrow the money to invest in plant and machinery by issuing bonds in a securities market. Householders' income is earned from selling their labour to entrepreneurs, and the income can either be spent on commodities or saved by buying bonds in the securities market. For ease of exposition, the production of both investment goods and consumer goods is counted as commodity production, so that the commodity markets are finding clearing prices and quantities for both categories of good. Finally, the money market is a residual market; cash balances accumulate here if transactors are holding cash rather than buying commodities, hiring labour, or investing in securities. The starting position is assumed to be one in which each individual market has 'cleared', so that not only is each market in an equilibrium but by definition so is the whole economy. Any disturbance to these equilibrium quantities will either take the form of excess supply (ES) (supply having risen or demand having fallen) or excess demand (ED) (supply having fallen or demand having risen); the analytic categories of excess supply and demand thus exhaust the description of any potential shock to the system.

The distinction between the two views of how the market can be expected to function is this: in the classical view any excess demand in one market will be exactly paralleled by excess supply in another market, and the price movement in the two markets will knock on round the system to produce a new equilibrium. At every stage in the process the sum of effective demand across all the economy's markets is equal to the sum of aggregate supply across those same markets. The effective demand may be taking place in different markets to the original market but it can never be 'lost'; if it were, the sum total would no longer equal zero. Prices move to bring about quantity adjustments and so bring the system to equilibrium.

In the Keynesian view the demand can get 'lost', the total of excess demand and supply need not sum to zero, and prices need not act to keep effective demand and supply permanently in balance once the initial position has been disturbed. The economy will be quantity-adjusting rather than price-adjusting.

Table 1

	Labour services	Commodities	Securities	Money	Sum
Initial Equilibrium state	0	0	0	0	0
Stage 1	0	ES	ED	0	0
Stage 2	0	ES	0	ED	0
New income equilibrium	ES	0	0	ED	>0

Source: Leijonhufvud (1979) *On Keynesian Economics and the Economics of Keynes*, p. 86.

In Table 1 at the initial stage all four markets are in equilibrium. Let us suppose that there is an increase in business pessimism following (say) a gloomy business survey. A number of entrepreneurs revise their expectations of future profits downwards and cut back their investment spending; immediately there is an impact in two of the markets. In the commodity markets there is an excess supply as demand for investment goods falls; and in the securities markets the entrepreneurs stop issuing as many bonds now that they have less investment to finance, and an excess demand for bonds appears as the same flow of savings find less bonds in which to invest. The question is: what is the process of 'adjustment' to this shock?

In the classical/Walrasian world, prices instantly react to keep the aggregate price/quantity relationship in the four-market economy exactly as it was before; that is, there is no fall in aggregate effective demand or supply. Leon Walras, for example, would argue that a fresh auction would now be held, and that different prices would then emerge in order to ensure that the same quantities of goods overall were traded. Because there had been a deterioration in confidence, prices of bonds would have to be higher to persuade entrepreneurs to issue them, and prices of commodities would have to be lower to persuade those same entrepreneurs to spend the proceeds on purchases of commodities. The relative price of bonds in terms of commodities would have to change in order to maintain the quantities produced/issued, given that expectations of future profits had fallen. In the Stage 1 part of the adjustment process, then, tâtonnement would translate the excess demand and supply into different relative prices, equilibrium is achieved and the quantities net out to zero – as in Stage 1 of Table 1.

If we do not feel happy with the idea of a *deus ex machina* descending on the four markets and trying out various combinations of prices on the market transactors until an equilibrium of intentions is achieved, then we can always trace an adjustment process solely through the price mechanism. Here it must be accepted that there will be transitional costs, frictional unemployment, and the like – but the fundamental mechanism is the same. Firstly, there has to be a ranking of how quickly prices will respond in the various markets to quantity changes. Inevitably one market will respond faster than another, and this market can become the locus of adjustment. Let us say it is the securities market.

As fewer bonds come on to the market so the price is bid up by savers who want to hold bonds in their portfolio; both their desire to save and their income remain the same, so that the flow of money into the security market remains as before. Those who issue bonds find that the receipt from any issue is higher now that the price is higher, so they have more potential spending power.

In the commodity markets prices are still unchanged, or only beginning to fall as producers, feeling the shortfall in effective demand, attempt to price their production back into the market. This process is inevitably slower than the adjustment in the security markets, but the lower prices tease those entrepreneurs who have issued securities at the new higher prices into the commodity market. Their increased demand from their higher than expected receipts from security sales compensates for the fall in demand from elsewhere, and finally an equilibrium is achieved with a different set of relative prices to reflect the changing balance of risk but with full employment in all the economy's markets. The transitional costs flow from the time lag involved in producers finding the alternative demand, and in the trial and error in setting the prices that produce the equilibrium. During this period there are production cut-backs, lay-offs, and so on, but finally the market automatically generates the necessary compensating increase in demand. The destabilisation never gets beyond Stage 1.

This result is achieved by the assumption that all assets in a market economy are traded, whether they are stocks of bonds or flows of production. Money makes no difference, for the rules are essentially those of a barter economy. Transactors command a stock or a flow of wealth, and they necessarily want to find the price at which the assets can be exchanged so as to best meet their preferences (which we can assume is to maximise their advantage). Definitionally savers will bid up the price of bonds; definitionally producers will lower the price of commodities; and definitionally entrepreneurs, confronted with a 'cheap' offer, will be attracted into the market as their proceeds from bond sales are higher than expected. The system is pre-set to deliver the desired result.

The Keynesian objection is this: in a market economy the nature of exchange is commodity/money/commodity, and this forces each transactor to take a dual decision every time he buys or sells. If he buys, he needs to know how the purchase will be financed; if he sells, he has to decide how he chooses to hold the money receipts – in money, in a financial asset, or to be spent immediately. The purchase and the sale will almost certainly take place at different times, and so the transactor has to take a view on whether tomorrow's price will be the same as today's. In other words, he is unavoidably at risk as he tries to assess his likely pattern of money spending against his likely pattern of his money receipts. This arises because there is money (so the economy is not run on barter lines), there is time (tomorrow's market conditions will be different from today's) and uncertainty (to buy now, or later; to hold cash, or financial assets).

As a result the adjustment process cannot be as the classical economists suggest. In the first place, savers are being asked to bid the price of bonds up, which conversely means a lower interest rate, just at the moment there is a decline in business expectations. They are being expected to pay more to receive a lower yield as gloom descends on the investment and business community. Herein lies the importance of expectations and the unpredictable nature of the future. Suppose a saver believes that an interest rate of r is normal, and at *r* he is accustomed to purchase *n* bonds. Why should he choose to hold more bonds at a lower interest rate? This only makes sense if he believes that *r* is no longer normal, and that *r* has now made a once-and-for-all jump to a new low level. But the saver cannot be certain of this. Although the system needs him to believe it so that the price of bonds will rise, an alternative strategy is to hold his savings in cash pending a fall in the price of bonds and *r* returning to its former level. Thus a rise in bond prices and a fall in interest rates cannot be taken for granted; instead of bidding up the price of securities, investors may choose to hold their uninvested funds in cash, 'hoarding' as Keynes called it. It is quantity, not price, that responds to the change in expectations; as a result there is a Stage 2 where the bond market stays in equilibrium as savers hoard the cash that had formerly been invested in bonds. The money market now has excess demand for cash, the bond market is in equilibrium, and the commodity market has excess supply (Table 1).

In the commodity markets producers are beginning to feel the fall in sales, and are reducing their prices to try and encourage demand. But on this occasion there is no increase in firms' receipts from increased bond prices. Traders are unwilling to run up liabilities so production is cut. They may try and set reservation prices as they go out to 'search' for new business, but what they find is not the notional demand around equilibrium prices and quantities (as in tâtonnement), but the effective demand based on traders' now-lowered expectations of future receipts. In this world, price cannot pull the system back on the rails because the first reaction in every market is to hedge bets and cut back on quantities – whether the security markets, or the commodity markets. There are no stabilisers; the system is moving into a tail-spin.

At the end of Chapter 2 of the *General Theory*, Keynes (1978: 21) claimed that classical theory depended on the assumptions:

(1) that the real wage is equal to the marginal disutility of the existing employment;

(2) that there is no such thing as involuntary unemployment in the strict sense;

(3) that supply creates its own demand in the sense that the aggregate demand price is equal to the aggregate supply price for all levels of output and employment.

These three assumptions, however, all amount to the same thing in the sense that they all stand and fall together, any one of them logically involving the other two.

If we follow through this quantity-responding adjustment process, we can get some grasp of what Keynes meant. At the end of Stage 2 the four-market economy is spinning downwards: there is hoarding in the money market as savers refuse to believe that interest rates can fall; in the commodity markets traders are concerned to protect their balance sheets and their budgets so they are cutting production; and in the labour market the fall in sales means that labour's marginal physical product is no longer equalled by marginal revenue. Demand, like the tide, is rolling back and leaving labour beached. In these circumstances labour is too costly given the money wage, and gradually an excess supply of labour appears; unemployment rises.

It is in this sense that the first of Keynes's postulates must be assessed. His claim was that the classical theory requires that the real wage be equal to the marginal disutility of existing employment; that is, the price paid to labour to forego leisure, the assumption being that as all the other markets in the economy are in equilibrium there can be no other obstacle to labour's employment than its refusal to give up leisure. But if the economy is quantity-adjusting then labour's marginal product falls willy-nilly through factors beyond its control, namely the fall in effective demand. The real wage, the commodities that an hour of labour time will buy, falls because sales fall; but this does nothing to price labour into work because it is only an increase in effective demand that will make labour's effort marketable and worth while re-employing.

This lead Keynes to the second postulate of classical economics which he believed to be wrong, that it denied the existence of involuntary unemployment: a state where workers cannot price themselves into jobs however low they offer to cut their wages. But it is impossible in a quantity-adjusting world for labour to price itself into work. Workers looking for work ask for a wage to be paid in money – this much is obvious. With that money they will then demand commodities. If the unemployed workers as a group asked for commodities directly, then producers would comprehend that there was an unsatisfied demand for commodities; but if workers ask for money, at whatever price they charge for their labour, it is not apparent to the producer that this request for work will translate into demand for his product. A money economy does *not* operate in the same way as a barter economy. To follow Leijonhufvud (1979: 90),

the fact that there exists a potential barter bargain of goods for labour services that would be mutually agreeable to producers as a group and labour as a group is irrelevant to the motion of the system. The individual steel-producer cannot pay a newly hired worker by handing over to him his physical product (nor will the worker try to feed his family on a ton and a half of cold-rolled steel a week) . . . the dynamic properties of an economic system depend upon 'its transaction structure'.

And what does Leijonhufvud mean by the 'transaction structure'? Consider the employers' balance sheet. If they hire workers at the current money wage then they immediately incur increased liabilities; but can they anticipate any possibility of an increased inflow of income to compensate, an increase in sales? Although it is true that the hiring of the additional workers will lift monetary demand for the system as a whole, an individual employer cannot know this, nor can it be expected given existing expectations of demand. The classical solution is for money wages to be lowered in an attempt to price unemployed workers back into work. But this implies a compensating fall in monetary demand which perversely has the contrary affect through its lowering of expectations. Then take the workers' notional balance sheet. One solution would be for them in aggregate to increase their liabilities, raise their spending, and so lift entrepreneurs' expectations of sales. Thus emboldened employers would hire labour, who could then pay off their liabilities with their wages. But labour, even less than employers, cannot be certain that the increase in liabilities is likely to be only temporary. The market is deadlocked.

The solution is for the price of real wages to fall while money demand remains constant, so that the cost of labour falls while expectations remain unchanged. But this solution is impossible for either employers or labour to organise, because the only price under their control is the money wage. The real wage is the relationship between the money wage and the price of wage goods, and the price of wage goods is not at issue in the labour bargain. Not only does the 'transaction structure' of the economy – how 'dual decision'-making transactors actually interact – imply quantity rather than price adjustment when an equilibrium is disturbed, it also makes it difficult for markets to clear without unused resources.

The settling point of this adjustment is the 'New income' equilibrium (see Table 1) and brings us to the last of the classical postulates whose assumptions Keynes disputed: the Walrasian view that supply creates its own demand. Output contracts to a point where it reaches a 'core' level of demand, and so the commodity markets find a level where there is an identity between supply and demand. The problem of excess supply has been solved by producing less. The fall in income equally solves the problem of hoarding in the money markets; it becomes purposeless and the excess demand for money disappears. Security, commodity, and money markets all find an 'identilibrium' where quantities of supply and demand in each individual market reach an identity, albeit well below a full employment of resources equilibrium. In the labour markets there is an excess supply of labour unable to price itself back into work because at the 'identilibrium' levels of output any additional production has no value to the entrepreneur, whatever the price of labour.

We have arrived at an equilibrium where notwithstanding the fact that there is excess supply of labour, there is no sign of any excess demand: excess demand and supply do not cancel each other out and sum to zero – the value of the sum is greater than zero. It is this above all that characterises the Keynesian view of how the market economy functions. In the words of Robert Clower (1965: 122) 'Contrary to the findings of traditional theory excess demand may fail to appear anywhere in the economy under conditions of less than full employment.' This is a phenomenon that classical theory cannot admit, but which we know from the real world is commonplace.

The only way out of the deadlock that our four-market economy has found itself in is for a Walrasian auctioneer or some guardian angel to descend and to ask all the agents what their plans are. He would begin by inviting the unemployed workers to reveal what expenditures they would undertake if they were employed at a given range of wages, and to what extent they would rebuild their portfolios of securities. He would then approach the producers, and indicate that a higher level of demand and thus output would be possible if they were to employ more workers. In the money markets the auctioneer would invite savers to reveal the terms on which they would cease hoarding money and buy the securities that the producers needed to issue in order to increase production. By constantly trying out different ranges of prices the auctioneer would finally arrive at a 'vector' which matched all the intentions of the actors in the system – and a full-employment equilibrium could be created.

In fact no *deus ex machina* in the form of a godly auctioneer is likely to rescue the economy, so the agents have to struggle with the situation as they find it – and the chances of success are not very promising. The question as to whether the markets are competitive, or solely responsive to the two axes, price and quantity, is beside the point; the issue is whether price alone is sufficient to bind them together so that all resources are fully employed. Unemployed labour cannot communicate what its demand intentions would be were it fully employed, and as a result there is no reason for producers to step up their production and hire new workers for a nonexistent demand; equally in the money markets, hoarders of money are preventing security prices from reaching a price that might persuade producers in their guise as investors to re-evaluate their decision and borrow money in order to invest. In a barter economy each agent would be obliged to reveal his intentions and plans as he traded, and the existence of unemployed resources would become quickly known. In a money economy relying on prices there can be no certainty as to what quantities would be traded with a different structure of prices. Workers need to let it be known that they are consumers as well as wage earners; producers need to let it be known that they are borrowers of money as well as investors of it; and hoarders of money need to let it be known that their decision to hoard would be different if producer/investors and worker/consumers were able to organise a higher and more profitable level of output. But it is just this kind of information that price is unable to convey – and there is no *deus ex machina* to bail the system out. Instead of the Marshallian analysis where price leads and quantity follows to produce an inevitable equilibrium, the equation is turned on its head – quantity leads and price follows, and there is no necessity for equilibrium, certainly not at full employment. There is no harmony and we do not live in the best of all possible worlds.

Notes

1. Axel Leijonhufvud, (1979: 394, fnote).
   See also Bastiat's remarks in *Harmonies Economiques* quoted by Keynes in *The End of Laissez-Faire* (Hogarth Press, 1926: 24, 25.) 'I undertake,' he says, 'to demonstrate the Harmony of those laws of Providence which govern human society. What makes these laws harmonious and not discordant is, that all principles, all motives, all springs of action, all interests, co-operate towards a grand final result. . . . And that result is, the indefinite approximation of all classes towards a level, which is always rising; in other words, the equalisation of individuals in the general amelioration'. And when, like other priests, he drafts his Credo, it runs as follows: 'I believe that He who has arranged the material universe has not withheld His regard from the arrangements of the social world. I believe that He has combined and caused to move in harmony free agents as well as inert molecules. . . . I believe that the invincible social tendency is a constant approximation of men towards a common moral, intellectual, and physical level, with, at the same time, a progressive and indefinite

elevation of that level. I believe that all that is necessary to the gradual and peaceful development of humanity is that its tendencies should not be disturbed, nor have the liberty of their movements destroyed.'

2. In 1951 K. Arrow published *Social Choice and Individual Values* setting out what has come to be known as 'Arrow's impossibility theorem'. With four restrictive assumptions, Arrow shows that it is impossible for a set of individuals who have different preferences between three outcomes to organise a choice consistent with these constitutional constraints. As the constraints correspond exactly to the claimed attributes of a competitive equilibrium this suggests that if a set of individuals were to vote on which of three goods they wanted to use as money they would be unable to come to an agreement. The constraints are:

(a) *Collective Rationality*. The system, like a competitive market, should be able to handle any number of voters and any combination of preferences and still produce an outcome that was rational for all voters.

(b) *Independence of irrelevant alternatives*. The system should be able to produce its results entirely from its own mechanisms and preference rankings: there should be no recourse to an extraneous agency to solve any problems. Again, this assumption is no more than claiming that a competitive market should be able to co-ordinate economic agents' plans spontaneously.

(c) *Non-dictatorship*. No outcome should favour one voter or set of voters. This is parallel to saying that in a competitive market all agents should be price-takers.

(d) *Pareto Principle*. No participant should be worse off for having contributed to the final and binding decision. This corresponds to the claim of Pareto optimality for a trading system.

There can be no Constitution which satisfies these four constraints; and it would be impossible to find agreement in a system in which these constraints held. Finding a good that would stand as money if there were different preferences as to which good it would be, is therefore impossible – if the market were to correspond to a competitive market. Money therefore may embody the fact that competitive equilibria are impossible; its very existence could be a proof of the inability of the market to arrive at a competitive equilibrium. I have not pursued this line of enquiry any further, but I believe it holds important insights. For a good account of the impossibility theorem see Alfred Mckay (1980) *Arrow's Theorem. The Paradox of Social Choice*. Yale University Press.

3. There is an analogous idea in R. H. Coase's (1937) 'Theory of the firm' (*Economica*, Nov.). The firm comes into existence as a consequence of transaction costs. At some level of output it becomes cheaper to organise production in a firm rather than contract everything out to the market. The co-ordination of production within

a firm (where relations do not change constantly with market conditions) is cheaper than co-ordination by the market because of the administrative and managerial problems of organising many hundreds of market decisions into one productive effort.

References

Clower, R. W. (1965) 'The Keynesian counter-revolution: a theoretical appraisal', in F. H. Hahn and F. P. R. Brechling (eds), *The Theory of Interest Rates*. Macmillan.

Diamond, P. (1982) 'Aggregate Demand Management in Search Equilibrium', *Journal of Political Economy*, (Oct.)

Hart, O. (1983) 'Optimal Labour Contracts Under Asymmetric Information: an Introduction' *Review of Economic Studies*, (Jan.)

Hellwig, M. E. (1976) 'A Model of Monetary Exchange' *Research Memorandum* No. 202. Econometric Research Programme Princeton Univ.

Hicks, J. R. (1978) *Value and Capital*. Clarendon Press.

Keynes, J. M. (1937) 'The general theory of employment', *Quarterly Journal of Economics*, (Feb.)

Keynes, J. M. (1978) *The General Theory of Employment, Interest and Money*. Macmillan/Royal Economic Society.

Leijonhufvud, Axel (1979) *On Keynesian Economics and the Economics of Keynes*. Oxford U.P.

Lipsey, R. G. (1980) *An Introduction to Positive Economics* (5th edn) Weidenfeld and Nicholson.

Lucas, R. E. & Prescott, E. C. (1974), 'Equilibrium Search & Unemployment', Journal of Economic Theory (Feb).

Walras, Leon (1954) *Eléments d' Economie Politique Pure*, trans. William Jaffé. Allen and Unwin: London. Irwin: Homewood, Illinois.

Chapter 6

Time and money

Summary

This chapter attempts to sketch the detail of Keynesian theory; in particular the key role played by liquidity-preference in driving the market economy along, and the importance of consumption, saving, and investment operating in the economy as 'aggregated' categories. The chapter begins with a brief review of how economists, both 'Keynesian' and classical, have managed to misinterpret the Keynesian 'vision'. The functioning of the labour market has tended to dominate economic debate rather than the question of liquidity-preference and the portfolio preferences of the financial institutions. Keynesians have allowed the agenda, and thus the discourse of debate, to be set by the orthodoxies of economics. The use of IS/LM analysis has accelerated this process. On the other hand, the proffered counter-arguments of the classical traditionalists would suggest that they have substantially misunderstood the essence of Keynesian theory.

The chapter then turns to the core of the Keynesian system: liquidity-preference. The rate of interest cannot be determined by the interaction of two schedules; a demand for and supply of money. The problem is the same as price and quantity determination in any market; plans depend on prices and expectations of prices, but price, if it is to co-ordinate plans, requires a stable and converging intention in relation to price. But this it cannot have in a money exchange economy because not only are agents' expectations unstable and potentially non-convergent, but so are their actions. The fact that quantities traded *ex post* are in an identity does not mean that plans have been co-ordinated by price; plans may still be very disparate, but, like two sides of a balance sheet, must be in an identity. Savings and investment decisions, dominated by expectations, are the most volatile of all; and the idea that plans are co-ordinated by the rate of interest, proven by the fact the market always clears – which it must *ex post* – seemed to Keynes to be 'circular reasoning' at its worst.

Liquidity-preference is at the heart of the market economy. It is not a 'demand for money' function because it has no stable, plottable relationships by definition. Investment and the level of economic activity thus adjust to liquidity preferences – the rate of interest and the portfolio preferences of savers. At the macro-level consumption, savings, and investment are categories that cut across sub-market systems and which provide the market system with its motion. The classical notion of the market as a series of interconnected sub-markets, all tending to clear, is thus highly misleading as an interpretation of the market economy.

Uncomprehending economics

The 'Keynesians'

It is said that Keynes's *General Theory* is a badly organised and badly written book which allows for any number of interpretations, and certainly there have been no shortage since its publication. But if we take an understanding of the notion of involuntary unemployment and the adjustment process as outlined in the previous chapter as a kind of base line from which to judge the degree of comprehension, it is clear that there has been very little. In the years after the Second World War the message was simple: the old classical/Walrasian view that an economy (given the free movement of prices) could only arrive at a full employment equilibrium was wrong, and therefore the Government had an obligation to influence economic magnitudes to yield full employment. But there was no accompanying intellectual effort to explore just why.

So it was that Klein (1949) could write that the Keynesian supply curve of labour and definition of involuntary unemployment were unimportant to the *General Theory*, and that explaining un-employment in terms of imperfections in the labour market was easy. Keynes 'did not really understand what he had written' and the real importance of the *General Theory* was the proof that interest rates do not act as they do in the classical system to make investment and saving reach an identity at full employment.

It was this kind of interpretation that began a weakening in the post-war comprehension of what it was that the Keynesian revolution implied. A further nail in the coffin was provided by the

'IS/LM' curve analysis developed by Hicks and Hansen, to show how the investment and financial markets yielded equilibrium at non-full employment levels of income: its objective was sincere, but the result was (as we shall argue later in the chapter) to reintroduce classical economics through the back door. The whole point of liquidity-preference theory is that there is no stable relationship between a given interest rate, the classes of financial asset held, the level of saving, and the level of investment; but to box this into the IS/LM approach, and to assume that expectations are *given* – this is to traduce Keynes to the point of betrayal.

Keynesianism became understood as 'demand management' – to make good the shortages of demand that the market could not spontaneously provide itself; and 'incomes policy' – to provide the cut in real wage levels that the markets again could not produce themselves. But this is Hamlet without the prince. What of liquidity preference and the portfolio preferences of the financial institutions (see the latter part of this chapter and Chapter 8)? Partly out of intellectual failure and partly because the pressing policy problem was inflation, Keynesians became more and more obsessed with the wage-determination element in the *General Theory*; the fact that Keynes argued that wages tended to be inflexible and that trade unions resist cuts in money wages has married neatly with the more contemporary observation that trade unions use their market power to insist on money-wage increases that are well beyond any likely increase in their marginal money product. Thus Keynesians in Britain – notably Meade, Matthews *et al.* – have become increasingly interested in how the State can intervene effectively in the labour market to regulate both unemployment and inflation, so that demand management and the conventional tools of Keynesian intervention in the economy can once again become operative.

There has been a parallel development in the USA with a whole school (Okun, Lerner, Weintraub) drawing attention to the wage-cost element in inflation, and arguing for some form of public policy towards wages and salaries so that the labour market will yield the variations in real wages over the business cycle that can sustain full or near-full employment. But whether the object of criticism is the structure of wage bargaining (Vines *et al* 1982) or just plain old institutional sclerosis (Okun 1981) the focus is the same; it is the inflexibility of money wages that is at the root of the market economy's difficulties. The problem with this direction of enquiry is that it drifts closer and closer to the discourse of economics that Keynes was challenging. It is true that the processes of wage determination are inefficient; but contemporary Keynesians have got

113

stuck in the foothills, and their near obsession with mechanisms to improve the working of the labour market almost completely obscures from view the summit that Keynes invites us to climb. The observation about the relative inflexibility of money-wages is only the starting point – not the end.

The confusion begins with Keynes's acceptance that not only do workers resist cuts in money-wages, but further that it is not irrational on their part to do so. As far as labour is concerned, a fall in money-wages implies a fall in real wages because there can be no certainty that the price of wage-good will fall by the same proportion; nor can this fall be supposed by economic theory. It may be rational as far as the market system is concerned for money-wages to be flexible; but that rationality cannot be assumed for the behaviour of wage-bargainers. The price of wage-goods is not under their control; they cannot organise their bargaining stance around the assumption that wage-good prices will fall, nor can they be expected to penalise themselves for a general interest that in the last resort cannot be guaranteed. Thus in any market system the price of wages can be expected to be slow to respond to any quantity changes, so expecting real wage cuts to be the locus of any adjustment to changing conditions in the labour market or in the overall level of economic activity is likely to be slow, laborious, and painful. And in the long run, declared Keynes, we are all dead.

From this observation, which clearly matches the behaviour of wage-earners in the real world, Keynes went on to launch a fundamental assault on the basis tenets of classical economic theory. Classical economists could accept that wages were 'sticky', but what they could not admit was that even if wages were not sticky then there could still be *involuntary unemployment*. The wage bargain in classical theory was a trade-off between labour's desire for leisure and labour's value to the entrepreneur. Yes, it was true that in real life there were deviations from the model, but that was only because of unenlightened behaviour by trade unions and workers; if they behaved like economic man the problem of involuntary unemployment could not exist. It was this postulate of classical economics that Keynes wanted to challenge (Keynes 1978: 15).

Men are involuntarily unemployed if, in the event of a small rise in the price of wage-goods relatively to the money wage, both the aggregate supply of labour willing to work for the current money-wage and the aggregate demand for it at that wage would be greater than the existing volume of employment.

This definition has been attacked for being unnecessarily cumbersome but the wording is vital if the Keynesian message is to be put across. The cut in real wages has been defined as resulting from a rise in the price of wage-goods relative to the money-wage, that is, as a cut that happens to the labour force rather than being produced by any cut in money-wages. It is only in this way that labour can 'reveal' its willingness to work at a lower real wage, because what was called in the last chapter the 'transaction structure' of the labour market prevents labour pricing itself into work through lowering its money-wage.

What prevents employers hiring unemployed labour is not the level of money wages, but the level of existing demand and *expectation of future demand*; lowering money-wages lowers effective demand now, without doing anything to promise an increase in monetary demand in the future. Labour cannot price itself into work; it is only when adjustment takes place around the same level of effective monetary demand that labour can be rehired; in other words, real wages have to fall at the same time as effective demand stays constant. This can only be achieved if the current money-wage buys fewer wage-goods because the price of wage-goods rises; if in these conditions the supply of, and demand for labour rises then we know that the lower real wage will produce a higher level of employment, and conversely at the old wage there was involuntary unemployment. It is because the price mechanism alone cannot overcome the transaction structure of the labour market that the problem of involuntary unemployment can come to exist.

It is exactly this view of the world that is lost in the concern about incomes policies, etc. The issue is not whether wages are inflexible but if they *were* flexible whether there could still be involuntary unemployment. The fact of their inflexibility gives the system an inbuilt bias; but can the price mechanism or any adaptation save it? By concentrating on how to regulate the level of real wages through State intervention, the contemporary Keynesian is conceding the classical case, and attempting to produce the real wage cut that the markets themselves cannot organise: the object being to price labour back into work. Typically some form of 'demand management' is advocated alongside the incomes policy, so that the overall effect is to cut real wages and increase effective demand.

This is a laudable objective, but it loses the essence of the Keynesian theoretical position, which is why should such action become necessary in the first place? It becomes necessary because of transaction structure of the labour market and the limits of the price mechanism to 'broker' expectations (see Ch. 3), and wage-bargainers are no less likely (in any case) to resist a state initiative to cut their money and thus their real wages than they are to resist an employer's initiative. Economists like Meade, for example, seem to have shed the Keynesian perspective on how the wage bargain must be located in terms of *the motion of the market as a system*. As a result of their concentration on the problems of collective bargaining (which undoubtedly exist) they see the world in much the same way as the classicists.

This, to follow Hahn (1980), is the litmus test between the classical/Walrasian/monetarist view of the world and the Keynesian. As soon as an economist argues for (say) an incomes policy on the grounds that the labour market has imperfections in setting the 'clearing price' of labour, he is leaving the Keynesian camp. The idea of involuntary unemployment marks a complete break with the Walrasian view of how markets operate. The Keynesian interpretation of markets emphasises, as argued in the previous chapter, the manner in which uncertainty, changing expectations, time, and money all combine to put the load of adjustment in markets on quantity rather than price. In the labour market this manifests itself as involuntary unemployment; in the financial markets as the hoarding of money; and in the product markets as the cutting of production. For the system as a whole, adjustment to a change in expectations and the consequent revision in quantities will be shouldered by output, income, and employment rather than relative prices moving to bring the system back to equilibrium after the initial shock. This is the Keynesian 'vision' which is muddied by the contemporary concern among Keynesians of how 'rigidities' in the labour market can lead to inflation and unemployment; a concern shared by Walrasians. We may agree with Klein (1980: 83) that it is not hard to describe unemployment in terms of 'various frictions, imperfections and rigidities of the real world' either in the classical or the Keynesian system; but to go on and dismiss the concept of involuntary unemployment as he did is actually to miss the whole point.

Keynes himself was anxious to drive the argument home; a Keynesian system is not just one where the economy may quite easily settle at a non-full employment equilibrium; it is a system which insists that there are many potential resting places for the economy, and the actual path the economy will take in practice depends on a series of subtle and complicated relationships that centre around expectations, the rate of interest, and the portfolio preferences of the financial institutions – about the last of which

116

especially, there is currently a marked lack of interest in 'Keynesian' circles.

The degree of instability of the economy depends on the price inelasticity of the various markets; that is, if quantities take the principal burden of adjustment and prices are largely ineffective then the economy will be very volatile indeed, with the price level and the level of output oscillating hugely. Suppose, for example, one were to fix the level of money and real wages by pre-ordaining that wage earners were to receive a fixed quantity of 'wage-goods', then in this hypothetical situation the whole burden of adjustment would be shouldered by quantities – and even violent movements in prices would be ineffective in changing the motion of the economy; in fact, Keynes argued (1978: 239), there *would* be a 'violent oscillation of money prices'. In the event of entrepreneurs experiencing a fall in quantities sold, and being obliged to remunerate labour with the pre-ordained quantities of wage-goods, the only response could be to reduce the quantity of labour employed while lowering prices in an attempt to stimulate sales. But lowering prices would bring forth no extra sales because the potential market would have been reduced as the result of the increased unemployed – thus a fresh round of unemployment, falling prices, and falling sales; and labour helpless to change anything because of the pre-ordained and fixed real wage. 'For every small fluctuation in the propensity to consume or the inducement to invest', wrote Keynes (1978: 239), 'would cause money prices to rush violently between zero, and infinity.' The tendency to quantity adjustment is so strong that in this special (contrived) case the price mechanism is rendered useless: it has no impact on expectations and on the behaviour of market agents – indeed it is for this very reason that the oscillation of money prices is so wild.

The Keynesian claim that the market economy is inherently unstable, and that there is no guarantee that it will either arrive at or even tend to a point of balance which ensures full employment or the 'best' use of resources, is a very shocking one. In these terms it is as much a watershed between nineteenth- and twentieth-century thought as Einstein's contribution to physics or Freud's to psychology: Keynes shifts economics from the classicists' world of harmonious and natural laws which inexorably exert a 'gravitational' pull towards balance to a much more twentieth-century conception of the economy as a dynamic process with instability and uncertainty the rule. Just as cybernetics challenges head-on the vision of Newtonian physics, so Keynesianism challenges the vision of Adam Smith: but whereas Newtonian physics has given way before the face of new insights and discoveries, economics continues to embody a view of the world that would be unsustainable if it were launched today. The Keynesian critique has made nothing like the progress of its intellectual parallels in other disciplines.

Some of the responsibility for what has happened must fall to the economic establishment – represented for example in its unreflecting use of the IS/LM framework, but there is also a fair measure to be borne by Keynes's political reception. By bastardising Keynes into the simple advocacy of high government spending, both the Right and the Left secured important political objectives. The Left were given the means to temper the Marxist/Socialist tradition in British politics into a devotion to the idea of a high public spending social democracy, while the Right translated Keynesianism straight into the tradition of paternalistic intervention to preserve the status quo. It suited neither to interpret Keynesianism as it actually was: a demand for the State to change the behaviour of financiers and businessmen by prosecuting an active fiscal policy in tandem with an assault on the portfolio preferences of the financial institutions – perhaps even their socialisation. For the Right the City was sacrosanct; for the Left the City was a sanctum that could only be stormed at the risk of colossal loss of financial confidence – and in any case the prime objective of policy was never to make the market system function well. The end result has been that Keynes has fallen into disrepute, indeed in some quarters become a pariah; but what post-war Keynesianism – in theory and in practice – has had to do with the economics of Keynes is another matter.

The classical tradition and the 'real-balance' effect

In a sense the two worlds – the Keynesian and the classical – were so far apart that it was always unlikely that the latter would comprehend the challenge to the very discourse of economics that Keynes represented. And this incomprehension is on display in one of the first critical reactions to Keynes; that of Professor Pigou. The idea that the economy had no tendency to equilibrium was inadmissible; it just could not be possible. Even if one conceded that quantities might be the first to adjust to any 'shock', and that prices would be weak in turning around any fall in quantities traded in the economy, that did not mean that the ultimate point at which the economy would settle was entirely a matter of caprice. The idea that the price level might theoretically shoot from zero to infinity or vice versa and that prices might have no impact on the quantity adjustment at work in a market economy, or on the tendency towards stabilising expectations, seemed economic lunacy to Pigou. There had to be stabilising influences at work; and Pigou provided an answer, the so-called 'Pigou effect'.

Suppose there is a downward movement of expectations, and the economy begins the adjustment process outlined in the previous chapter. Now, if the money stock is given and banking policy is such that the money stock is not allowed to contract in proportion to the fall in the price level, then the quantities of money 'hoarded' as the price level falls must at least stay constant. As a result the exchange ratio between the quantity of money and the quantity of commodities must improve in terms of money; a pound note buys proportionally more commodities than it did before the price level fell. At some point this increase in the value of money will lead to money being transformed into holdings of commodities. Or in plainer language, the increase in the value of money in a deflation will make people progressively less willing to hoard it and progressively more willing to spend it; thus stabilising and ultimately turning around the economy. There must come a point where hoarded money will be traded for commodities and thus stimulate demand for labour: it may not come from the price mechanism directly but from the increase in the value of real 'balance' of money as the price level falls. As goods *must* be traded, so money will be traded for goods as goods become cheaper. The idea of equilibrium is safe again.

The first problem with the Pigou effect is its fundamental view of how a money exchange economy works. There is an explicit denial of both what we have labelled the 'dual-decision hypothesis' and the 'transaction structure' of the market economy. In Pigou's world-view transactors are predefined as wanting to trade whatever their view of the future; because there must be trade, money will be traded for goods once they have become cheap enough to warrant their purchase given the changed expectations. For the real-balance effect to work, holders of money are assumed to drop the expectations that made them hold money in the first place, and translate their holdings of money into commodities as relative values change. But the expectation that asset and commodity prices are falling, which made them hold money in the first place, is now being borne out by events – why should they change their mind? The real-balance effect is at bottom a Walrasian device playing the Keynesian quantity game. It is now a change in relative quantity values that brings the system back to equilibrium; a device which the whole Keynesian argument is aimed at overturning.

But if the system is quantity- rather than price-adjusting then even the initial assumption of the real-balance advocates is inadmissible; namely, that the money stock remains unchanged. If the authorities act in a neutral fashion, then the very decline in income will lead to a decline in the money stock, *because banks are quantity adjustors too*. As the level of activity falls, so also does the number of bills the banking sector is asked to discount; as cash is mediated into the system via the number of bills that are discounted, a fall in the number of bills will lead to a fall in the money stock. Even if the banks lower the interest rate to encourage the flow of new bills, if quantities are falling in the economy as a whole then a price change of this type will have only a marginal or negligible effect on the quantity of bills demanded because there is no reason for any borrowers to revise their depressed expectations. Consequently the concomitant of a fall in output and the price level is a shrinking of the banking sector's balance sheet, and the money supply declines in the same proportion as prices.

Even if the assumption that the money stock remained unchanged over the cycle were plausible, then there is a further problem over exactly what part of the money stock is supposed to have its terms of exchange improved by a general fall in commodity prices. The money stock is taken not just to mean cash but all means of holding a financial claim on others, i.e. credit lines. If prices fall the exchange ratio of credit in terms of commodities may improve for lenders, but it will fall by an exactly equal amount for the borrower. In other words, any increase in spending by creditors will be exactly compensated by a decrease in spending by debtors. The only 'real-balance' boost to spending will be the extent to which the money stock is held in cash rather than credit (inside money).

For the real-balance effect to work we must therefore assume four things. Firstly that transactors must trade money for commodities if the terms are right, thus 'hoarding' because of expectations is disallowed and conceptually there is a structure of exchange values at which the economy can find an equilibrium. Secondly that transactors will abandon the expectations of falling prices that made them hoard at just the moment prices are falling. Thirdly that the banking sector is not quantity-adjusting; that is, the money stock will remain constant throughout a fall in economic activity. Fourthly that there is a sufficient proportion of the money stock held in cash rather than credit for the real-balance effect to have some impact on levels of effective demand. Presumably there exists a theoretical point where notwithstanding a small amount of cash held in relation to the total volume of commodities, the deflation in commodity prices is such that the sheer scale of the increase in the value of money balances demands that they be transformed into holdings of commodities. It may be true that such a point exists, but like the prospect of labour pricing itself into work, and removing unvoluntary unemployment, finding it is likely to be a time-consuming and uncertain process.

The debate over whether the money exchange economy has the stabilising tendencies the 'real-balance' advocates claim has been conducted with much sound and fury over the years, but the issue is unresolvable. Of course there is a 'real-balance' effect if we can make the qualifying assumptions listed above; but it is precisely those assumptions that Keynes sought to challenge. The rules of an exchange economy do not stay the same once money is used. Transactors are not compelled to trade money for commodities; money may be hoarded because of the 'dark forces of time and ignorance'. Exchange values do not necessarily drive the market economy to an equilibrium of full employment because the economy is fundamentally quantity-adjusting rather than price-adjusting. Thus it cannot be assumed that the money stock will stay the same throughout a decline in economic activity: it must fall because the banking sector is quantity-adjusting too. The future does intrude into the present; thus expectations can prevent prices from co-ordinating the actions of market transactors into a beneficent whole. At these assertions the classicist responds with dull incomprehension. This will surely 'wreck the body of economic theory'. It cannot be true. To the barricades: the theory of the market must be saved!

The classical 'vision' of how the market economy can be expected to function is represented today in an extreme form by the so-called 'monetarist' economists, and the real-balance effect has resurfaced as a wealth effect (Laidler 1980). The phenomenon that requires explanation is inflation, and all the same assumptions about the rationality of market transactors and the constitutional properties of the market have been reburnished and wheeled out again for display before a credulous world. If the quantity of money expands then transactors trade their money for goods; because no concomitant expansion of goods has been allowed for, all that can happen is that the price of goods is bid up: hence inflation. The 'wealth effect' describes the disposition transactors have for holding their assets in a certain preference order; if that ranking is disturbed by an exogenous increase in the quantity of money and the price of some assets unexpectedly rise in consequence, then they will rearrange their portfolio so that it has the same distribution after the increase in the money supply as before; that is, the money will be exchanged for other assets whose relative price has fallen. In this way an increase in the money supply may cause consumption to increase, and if the supply of goods is fixed, *ceteris paribus*, the price level to rise. Again the point at issue is not the internal logic of the argument, but whether the market *does* possess these constitutional properties that automatically produce inflation for a given increase in the money supply. The Keynesian position is that it does not: but that these can be circumstances in which inflation may happen in this way.

Yet this does not mean that 'money does not matter' in the Keynesian perspective; on the contrary, it matters so much that it transforms the nature of the exchange economy. Already we have examined the broad manner in which the economy and its participants might behave if we change the basic conceptions of classical economics; but how in detail does the Keynesian system operate?

Money and the rate of interest

We make our starting point the role of time.

All production is for the purpose of ultimately satisfying a consumer. Time usually elapses, however – and sometimes much time – between the incurring of costs by the producer (with the consumer in view) and the purchase of the output by the ultimate consumer. Meanwhile the entrepreneur (including both the producer and the investor in this description) has to form the best *expectations* he can as to what the consumers will be prepared to pay when he is ready to supply them (directly or indirectly) after the elapse of what may be a lengthy period; and he has no choice but to be guided by *these expectations*, if he is to produce at all by processes which occupy time. (Keynes 1978: 46) [my italics]

The production of commodities involves locking up resources over time with no certainty that the end-product will actually sell for more than the cost of production; an entrepreneur, in short, is at risk. Because production takes time, an entrepreneur must necessarily make a judgement about market conditions in the future when finally his commodities will be offered to the market; 'he has no choice but to be guided by *these expectations*, if he is to produce at all by *processes which occupy time*'. We can visualise the producers of commodities as continually evaluating prospects, making decisions about what level of production they think they should organise given their expectations of future sales.

Now herein lies an important distinction: between the production of goods for immediate consumption (consumer goods), the demand for which can be reckoned to exist in the present or near-present, and the production of goods (capital goods) which contribute to the production of other goods, the demand for which will depend on a calculation about what market conditions will be when those other goods will be sold. The production of a car, for example, is for immediate use; the production of machines with which cars are made depends on how many cars the entrepreneur believes he can sell if he were to order the relevant machines. In a sense, time intrudes into both sets of decisions, because even the production of cars involves some lapse of time before they are finally delivered to car showrooms, during which time market conditions might have changed. The distinctive attribute of a capital good is not so much that the time horizons for its use are longer than a consumer good, which is *fully* used immediately, but that it will produce *a flow of income over time* – a flow of income, moreover, that will fluctuate with changing market conditions. The decision to invest in a physical capital asset, argued Keynes, is parallel to investing in a financial capital asset. Indeed, he postulated that the owner of wealth, 'who has been induced not to hold his wealth in hoarded money still has two alternatives between which to choose. He can lend his money at the current rate of money-interest or he can purchase some kind of capital asset.' (Keynes 1937a: 217) In other words, the attributes of a physical capital asset and a money capital asset are identical as far as a wealth-holder is concerned: both require the outlay of a capital sum; both yield a flow of income over time; and the price of the asset can change.

There are, however, a couple of important differences. A physical capital asset is capable of being newly produced, and the anticipated flow of income depends crucially on the expectations of market conditions in the future. A financial capital asset, a money-loan or bond, has no production cost; its valuation depends on the rate of interest and *expectations* of the rate of interest.

These differences are not important, however, from the point of view of the wealth-holder. As far as he is concerned both assets provide a stream of income over time in return for the initial outlay of a capital sum. He is confronted with a choice, and at any equilibrium point we can expect the money price of the two assets to be pitched at a level at which the expected yield is identical – allowing for all the reasons of convenience, ease of sale, etc., that might make one class of asset more attractive than the other and thus marginally differently priced.

Herein lies the conundrum that teased Keynes for years; the same conundrum we examined in the theory of value when assessing the classical construction of the demand curve. In the classical theory the rate of interest mediates the flow of saving and investment in the economy; if savings are high and investment is low then the rate of interest is supposed to fall to encourage more investment, and if savings are low and investment high the rate of interest rises to encourage saving. The rate of interest equalises the supply and demand for credit in the same way that price equalises quantities in any competitive market.

But the problem facing Keynes was that a financial asset and a physical capital asset can only be valued *once the interest rate is known*, valuation requiring an interest rate at which income can be capitalised. How are interest rates to determine the capital value of these assets and at the same time be determined by the interaction of their capitalised values? The level of investment in capital goods will depend on their cost; but that cost must equal the capitalised value of their income stream and that depends on expectations of future income and the rate of interest. Equally, the level of acquisition of financial assets depends on their cost: but their cost/price can only be arrived at if we know the interest rate at which to capitalise the dividend stream. Thus in order for the classical system to work we must know *beforehand* the interest rate which the theory tells us is the *outcome* of the process we are analysing.

This situation is parallel to the problem of price and quantity determination outlined in Chapter 4. The rate of interest cannot be determined by the interaction of two schedules; a demand and supply for money. In the classical view the plans of savers and investors are supposed to be made convergent by the rate of interest, but this is impossible because investors must make their demands on savers in the light of what they expect the interest rate to be; and their expectation may not be the rate that makes their plans converge with savers' plans. The identity of savings and investment after any market period does not mean that the savings and investment markets have been cleared by the rate of interest; it simply means that they are in an accounting identity, as they must be. The line of approach, declared Keynes, seemed to be 'circular reasoning' (1937b: 250) and the only way out was for the rate of interest to have its origins elsewhere, rather than in the interaction of the supply and demand for credit – but where?

It was this brain-teaser that obsessed Keynes between the writing of the *Treatise on Money* and the *General Theory*, and his resolution of the problem lay within his view of the role of money. By now there should be no need to labour the point; it is money that transforms the character of the exchange economy by permitting uncertainty about the future to wreak havoc on the neatly functioning markets of a barter economy. Money can either be spent now, or not, depending on the view of the future course of market prices as formulated by money-holders. The rate of interest for Keynes therefore must be, as he himself put it: 'a purely monetary phenomenon – in the sense that it is the *own-rate of interest on money itself*. The rate of interest equalises the advantages of holding *actual cash* and a *deferred claim on cash*'. (1937b: 245 [my italics]) Or put another way, if uncertainty about the future is reflected in a need to hold money rather than other assets, then fluctuations in confidence will be reflected in greater or lesser desire to hoard money. Interest rates are then the premium that has to be paid in order to persuade people not to hoard – 'The rate of interest obviously measures the premium which has to be offered to induce people to hold their wealth in some form other than hoarded money.' (Keynes 1937a: 216)

This is all very well as far as it goes, but as Keynes (1937b: 250) was the first to admit, it does not take us very far. Interest rates are about the willingness to hold money rather than the supply and demand for credit, but that still leaves a lot of explaining. Why should interest rates arrive at one level rather than another? It was the attempt to answer this question that lead to the theory of liquidity-preference.

The theory of liquidity-preference

The first point to make about liquidity-preference is to make clear what it is not. It is not a demand for money function, as some Keynesian economists would have us believe, dependent on two key variables: the rate of interest and the level of income, whether real or money income. The liquidity-preference theory is an explanation of the *motives* that lie behind decisions on liquidity, so that Keynes can get nearer the dynamics of interest rate determination. The word liquidity is important because it gives the clue as to how Keynes saw the interest rate setting process; wealth-holders and savers have to decide how they are going to hold their claims on future resources, and there is no point in holding a claim on a future resource if that claim is not realisable into cash. Thus this category of decision making is about just how *liquid* claims on future resources should be; the most liquid claim is cash, the least liquid is a long-term bond, which only becomes cash at the end of its life. Over the life of the bond the capital value will fluctuate with interest rates so that in the event of a sale before redemption there is a risk that the realised cash will be less than the final cash value of the bond. Thus the longer a financial asset is held, the higher the rate of interest must be in order to compensate for the uncertainty over the course of future interest rates, and the risk of disappointment if the asset has to be sold at a lower cash value than the holder could have expected if he or she had held the asset to redemption.

Keynes discerned three *motives* for holding cash: *the transactions motive*, or the need of cash in financing the current level of personal and business activity; *the precautionary motive*, or the need to hold cash so that the holder can be absolutely certain that he can command a certain proportion of resources in the future; and, *the speculative motive*, the object being to make a profit by taking a different view from the market over the future pattern of prices. A speculator (say) will build up a holding of cash if he expects bond prices to fall (that interest rates will rise); or run down his holding of cash if he expects interest rates to fall and bond price to rise. The prospect of a capital gain can only exist if he is right and the market wrong, because the market price will already contain the consensus judgement over the future course of prices.

In the textbooks (Rowan 1979; Lipsey 1980; Samuelson 1980) these definitions are not described as motives, but as demand functions: there is a transactions demand for money, and so on. Expectations, that is liquidity-preferences, are assumed to be given. This allows the respective author to go on and build a demand-for-money function; there is a demand for money as an 'active balance' to finance any given level of economic activity, and there are 'idle' balances which rise mechanistically as interest rates fall (the rate of interest usually being defined as some rate on short-term money). As the rate of interest falls it becomes less and less costly to hold financial assets as cash, and so idle balances grow. The demand for money can be constructed from the two schedules plotting these relationships; by going on to assume liquidity-preferences as given, a further schedule can be drawn in which the money markets are in equilibrium (the LM curve) at varying levels of real income and the rate of interest (Fig. 1).

This is the beginning of the bastardisation of Keynes. The whole point about expectations is that they change, and they may change at any point along the schedule, to the extent that the very concept of a schedule in which rates of interest and income correspond to certain levels of demand for money is bogus. The most Keynes would claim for liquidity-preference was that it suggested, *ceteris paribus*, that the

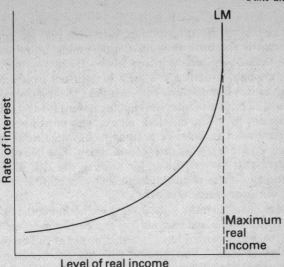

Fig. 1

greater the quantity of money, the lower the rate of interest, but even this was no more than a tendency, and that 'there were several slips between cup and lip' (Keynes 1978: 173), i.e. if the liquidity-preference of the public changed faster than, say, the increase in the quantity of money, then interest rates could rise, not fall. To build a demand-for-money schedule as a function of interest rates and income was absolutely impossible, because given the money stock almost any level of interest rates could be hypothesised. Interest rates could only be calculated once the liquidity-preferences of the public were known; and moreover those preferences could change frequently, depending on the state of expectations. Hence the importance of the label 'motive' to the various definitions of why cash should be held.

However, the theory is not so nihilistic as might first appear. The transactions and precautionary motives for holding cash are actually far less subject to volatility than the speculative motive. The transactions motive could be regarded as having a fairly stable relationship to the level of income, it being assumed that a certain level of activity required a fairly fixed proportion of financing via cash. The precautionary motive is a little more subject to expectations, because holders of cash are required to take a view on the *future* level of activity so they can put aside the proportion of cash they anticipate that they will need: it is an intermediate stage of volatility, before we arrive at the speculative motive for holding cash, which is wholly subject to expectations. It is the speculative motive that is the mainspring of the determination of the rate of interest, because – given the money stock – the rate of interest has to be high enough to persuade holders of cash not to hoard, but to invest in money-loans which can then finance the planned level of investment. The rate of interest is not the reward for abstaining from consumption, as in the classical theory, with borrowers having to pay interest rates as the price of using money now while savers are compensated for deferring their consumption. The rate of interest is the reward that savers receive for running the risk of not being liquid, because there is uncertainty about the future and about the future course of interest rates.

We have begun to make some progress in outlining the links in the chain. As a first step, income, output, and employment are assumed to have reached a certain level, whether or not at full employment. That level of output and income will, via the banking system, produce a certain money stock. The money stock will be divided into various categories of financial asset according to the current state of liquidity-preference so that there will be a proportion of the money stock held in cash, and a proportion held in liquid financial assets, principally bonds. If the supply of bonds is fixed, the rate of interest will be determined by the amount of savings that wealth-holders are prepared to divert into bonds – and that will depend on their expectations of future yields; or more correctly of future interest rates. However, there is another class of asset in which wealth-holders may invest; physical assets, capital machinery which like bonds will produce a flow of income into the future. The yield on the two classes of asset will be the same, because in the words of Keynes (1937a: 217),

the prices move until, having regard to their respective yields and account being taken of all those elements of doubt and uncertainty, interested and disinterested advice, fashion, convention and what else you will which affect the mind of the investor, they offer an equal apparent advantage to the marginal investor who is wavering between one kind of investment and another.

And of course 'opinions as to their prospective yield are themselves subject to sharp fluctuations, . . . (because of) the flimsiness of the basis of knowledge upon which they depend'. (Keynes 1937a: 217)

The next step is to link the decisions taken in the financial markets with those who actually order and produce capital assets. This is the important distinction between financial and physical assets; the latter can be newly produced. The scale of production of capital assets depends on the relation between the costs of production and the price they can command in the market; the higher the valuation of capital assets, then *ceteris paribus*, the more will be produced. In other words, investment will be higher if the rate of interest which capitalises the profit flow is lower, because the lower the rate of interest, the higher the capitalised value and the greater will be the production of capital goods.

However, while producers of capital goods will step up their production as the price of their commodity rises, this as yet gives no clue as to the process of evaluating whether or not to place an order for a capital good. Here Keynes developed the concept of the *marginal efficiency of capital*, which is nothing more than that discount rate which makes the present value of a flow of income equal to the supply price of the asset which will produce that income. The interest rate as fixed in the financial markets for bonds is also applied in the market for physical assets as the discount rate. If the discount rate falls, as interest rates fall on financial assets, then the capitalised value of the income stream will rise above the current supply price of the capital asset. Hence more will be ordered and orders will continue until the supply price has been bid up to equal capitalised value of the income stream again. We may quote Keynes himself (1937a: 218 [my italics]),

Capital-assets are capable, in general, of being newly produced. The scale on which they are produced depends, of course, on the relation between their costs of production and the prices which they are expected to realise in the market. Thus if the level of the rate of interest taken in conjunction with opinions about their prospective yield raise the prices of capital-assets, the volume of current investment (meaning by this the value of the output of newly produced capital-assets) will be increased; while if, on the other hand, these influences reduce the prices of capital-assets, the volume of current investment will be diminished.'

There are two important points to be made immediately. One concerns the role of expectations; the other the determination of the rate of interest. Taking the last point first, it now becomes perfectly obvious why interest rates must have their origin elsewhere than in the supply and demand for credit. To quote again from Keynes (1978: 137),

I would . . . . ask the reader to note at once that neither the knowledge of an asset's prospective yield nor the knowledge of the marginal efficiency of the asset enables us to deduce either the rate of interest or the present value of the asset. We must ascertain the rate of interest from some other source, and only then can we value the asset by 'capitalising' its yield.

In other words, it is impossible to posit investment demand unless we already know the rate of interest; but if the rate of interest is the result of the interaction of the demand for investment finance with the supply of that finance, then the rate of interest has to be determined by a value that it itself is determining. And that is 'circular' nonsense.

The other point is the importance of expectations. The entrepreneur has to formulate a potential demand for the product the capital asset is going to produce, and if his expectations change then that will lead to a different projection of the future income stream, and thus of the capitalised value of that stream. Investment is thus subject to no less than

two sets of judgement about the future, neither of which rests on an adequate or secure foundation – on the propensity to hoard and on opinions of the future yield of capital assets. Nor is there any reason to suppose that the fluctuations in one of these factors will tend to offset the fluctuations in the other. (Keynes 1937a: 219)

We have arrived at the heart of the matter, because we know that we operate in a quantity-adjusting system. Investment, subject as it is to two sets of guesses about the future, is likely to be the most volatile component of national income. Once it moves there is no saying at what level of income the values in the economy will find equilibrium, because the rate of interest in the financial markets and the discount rate in the investment markets could easily equal each other at almost any potential level of output and employment. There is no reason why the rate at which the capital values in the two markets reach an identity should be one which produces full employment.

Suppose for example that an entrepreneur downgrades his projection of an income stream produced by a capital asset. Necessarily that produces a lower capital value if the discount rate is unchanged. He lowers his purchases of capital assets. Now, what is required to keep the system at full employment (assuming the initial shock occurred at full employment) is that the discount rate that capitalises that stream should fall, so lifting the capitalised value back to the supply price of the asset. But the same pessimism about the future will make wealth-holders anxious to hold more cash: as the quantity of cash increases, bond prices fall and interest rates rise. This has the perverse effect of compounding the initial shock by raising the discount rate, lowering the capitalised value of the income stream on capital goods, and cutting still further the orders of capital goods producers. It is only when the fall in output leads to less transactions need for cash that the possibility opens up of idle cash balances accumulating to such a level that finally bonds are bought, notwithstanding the hoarding in the expectation of further falls in bond prices. As asset values start to rise, so orders are placed for capital goods and the recessionary influences in the economy are dispelled.

Now, contrast this explanation of income determination with that on offer in the textbooks. The typical device is the IS/LM analysis in which two schedules are constructed: one representing equilibrium in the money markets (the LM curve), the other in the real economy (the IS curve) – and at the point of intersection of the two schedules the system supposedly yields an overall equilibrium.

A graph is drawn with the rate of interest on one axis, the level of real income on the other (see Fig. 2). The trick is to hold every other variable constant and build a schedule that is dependent on the variables depicted by the two axes. The LM schedule traces the level of interest and real income at which the money markets clear, so that at higher levels of real income (given an unchanged money stock) a higher rate of interest is required to clear the money markets. The idea is that as real income grows, so the quantity of cash grows that is required to finance the higher level of transactions: that reduces the level of potential idle balances, so given the money stock interest rates are bid up.

The IS schedule traces the level of interest rates and real income at which the 'real economy' is in equilibrium, which is assumed to be where investment equals savings. Again the idea is that as real income rises so there is an associated need for higher investment and lower interest rates. Higher investment can only happen if the marginal efficiency of capital is lowered; that is, the discount rate at which income streams are capitalised has to fall progressively in order to induce the required levels of higher investment. The point of intersection E is the equilibrium position (with an equilibrium rate of interest, r^e, and of real income, Y^e), and if the intersection point is elsewhere than full employment, then external action – either fiscal or monetary policy – is needed to push the two schedules to that point.

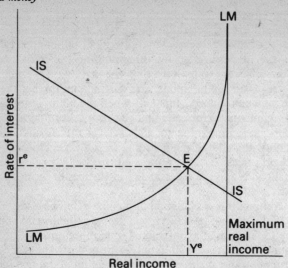

(*Source*: D.C. Rowan, *Output Inflation and Growth*
(2nd edn) 1979, p. 243.)

Fig. 2

IS/LM analysis has become the accepted paradigm of economic debate to the extent that it is entirely possible for contemporary Keynesians and classicists to have their dispute cast not in terms of their 'vision' of the dynamics of a money exchange economy, but the degree to which they are 'Walrasian' (Hahn 1980). The neo-classicist argues that the slope of the IS curve is gentle; the neo-Keynesian that the slope is steep: the bone of contention being just how sensitive one can expect the level of savings and investment to be to interest rate changes, a Keynesian denying that interest rates are effective means of changing quantities of either saving or investment. As to the LM curve, the neo-classicist argues that its slope is steep, while the neo-Keynesian insists it is gentle; here the issue is whether one can expect there to be a stable demand for money function over various ranges of real income. The neo-classicist view is that this function is stable, depending as it does on wealth, and portfolio preferences – so that there can be little variation with either income or interest rates. The neo-Keynesian insists that cash holdings vary with income, so that *ceteris paribus* the higher the level of income, the higher the interest rate. Both schools can agree that price rigidities may prevent the intersection point from yielding full employment, so the debate centres on the relative importance of money and the rate of interest in shaping the slope of the two curves (Gordon 1977).

This is all very well but it has nothing to do with Keynes; IS/LM analysis fundamentally misrepresents the Keynesian position in a number of critical respects. Firstly, it is only operational in so far as it assumes liquidity-preference as *given*, that is, it turns liquidity-preference into a demand-for-money function. But the whole point of liquidity-preference is its insistence that the motives that lie behind the wish to hold liquidity cannot be given, and are in reality highly volatile. Secondly, IS/LM analysis suggests that the rate of interest *alone* can yield a given level of investment; this can only be done if expectations are assumed to be constant – an assumption that the entire thrust of the *General Theory* is aimed at displacing. In fact, IS/LM analysis assumes away the two sets of guesses that Keynes saw as the heart of the market economy: the guess over the future level of interest rates and the guess over future income streams from capital assets.

But more seriously still, it ignores how the transaction structure of an exchange economy based on money leads to quantity rather than price adjustment (Hahn 1980). The key difference between the Keynesian and Walrasian view of the world – that price cannot successfully co-ordinate the plans of all the traders in a market economy – is obscured. The suggestion is that interest rates, acting as price signals in the money markets and the goods market, can have the potential to co-ordinate the two markets into a full-employment equilibrium. But this is utterly at odds with Keynes's entire argument: it was to disprove this notion that he devoted his life's work. IS/LM analysis is not even useful as a heuristic device, at least as far as the Keynes of the *General Theory* is concerned, because it either assumes away or ignores the entire base of the Keynesian system.

The market as sub-markets v. the market as a system

The measure of Keynes's achievement is the measure of the classicists' failure. At the end of Chapter 4 orthodox economics within the classical tradition was shown to have demonstrable weaknesses. A determinant equilibrium of output consistent with full employment appeared to rest on a series of questionable assumptions about rational economic man and the constitution of an exchange economy. Even that limited success was qualified by the evident lack of robustness in the whole approach to price and quantity determination *as a process*, i.e. how to circumvent the problem that market clearing needs to be instantaneous if the price mechanism is to be deemed consistent with time, expectations, and the notion that demand and supply are independent schedules.

Economic theory seemed at loss as to how to explain the economic world as it is, explaining economic phenomena like monopoly and unemployment as departures from how the world *should* behave rather than how it *does* behave. Keynes pitchforks us into a world of uncertainty, where changing calculations about the future operate in key markets so as to produce economic values which may do anything else but produce full employment and price stability. Suddenly unemployment, inflation, and recession, rather than aberrations from the rule, become the rule: and moreover we have some clues as to which market values policy-makers should try and influence if the system is to deliver less distressing results.

The result is, of course, to look at the functioning of the system as a whole rather than of the parts of the system. The attempt to build a model from the parts leads to all kinds of blind alleys, contrivances, and circularity of argument in order to reach the desired destination: namely, to prove that a market economy is 'best'. The concept of aggregate demand is a good illustration. For the classical school aggregate demand is the sum of the demands in all the sub-markets in the economy; for Keynes aggregate demand cuts across all the sub-markets and falls into two essential categories: investment expenditure, which turns on the liquidity-preference/marginal efficiency of capital relationship, and consumption expenditure, which turns chiefly on the level of income. The motion of the market is seen to turn not on the degree of price flexibility in the system's sub-markets, but on the axis of savings, investment, and consumption. This brings into consideration a propensity to consume which rests on a simple but none the less vital psychological law – that when income increases, people will tend to spend more rather than less. The motor of overall expenditure is the investment component, and out of the income thus generated there is a decision to consume or save.

Keynes listed six 'objective' influences on what he termed the 'propensity to consume', and eight 'subjective' influences that influenced individuals in refraining from spending. The object was to turn the classical analysis on its head: instead of attempting to build a model of aggregate demand from the bottom up, and which had to explicitly assume a functioning whole with a set of prices and quantities as given, Keynes tried to explain how the whole functioned as a system and thus how prices and quantities were *derived*. Already he had located the instability of the economy in the volatile state of expectations that can be expected to exist in the money markets, via liquidity-preference, and in the investment markets, via the marginal efficiency of capital. Investment expenditure, and in particular changes in investment expenditure, drove the level of income up and down: but what happened to consumption-expenditure, by definition the other component of income?

The theory of consumption lay in a simple psychological law: that 'men are disposed, as a rule and on the average, to increase their consumption as their income increases'. (Keynes 1978: 96) As Keynes said, it was a little-noticed part of his thinking, but that did not mean it was any less important. For if it is true – and as a psychological law it seems pretty unexceptional – then two important consequences follow. First, consumption can be made a function of income rather than an aggregation of lots of individual demand curves; second, consumption becomes essentially a dependent variable, dependent that is on the level of income – a level of income that is generated by the interplay of liquidity-preference and the marginal efficiency of capital and their impact on investment.

That is not to say that consumption is unimportant. In fact consumption, declared Keynes, is the principal object of economic activity. It is to meet anticipated consumption that investment is undertaken. However, the other side of consumption is non-consumption, savings, and here those 'subjective' influences come into play. Precaution, foresight, calculation, improvement, independence, enterprise, pride, and avarice all motivate saving, and notwithstanding the overall level of income these subjective motivations can clearly affect the allocation between consumption and saving. If the level of saving were to increase, then that is all saving that the liquidity-preferences in the money markets will have to mediate – and there is no certainty that the knock-on effects on interest rates will be strong enough to persuade investors to use all the savings in investment projects. In this case underconsumption, which is the other side of an increase in saving, will lead to underemployment of resources.

Explaining consumption as a psychological law, and admitting that the split between saving and consumption is subject to any number of factors that do not lend themselves to economic predictability, raises as many questions as it solves. Certainly it means the economist is offered a more satisfactory theory of demand than that provided by the classical school, but it also opens a Pandora's box of new problems.

In this new view of the world the economy is permanently on the horns of a dilemma. The investment component of aggregate demand lifts the potential of the economy to produce, a potential that will only be exercised if there is a comparable increase in the consumption component of aggregate demand. But this, we know, is the last thing upon which we can rely. Moreover, if it does not prove forthcoming, or even if it is not *expected* to be forthcoming, the disappointment of present and future expectations lowers the marginal efficiency of capital, reduces the price entrepreneurs are prepared to pay for capital goods, and sets in train the whole process of downward quantity adjustment to which the market economy is constantly prone. The key element is not only that consumption and saving are fickle, but that so are our expectations of them; and once the system is thrown out of kilter the transaction structure of the economy amplifies any initial disturbance and the price mechanism is helpless to turn the system around. To avoid the disturbance the prime object must be to sustain consumption, and even more importantly our *expectation* that consumption will continue. 'We are reminded of "The Fable of the Bees"', wrote Keynes (1978: 105) '– the gay of tomorrow are absolutely indispensable to provide a *raison d'être* for the grave of today.'

The dynamic of the market economy is thus immensely subtle. Each individual transactor faces a 'dual decision' in his actions; he juggles his money inflows with his money outflows and confronts uncertainty in the very nature of things. Thus, as we argued in the previous chapter, the quantity-adjusting bias in the economy. But overlaid on this are the attributes of the aggregated elements in the system. Investment expenditure is subject to two sets of guesses about the future. The rate of interest is determined by savers' 'desire for liquidity'. And now we find that the split between consumption and saving is organised around psychological factors which brook no prediction, but which none the less are critical to the stability of the system. There is a further twist. It is not just that our expectations of consumption may be disappointed and are volatile, but that the market economy has no means to reintegrate a decision over non-consumption (i.e. saving) back into the system once it has been taken. The transaction structure of the money exchange economy permeates it at every level: from the individual's balance sheet to the split between consumption and saving; from the process of interest-rate determination to the means by which savings and investment are made equal. The end result is chronic instability; but let Keynes (1978: 211) himself describe the savings/consumption conundrum.

An act of individual saving means – so to speak – a decision not to have dinner today. But it does *not* necessitate a decision to have dinner or to buy a pair of boots a week hence or a year hence or to consume any specified thing at any specified date. Thus it depresses the business of preparing today's dinner without stimulating the business of making ready for some future act of consumption. It is not a substitution of future consumption-demand for present consumption – it is a net diminution of such demand . . . If saving consisted not merely in abstaining from present consumption but in placing simultaneously a specific order for future consumption, the effect might indeed be different. For in that case the expectation of some future yield from investment would be improved, and the resources released from preparing for present consumption could be turned over to preparing for the future consumption. The trouble arises, therefore, because the act of saving implies, not a substitution for present consumption of some specific additional consumption which requires for its preparation just as much immediate economic activity as would have been required by present consumption equal in value to the sum saved, but a desire for 'wealth' as such, that is for a potentiality of consuming an unspecified article at an unspecified time. The absurd, though almost universal, idea that an act of individual saving is just as good for effective demand as an act of individual consumption, has been fostered by the fallacy, much more specious than the conclusion derived from it, that an increased desire to hold wealth, being much the same thing as an increased desire to hold investments, must, by increasing the demand for investments, provide a stimulus to their production; so that current investment is promoted by individual saving to the same extent as present consumption is diminished.

Savings would not be 'lost' to the system if the build-up of financial assets and/or money that saving represented was paralleled by some conpensating increase in expenditure, either consumption or investment expenditure. In the classical literature this outcome is achieved by the rate of interest, which coaxes borrowers and lenders into a community of activity; the rate at which money is lent, or financial claims issued is such that those who wish to supplement their current expenditure do so at exactly the same rate as those who reduce their current expenditure through saving. The level of effective demand thus remains the same. The problem is that saving does not imply 'placing a specific order for future consumption'; those who use savings to invest in capital assets have no idea of when that saving will be translated into future consumption, but in the meantime there is a net loss of demand today. As a result their expectations of *future* demand become all important, and the only mediating mechanism is the rate of interest – but that does not perform as the classicists insist.

The reason the rate of interest proves ineffective is that it is not the 'price of money' as the classicists claim; rather it is the price that has to be paid to persuade wealth-holders not to hold money – and that price turns on their confidence about the future, their willingness not to be 'liquid'. The rate of interest spans the money market and investment market, because once it has been set it is the rate at which expected flows of income from physical assets are capitalised and it is the rate at which wealth-holders will invest in financial assets. But the fact that there is a common rate at which investment and financial assets are valued does not mean that the resulting valuation will produce the level of investment that will in turn produce full employment of resources. There is no reason why that should happen at all. Indeed, given the structure of the saving and investment markets there is every reason why it should not.

They are two distinct groups of people whose judgements about the future are independently formulated: one is making a judgement about liquidity; the other about future levels of income. What mechanism is there to co-ordinate their view? The answer is that there is none, except adjustments to the level of income and thus the quantities of savings and investment that take place. It is only after the event that the necessary identity between a community's non-consumption (i.e. saving) and investment can happen: there is no simultaneous equilibrium, with interest rates instantaneously co-ordinating the supply of investment finance and the demand for investment goods.

The same conundrum exists for the labour force. A downward move in income throws them out of work, and they become involuntarily unemployed. They look for a job, not a wage, and employers cannot offer a job because there apparently is no prospect of the marginal addition to output having any value given the prospect for sales. The problem is exactly the same as in the savings/consumption equation. Just as an act of saving does not bring about a corresponding act of consumption or promise of future consumption, so unemployed workers are unable to bring about their employment because they have no means of showing that the payment of wages would justify their jobs through lifting the demand for the entrepreneurs' products. There is no ticket saying 'I save, and I promise to spend at some date in the future': nor is there a ticket saying 'if I am paid a wage I promise to spend it – thus warranting my job'.

It is the uncertainty about everyone's intentions that makes wealth-holders hold cash, and entrepreneurs downgrade their expectations of profits: it is money that separates their plans and permits market valuations to reflect uncertainty. It is the rate of interest that creates capital values, but its origins lie in the willingness to hold money rather than liquid financial assets. It is the level of income and output that produce equilibrium in the component markets of the economy: it is not the component markets of the economy that produce overall equilibrium. And if income changes produce the identity of quantities that allow the economy to stabilise, then unemployment follows in its wake; for in the labour market too it is quantity rather than price that shoulders the burden of adjustment, and as in the other markets, prices are helpless. Keynes's theory truly is a theory of employment, interest, and money.

References

Gordon, R. J. (ed.) (1977) *Milton Friedman's Monetary Framework: A debate with his critics*. Chicago U.P.

Hahn, F. J. (1980) 'Monetarism and economic theory', *Economica*, vol. 47, no. 185, (Feb.).

Keynes, J. M. (1937a) 'The general theory of employment', *Quarterly Journal of Economics*, (Feb.).

Keynes, J. M. (1937b) 'Alternative theories of the rate of interest', *Economic Journal*, (June).

Keynes J. M. (1978) *The Collected Writings of John Maynard Keynes*; vol. VII. *The General Theory of Employment, Interest and Money*. Royal Economic Society.

Klein, Laurence R. (1980) *The Keynesian Revolution*. Macmillan.

Laidler, David (1980) in R. M. Grant and G. K. Shaw (eds) *Current Issues in Economic Policy*. Philip Allen.

Lipsey, R. G. (1980) *An Introduction to Positive Economics* (5th edn). Weidenfeld and Nicholson.

Okun, A. M. (1981) *Prices and Quantities*. Blackwell.

Rowan, D. C. (1979) *Output, Inflation and Growth* (An Introduction to Macro-Economics). Macmillan.

Samuelson, P. (1980) *Economics* (11th edn). McGraw Hill/Macmillan.

Shackle, G. L. S. (1967) *The Years of High Theory*. Cambridge U.P.

Vines, D., Maciejowski, J. & Meade, J. (1982) 'Stagflation' vol. 1 *Wage-fixing*. Allen & Unwin.

Chapter 7

Liquidity-preference and the financial system

Summary

Keynesianism is now seen by many as close to the root of all economic evil, and the reaction against government attempts to manage the economy has included a reaction against not just Keynesianism as it was practised, but even the very precepts upon which it was based. Yet Keynes was no enemy of the market, and the current enthusiasm for market economics, and in policy for 'letting the market go free', is unwise if it ignores the objections he raised to the theoretical basis of classical economics.

After a brief survey of the current attack on the Keynesian 'incubus' and the validity of its claims, the chapter attempts to pull together the main elements in the reassessment of Keynesian economics from Chapters 5 and 6. The heart of the instability of the market economy lies in the tension between the financial system's desire for liquidity – and the need for illiquidity in order for the real economy to finance the acquisition of physical capital assets. Interest rates are the results of the financial sector's liquidity-preference function. Moreover, the portfolio preferences it expresses, especially for long-term debt instruments, will be a key determinant of the level and rate of investment. As the level of instability in the economy is consequential upon the financial sector's liquidity-preference decisions, there is a possibility of counteracting those decisions. The Central Bank and the banking system can lean against the upward and downward cyclical movements in the economy, represented as they are by interest rate movements and *changes in the class of financial asset that are held*.

This leads to a brief assessment of the characteristics of the British financial system today. It remains as preoccupied with liquidity as it was in the 1930s. In particular, illiquidity, in the shape of long-term debt instruments, is comparatively scarce, while there appears to be a propensity to hold short-term financial assets. This gives the system a bias away from investment and towards consumption and inflation.

The Keynesian 'incubus'?

Hayek (1975: 43) has talked of the urgent need to 'exorcise the Keynesian incubus' in order to restore the body economic to health, and other writers in the tradition of the classical economists have said that 'Keynesianism represents a substantial disease' (Buchanan *et al*. 1978: 27). Sam Brittan (1981) has coined the phrase 'counter-revolutionaries' to describe those economists who challenge the Keynesian orthodoxies. The reaction to Keynes is now hostile and if anything gathering pace – he is regarded as the enemy of the market's spontaneous adjustment processes, the proponent of careless government spending and large budget deficits, the author of the doctrine that 'money does not matter', and as such the mindless sponsor of inflation, low growth, high taxes, and rising unemployment. As in his private life (where he appears to have conducted a homosexual affair for at least part of his adult life), so in public life he is charged with advocating the destruction of natural rules and natural disciplines. The one-time 'revolutionary' is now the object at worst of contempt; at best of patronising condescension – what he had to say corresponded to a particular market structure (with relatively inflexible money wages) at a particular moment of time (Britain in the 1930s).

The 'counter-revolutionary' argument starts off with a view of the market and its properties, and then runs to the appropriate policy responses. Let us briefly examine this view of the world, and the nature of its understanding of Keynes.

Of the basic assumption there can be no doubt: it is that markets do work, and have a spontaneous tendency to stability. It is most clearly set out as follows: 'There is no evidence to suggest that market economics are inherently unstable. Economic research has shown that market economies are dynamically stable. The business cycle does not arise because of any inherent instability on the part of the economy, but apparently is caused by exogenous "shocks" that disturb its workings.' (Buchanan, *et al*. 1978: 85)[1] The shocks to the system? Those are provided by government: 'The most serious "shocks" that destabilise the economy are ill-considered and erratic policy actions by government.' (Buchanan, *et al*. 1978: 85) It is Government attempts, in the name of Keynes and his view that the market system was quantity-adjusting, that paradoxically upset the market and its natural processes. There is a 'natural rate of unemployment' (Brittan 1981) corresponding to some level of money-wage flexibility in relation to any given real wage; and a rate of inflation that accelerates if the Government attempts to manage the level of output beyond that consonant with the 'natural rate of unemployment'.

The reader will immediately recognise two claims that parallel those of classical economics: the tendency of the market system to produce an equilibrium; and that the wage bargain contains all the information rational economic agents need to know, so that opting for leisure rather than work is a rational response to a set of market valuations (see Chs 2, 5, and 6). The market is stable and there is a natural rate of unemployment.

Anyone who has persevered this far will know that the body of theory that stands behind those positions is profoundly suspect. There is no theory of expectations formation apart from the doctrine of rational expectations; and no theory of price determination. It is even possible to cast doubt on the hypothetical slope and properties of the curves that are supposed to make market experimentation produce convergent behaviour on the part of supply and demand. Above all the analogy is with 'natural' processes in a barter economy, where voluntary and free exchange is constrained by the constitutional properties of the system to produce a 'best' outcome. It was this discourse of understanding that Keynes challenged – and shattered.

But this did not mean that he was anti-market and pro-collectivism. The oldest truth in political economy is that a 'perfect' system of competition and of planning would equally produce a 'best' result; and the processes by which each would arrive at that result would be very similar – trial-and-error experimentation (Lange 1964). But that begs the question. There is an open value-judgement to be made; is trial-and-error experimentation best performed by many agents whose decisions are decentralised, or by a central planning authority? Suppose the question is pitched at the second-best out-turn; which is most *likely* to produce the best result? Even in these terms Keynes would have plumped unhesitatingly for the market (Keynes 1978: 380). In his view the 'animal spirits' of entrepreneurs are the driving force of economic progress; and a market which allows private profit, property, and individual decision-taking is the best means of harnessing those spirits. His message was plain: if we want the benefits the market can deliver, we must understand the dynamic of the market economy, understand it has no tendency to stability, and attempt through our collective institutions (for there are no other) to make up for the markets' proven inability to co-ordinate the actions of economic agents in the present and the future. The general equilibrium model built by Arrow and Debreu is a remarkable construct, but it depends on futures and contingent futures markets for its coherence (Hahn 1973: 324). Keynes was the first to see that the market system did not possess such markets, nor could it; therein lay the root of its instability and the State had to act in the place of the markets that did not exist.

This does not mean that the policies prosecuted by the State in the light of the theory have always been well informed, well judged, and well directed. The 'counter-revolutionaries' have performed a valuable service in reminding us of the limits of government action and the power of the market to unravel economic difficulties. Indeed there is some truth in the accusation that Keynesianism is a classic case of the 'misuse of economic theory for political profiteering' (Buchanan *et al.* 1978: 1). But although policy might have been poor, it is contestable whether it was as bad as is now claimed. The period between 1949 and 1973, the now-decried age of demand-management and 'fine-tuning', looks more and more like a golden age. Even if mistakes were made in the practice of policy and in the interpretation of the theory, that does not mean that Keynesianism is for ever bankrupt. This author charges the 'counter-revolutionaries' with launching not a counter-revolution, but a counter-reformation-based on the same very infirm foundations.

The most telling ignorance of the complexities of Keynes's economics lies in the criticism that he was the origin of the view that 'money does not matter' (Friedman and Friedman 1980: 70–1).[2] For Keynes money mattered very much – so much that it transformed the operation of the exchange economy, and made equilibrium price and quantity determination in markets a question of chance. Here 'Keynesians' have a measure of responsibility for the contemporary interpretation.

The problem was that the initial focus was on the quantity-adjusting properties of the market, rather than the *origins* of that process; and so post-war Keynesians found themselves advocating fiscal policy almost exclusively. But although fiscal policy is undoubtedly a key element in any Keynesian programme, so is action to counteract the changing and volatile liquidity-preferences of the financial system. At the very least this means an interest-rate policy focused as much on relative interest rates as on absolute interest rates, the object being to maintain as high a stream of

143

long-term debt instruments to the non-financial business sector as possible over the business cycle. Indeed, not just the rate of change of investment but the absolute level are crucially determined by the readiness of the financial institutions to offer long-term liabilities to investors. The propensity to do this in Britain was, and is, extremely low and in the absence of any spontaneous, self-correcting market action, Keynes was ready to compel such lending – even to the point of 'socialising' the financial institutions. Fiscal policy without any supportive policy towards liquidity-preference was never likely to be very successful; nor was it.

The exorcism of the Keynesian 'incubus' is now almost complete, and economic policy in most Western industrialised countries is once again organised around the perspectives of classical economics; the stable properties of the market, a fiscal policy aimed at reducing government deficits whatever the stage of the business cycle and a monetary policy in which the object is not to sustain a flow of long-term debt instruments but to control the growth of some measure of the money supply in the name of 'sound money'. But if the critique offered by Keynes of the classical tradition is right, these are inappropriate policies to be prosecuting.

It is to an overview of Keynes's theory that we now turn, in particular to an examination of the properties of the financial system that Keynes found so important. In urging that action on liquidity-preference is a vital concomitant of any contra-cyclical fiscal policy, we have slightly stepped ahead of ourselves. How is it that liquidity-preference and the portfolio decisions of the financial system loom so large in Keynes's theory?

Keynesian theory: an overview

The first step in Keynes's thought is to reinterpret *Homo economicus* as a creature who while driven by self-interest is not always certain how he should go about it and is subject to all kinds of hopes and fears. This is a character familiar to us all, and it is worth while recapping on why this creature differs so markedly from the man who inhabits classical and neo-classical economic theory – the theory of the 'counter-revolutionaries'.

The introduction of money into a system of exchange is another way of introducing time and uncertainty. It is because money has purchasing power over time that the option opens up of trans-actions not having to happen simultaneously as they do in a system of barter. So although a market transactor can be assumed to want

144

to pursue his self-interest, every time he contemplates a market transaction he is in effect contemplating a dual decision whose very nature is fraught with uncertainty. Every time he chooses to buy a commodity with an outlay of money he has to have some idea of where that money is coming from; and because the one decision cannot automatically be matched with the other he has to make a judgement about what is likely to happen in the future. Not only do transactors not know what is going to happen in the future, they are prey to all kinds of sentiment and influence when making that judgement.

This 'dual-decision' nature of the market economy makes it inherently unstable because it is likely that if expectations about the future change, as they will, transactors will want to preserve the structure of their balance sheets. This will mean that if (say) expectations about future market conditions deteriorate then transactors will revise downwards their expectations of future income, and unless they are prepared to increase their borrowings, they will reduce the quantity of goods they are currently purchasing because financing that level of purchases has become more difficult. The first reaction to a change in expectations is thus a quantity reduction, not a price reduction.

If the markets were simply exchanging stocks of non-wasting and non-produced goods then the quantity changes would be reflected in price changes that would equalise the value of money inflows and outflows. The problem is that in an industrial economy goods are produced, and existing goods are consumed. Thus in the middle of the quantity change those who organise the production of goods have to decide whether they will continue producing the same quantity of goods in the light of reduced expectations of money inflows, and what price cut would be required to persuade buyers to maintain their quantity of purchases allowing for the fact that they, too, have reduced expectations of money inflows. Because of uncertainty they will be obliged to revise downwards their quantities produced, and because their money outflows are somebody else's money inflows, that decision will intensify the quantity contraction. Spending is reduced around the system and prices have only a limited ability to 'price' quantities back into demand once the first round of diminished expectations has been translated into cut-backs in the level of *current production*. Once that has happened the expectation of a fall in money inflows has become a reality, and all because of a judgement about the future which today's prices are by definition not equipped to deal with. The amplification of the quantity adjustment that follows was called the 'multiplier' by Keynes; with current production falling, current incomes fall, and so spending falls, causing a downward revision in quantities produced that leads to a further fall in income – and so on down a vicious circle.

Of course, the whole process could be reversed if a *deus ex machina* were to descend from the skies and call a halt to any quantity adjustment until a range of prices was found that could allow all the markets to clear with no under-utilisation of resources. But no *deus ex machina* exists. It is the very 'trial-and-error' means of price and quantity determination in markets that gives them their quantity bias because as transactors make a dual decision every time they buy and sell, they must guard against 'error' by revising quantities rather than prices.

To sum up: the market is a network of economic agents all trying to juggle money inflows and outflows through their notional balance sheets; inflows may exceed outflows, or vice versa. What is least likely is that inflows will exactly match outflows, and it is how transactors distribute the build-up of their net money inflows, their money claims on others, and the degree and terms on which those money claims are accepted by those who have net money outflows, that gives the market economy its unique dynamic.

If the problem were simply one of money inflows and outflows not matching for individual transactors then there would be no difficulty, because the totals of money inflows and outflows across the whole economy must be equal and all that is required is for the economy to have an efficient banking system that swops money for those whose inflows are (temporarily) exceeding outflows to those who (temporarily) are in the opposite position. A business, for example, that is accumulating money balances as its production is sold will lend on, via the banking system, to a business that is in the process of production and whose money outflows in payments for raw materials and wages must necessarily exceed its money inflows, for it has as yet no goods to sell. It was this kind of function that London bill-brokers performed in the nineteenth century when they issued bills on behalf of cash-hungry Lancashire mill owners to cash-rich Hampshire farmers at harvest time. In this way no money demand is lost to the economy through the accumulation of idle balances, and because money flows are circular at the end of the period – say a year – the positions the banking system has taken are unwound: bills and credits are repaid, and the process begins again.

The area of difficulty for the money economy is when money balances are either accumulated or required for a period longer than that over which there is a straightforward mismatch of money inflows and outflows; i.e. there is saving or investment. Here there is a deliberate attempt to build up the stock of net money balances on the part of the saver through abstaining from current spending in order to have spending power in the future, and a deliberate attempt to build up the stock of physical assets on the part of the investor through the acquisition of goods that will not be consumed now, but will be used to produce goods and services in the future. The question is: can the system devise a mechanism that allows savers and investors to match their decisions about an incalculable future in the same way it does decisions that mismatch in the present? In other words, how is it that the volume of saving and the volume of investment come to be made equal as they must be; the money inflows and outflows in the economy in the present must be equal; thus even though savings and investment occur because of judgements about the future, the activity flowing from those decisions happens in the present – and as current consumption equals current production for consumption, so current abstention from consumption (saving) must equal the production of goods that will be used in the future (investment).

This leads us to consider the decision the saver is taking. He wants to be able to consume in the future, so his saving must be in a money form. On the other hand, if the saving is held in money it is 'lost' to the system; it needs to be held in a form which permits the investor to use it. The investor needs to tie the money up in physical assets, but the saver, because he does not know about the future, needs access to his savings as soon as the unpredictable event for which he is saving actually happens. He has a preference for *liquidity*, whereas the investor has a need for *illiquidity*. Both face an uncertain future, because the investor has to make a guess about the likely stream of income in the future, and the saver about his future needs.

· The only way the conundrum can be unravelled is if the saver parts with his liquidity and holds an asset that can be sold for a determinable amount of cash in the future: a financial asset. At the same time the investor claims title of the corresponding cash in the present, so gaining the wherewithal to buy the physical asset, but accepts responsibility for returning the cash at some date in the future. For example, the investor could issue a bond in exchange for the payment of cash: with the cash proceeds he purchases a capital asset, the capital asset produces income over time, and the income is used to gradually repay the buyer of the bond. The saver gets his money back in the future – which is what he wants – and

147

the investor gets purchasing power in the present – which is what he wants. Savings are not 'lost' to the system, the acquisition of capital goods can go on at the same pace as financial assets are acquired by savers, and the markets are squared with no loss of demand.

Explained in this way, it becomes quite clear what is the function of the rate of interest. It is the rate that is paid to savers not to hold money as cash but to hold a financial asset so that the money can be kept in circulation by being used by investors. It is a rate that reflects savers' need to hold their money in a liquid form and the system's need for the money to be held in an illiquid form.

It is in the term structure of interest rates – the fact that the rate is higher the longer the financial asset will be required to be held to redemption – that the preference for liquidity expresses itself. Interest rates can be seen as a continuum: from a zero rate on cash through to the higher rates on the longest-term financial assets. The sharpest discontinuity will be between the rate on cash and the rate on near-cash; but the determinant of any particular rate for any particular term of financial asset will be liquidity-preference, the preference for one class of asset over another given the expectations of future movements in rates in the light of current rates.

But the problem for the system is that at the same time as the rate of interest is performing this function, it is also functioning as the rate at which investors are capitalising the expected income streams from the capital goods in which they are investing. It is only by capitalising the income that investors can judge whether to pay the price that producers of the capital good are asking. So no sooner has the system created a mechanism to get it off the horns of one dilemma – how to ensure that savings can be held in a form that could be remediated into the system as investment – than it is impaled on the horns of another – how to make the volume of savings equal the volume of investment. For there is no reason why the volume of investment, or put another way, the quantity of capital goods that entrepreneurs feel they can order given a rate of interest and their expectation of future income, will equal the volume and categories of financial assets that savers want to acquire.

In the classical system the equalisation of the supply of financial assets by savers and the demand for financial assets by investors is equalised by the rate of interest, but, argued Keynes, this cannot be the case. The demand for financial assets, for the use of money *now* to buy capital goods, depends on the valuation of the capital goods and that valuation cannot be made without the rate of interest already existing. If it were true that the rate of interest equalised the supply and demand for financial assets then investors would be in the illogical position of simultaneously co-determining through their demand pattern a rate of interest and requiring that the rate of interest be determined so that they could calculate their demand for financial assets.

The fact that the rate of interest is the common basis of valuation for two classes of capital asset, one physical, one financial, does not mean that the volume of financial assets the public wants to accumulate will necessarily equal the volume of physical assets the entrepreneurial sector wants to accumulate as investment. In fact, the influences on the two classes of decision make it extremely unlikely that they could ever be equal as planned intentions; entrepreneurs must make a judgement about market conditions in the future when they evaluate a capital asset's probable income stream, and savers are making a judgement about their future spending plans and their confidence in the stability of value of the financial asset they are buying.

It is the very commonality of the interest rate as a basis of valuation that puts the system in motion, gives it its instability, for volumes of capital good purchases follow on from the interest-rate decision. If the resulting investment level is insufficient to create a demand for the financial assets that savers are willing to supply, it is not the rate of interest that falls *but the level of income as a consequence of the insufficient level of investment*. The price of investment goods, and thus the volume of investment demand, are continually adjusting to the price of financial assets as set by liquidity-preference; the level of investment, the volatile component of the effective demand in the economy because of the dual influence of the rate of interest and expectations upon the investment decision, drives the level of economic activity up and down, and the level of savings moves up and down with the overall level of economic activity. Savings equal investment after an income change that the rate of interest brings about. In other words, the economy is quantity-adjusting, and the interest rate does not 'clear' the supply and demand for financial assets but ensures their identity through income changes.

The question of liquidity is central to the working of the market economy. It is the concern to protect against the future that makes all economic agents anxious to guard against their 'balance sheets' becoming illiquid; it is this that gives the system its quantity-adjusting bias, and in the area of the economy where decisions are uniquely concerned with judging the course of future market

149

conditions the question of liquidity become paramount. The 'dual decision' that characterises market trading amounts to a decision about liquidity, and if there were no future an efficient banking system could broker the varying liquidity positions. It is the intrusion of the future, and its impact on current activity that presents the market economy with an irresolvable problem. The concern for liquidity by savers creates rates of interest that may not generate the investment commensurate with a full employment of resources, and once the system is out of kilter the 'multiplier effect', which itself originates in the transaction structure of the market and the liquidity needs of 'dual-decision' taking economic agents, amplifies the initial 'disequilibrium'. Herein lie the causes of the instability of the market economy, and the relative inability of the price mechanism to stabilise it.

The prime target for any corrective action by the managers of an economy is thus liquidity and the rate of interest. This even leads Keynes in the closing chapters of the *General Theory* to reassess usury laws and the theory behind mercantilism 'The faculty of economists', he writes, 'prove to be guilty of presumptuous error in treating as a puerile obsession what for centuries has been a prime object of statecraft' (Keynes 1978: 339) – namely to lower interest rates. Throughout history, states have attempted to protect their subjects from the consequences of liquidity-preference; usury laws, for example, which either ban or set a limit to the rate of interest, were a vital tool in permitting an adequate inducement to invest 'in a world which no one reckoned to be safe' (Keynes 1978: 351) – and where the premium needed to persuade wealth-holders not to hoard would have risen sky-high. Equally mercantilism, the object of which was to accumulate gold and silver through running a balance-of-payments surplus, had a similar effect. By attempting to guarantee that the economy never had a shortage of precious metals – which at that time were the principal means of exchange – the liquidity-preferences of a community living in a hazardous and tempestous environment could be satisfied at comparatively low rates of interest. In Keynes's own words (1978: 336) a favourable balance of trade was 'the only indirect means of reducing the rate of interest and so increasing the inducement to home investment'. In a society where there was no question of direct investment 'under the aegis of public authority', the only economic objects which the Government could reasonably try and influence were the domestic rate of interest and the balance of foreign trade. Interpreted in this light, both mercantilism and usury laws, far from being 'puerile obsessions', were sensible attempts to attack the problem of liquidity-preference – attempts which contemporary governments would do well to emulate.

It is this same theme that Keynes strikes in the *Treatise on Money* when advocating 'saturation' monetary policy – open-market operations *à outrance* (Keynes 1971: 347): the latter-day surrogate for usury laws and mercantilist hoarding of precious metals. It is via the financial system that liquidity-preference is expressed, and thus interest rates, investment, and income determination; the object of open-market operations *à outrance* is to lean against the financial markets' liquidity-preferences so that interest rates are prevented from rising in the event of a decline in business expectations. If savers are unwilling to increase their illiquidity and buy bonds so that interest rates fall, then the State in the guise of the Central Bank should increase its illiquidity. 'They (Central Banks) should combine to a very low level of the short-term rate of interest, and buy long-dated securities either against an expansion of central bank money or against the sale of short-dated securities until the short term market is saturated.' (Keynes 1971: 347) The Central Bank thus ends up with a portfolio that is the mirror image of the financial markets: when expectations are poor it will sell short-term financial assets – bills – to savers and use the proceeds to buy bonds. Savers have their liquidity-preference assuaged, but there will be no resulting increase in interest rates because bond prices will have been supported by the Bank.

Liquidity-preference does not therefore happen in a vacuum: it interacts with the willingness of the institutions of the financial system to meet that demand for liquidity by becoming illiquid themselves. In an article published after the issue of the *General Theory*, Keynes (1937: 666) quotes approvingly the idea that 'the rate of interest is determined by the interplay of the terms on which the public desires to become more or less liquid and those on which the banking system is ready to become more or less unliquid.' It is not enough to say simply that the rate of interest is the outcome of liquidity-preference; one has to examine how liquidity-preference is handled by the financial markets and the financial institutions. It is behind this process that the State stands watchfully.

The liquidity-preference of the *General Theory* should therefore be judged in the light of the financial markets and institutions of the 1930s. There was still an enormous rentier class, and it was their decision on whether to hold bonds or cash that was the prime determination of the rate of interest. In fact the *General Theory* can be read as a condemnation of the behaviour of the rentier class during the Great Depression. Instead of buying bonds they had accumulated large hoards of cash, which with commodity prices falling made a great deal of investment sense; the value of money was rising as prices fell. The return on holding cash – given falling commodity prices – was more certain than any potential return from investing in bonds. The problem was that the hoarding of cash caused monetary demand to fall to such an extent that business expectations collapsed; even though bonds could be issued on very low interest rates, there were very few issuers and very few buyers. The issuer was deterred by the prospect of falling prices, low demand, and poor profit expectations (a low marginal efficiency of capital); while the buyer was deterred by the fact that with interest rates already so low there was little prospect of bonds going up in value, and in any case money was increasing in value as commodity prices fell (the liquidity trap).

The liquidity-preferences of the rentier class were thus at the root of the recession. In the financial markets there was hoarding of cash and low interest rates. In the commodity markets there was an acute shortage of monetary demand – the counterpart of the monetary hoarding. Employers were unwilling to hire labour or issue bonds. Labour was involuntarily unemployed, and paradoxically any attempt to lower money wages and price labour back into work would only cause monetary demand to fall further.

But if the rentier class's liquidity-preferences had caused the recession, the reaction of the financial system and the Central Bank had only been to prolong it. In the stock markets there were no buyers of bonds; the rentiers because they wanted to hold cash, the speculators because any recovery would presage higher interest rates. The banks did not want to stretch their balance sheets by going illiquid just as their customers were in trading difficulties: they were unwilling to offer money loans to maintain the level of aggregate demand. The Central Bank under Montagu Norman took the view that its responsibility was to ensure that the system was sound, that is, that the financial institutions remained liquid. As for a policy of selling Treasury bills and using the proceeds to buy bonds, thus solving the liquidity trap, the Bank was set against it on the grounds of financial imprudence; not to say the Treasury's unwillingness to stand surety against the potential capital losses in such an enormous operation.

The only solution was for the Government to borrow the idle cash and by spending itself to make up the shortfall in monetary demand, even if the spending was on projects such as digging a hole in the road and filling it up again. This famous Keynesian dictum has been used repeatedly to show that Keynes was in favour of public spending at whatever cost, but he arrived at this prescription only after all the other avenues had been closed. Lloyd George and the Liberal Party were advocating a programme of public works, and it was through this vehicle that Keynes saw the best prospect of stimulating the economy, given the saving habits of the rentier class, the behaviour of the bankers, and the reluctance of the Bank of England to step into the breach.

Once the liquidity preferences of the public had been amplified by the financial system, and with the manufacturing classes sharing the same pessimistic view of the future as the rentiers, the price mechanism had no means of getting the economy out of its hole. Industry and finance shared the same gloom; the rentiers were oversaving, but low interest rates were incapable of unravelling the conundrum. In the language of the *General Theory* liquidity-preference had compounded the lowering of the marginal efficiency of capital, and a liquidity trap prevented the excessive holdings of cash from being turned into effective monetary demand. A programme of public works seemed the only solution, with the State using the idle cash: but this was a last resort. Had the financial system taken a contrary view, or had the Bank of England acted to produce a contrary view, then the crisis need never have started. It was because the market system was such an effective buttress to economic and political pluralism that the State was obliged to act to help the markets help themselves. On this occasion the remedy was to borrow and spend, but this was because other remedies had been abjured.

The portfolio preferences of the financial system

If this is the essential flavour of the *General Theory*, how applicable is it fifty years on? The special characteristics of time, money, and uncertainty that are the foundations of the Keynesian view of how markets work remain constants, while the interaction between the structure of liquidity in the various markets in the economy and the overall preference for liquidity remain as upsetting to price and quantity adjustment now as then. Given that liquidity and liquidity-preference are the key building blocks in any explanation of the dynamics of market behaviour, Keynes's theory of interest-rate determination and investment decision-making seem just as valid, as does his general view that it is income and economic activity that adjust to bring prices and quantities into equilibrium, rather than prices adjusting to bring quantities into equilibrium.

Savings and investment are no less uniquely affected by expectations which 'based on shifting and unreliable evidence – are subject to sudden and violent changes' (Keynes 1978: 315) and remain the volatile values in a market economy. The problem is not with the theory but how it is to be interpreted in the circumstances of the 1980s. It is clear that the financial system occupies the centre of the stage, because it is here that the liquidity-preferences of the public are expressed and translated into interest rates. But it is the financial system which has experienced the biggest change since the 1930s. The rentier class has suffered the euthanasia that Kenyes predicted (if not for the same reason) and in its place have grown enormous financial institutions. No longer is it a rentier class making decisions about whether to hold its deferred claims on the future in the form of cash or bonds, but banks, insurance companies, and pension funds. And with the rise of these institutions the form of financial asset has changed. Company debentures and bonds, which were one of the most important sources of finance in the 1930s, have declined to the point of extinction. The provision of finance in the form of money loans has become the almost unique preserve of the banks; although the loans are not tradeable they play the same role as bonds with the effect that the decision on whether to hold cash or bonds is no longer the 'rentiers' but the banks.

At the same time the rentier has been superseded as the principal *owner* of financial assets. Whereas in the 1930s savings were accumulated and invested largely by individuals, the operation of the tax system and the spread of the idea of the funded pension has led to a growing proportion of savings being managed by institutions. Over a third of the public's savings is in the form of contractual payments to financial institutions such as insurance companies and pension funds (Wilson Rep.)[3] and some two-thirds of the equity traded on the London Stock Exchange is owned by financial institutions. (See Plender 1982: 13)

This dramatic increase in the importance of institutions and the accompanying decline in the rentier is the principal change in the financial markets over the last fifty years, and is of immense importance. For whereas in Keynes's day the problem was to balance out the liquidity-preferences of the rentier with those of the financial institutions so that the valuation of investment in physical assets could be maintained, the problem today is the liquidity-preference of the institutions themselves. It is their decisions on how they will hold the community's deferred claims on the future that determine the valuation of investment and the rate of interest, because they now manage the bulk of the community's savings. Whereas before there were two sets of decisions being taken – the public's on how liquid it was prepared to be, and the financial system's on how illiquid it was prepared to be – now the two decisions are rolled into one. The decision on the part of the institutions about how they are prepared to structure their claims on the future has become the economy's liquidity-preference function. If the *General Theory* should be understood in terms of the interaction of the rentier class and the financial system, in the 1980s it must be interpreted largely in terms of the behaviour of the financial institutions.

In the classical scheme of things the financial system is fundamentally the creature of the money flows created in the 'real economy'; it accommodates the financial needs of investors with the savings thrown up by savers, and as far as possible it will do no more than match the maturity date of its liabilities to savers with those of its assets – its advances to borrowers. The process of matching money flows in the future – savings and investment – is no different to matching mismatched current money flows. Investment levels will be determined by 'real' factors such as profitability, while savings will be determined by the thriftiness of the community. The financial system is nothing more than an intermediary.

However, the point is that savers do not know when they will require their savings; they are uncertain, by definition, about the future and they need to guard against this uncertainty by having the option of always being able to turn their saving into cash at the drop of a hat. This is what Keynes meant by liquidity. Savers will only commit themselves to non-consumption for specified time as long as they are able to unravel this commitment if their circumstances change. Because they 'cannot defeat the dark forces of time and ignorance which envelope our future' they take refuge in the liquidity that the financial markets provide.

This liquidity is illusory. There can be no liquidity for investors collectively, because not all investors can sell at once; but it allows each individual investor 'to flatter himself that his commitment is liquid . . . calms his nerves and makes him much more willing to run a risk.' (Keynes 1978: 160) The financial system's role of confidence trickster, giving the appearance of liquidity where in fact there is none, is critical: it allows the economy to meet the otherwise irreconcilable need of savers for liquidity with the need to carry and accumulate an illiquid capital stock. Axel Leijonhufvud (1968: 302) writes: *'In Keynes's grand conception, the basic function of "Finance" in modern systems is to reconcile the desire of households to be "liquid" with the technological necessity for the system as a whole to carry vast stocks of "physically illiquid" capital goods.'*

The struggle for liquidity is not just the feature of the security markets; it is the feature of the entire system. Whereas in the *General Theory*, Keynes focused on the trade-off between bonds and cash, which in the England of the 1930s was a trade-off that dominated the valuation of investment through the importance of the bond market, he was equally aware that the financial institutions themselves are making a similar trade-off within their own balance sheets. Just as the function of the security markets is to provide the appearance of liquidity, so banks function on exactly the same principle. If all depositors withdrew their deposits at the same moment, the bank could not honour its commitments, because the bank is no more broking between savings and investment than the financial markets. The bank gives its depositors the assurance that the individual deposit can be withdrawn at any moment – an assurance which cannot be true for all depositors collectively. But with the surety of this assurance the depositor happily leaves his deposit with the bank, which in its turn advances that deposit to those who are in need of cash. Once again the comfort of apparent liquidity allows the system to function; the banks can transform money into debt only if the money holders are individually persuaded that their money is withdrawable on demand; and without bank debt any more than bonds the economy could not carry the fixed and illiquid assets it needs to carry if it is to function.

Keynes sees one of the responsibilities of financial institutions as to operate against the liquidity-preferences of the system; to be the 'bulls' against the 'bears'. If portfolios of assets are moved towards the short, liquid end of the security market, the financial institutions must step in to prevent the consequent rise in interest rates; and this is how he explains it:

If, however, the banking system operates in the opposite direction to that of the public and meets the preference of the latter for savings-deposits by buying the securities which the public is less anxious to hold and creating against them the additional savings-deposits which the public is *more* anxious to hold, then there is no need for the price-level of investments to fall at all . . . A fall in the price-level of securities is therefore an indication that the 'bearishness' of the public . . . has been insufficiently offset by the creation of savings-deposits by the banking system. . . . (Keynes 1971: 142–3)[4]

If financial institutions will take the contrary view to the public, then there is some hope at least of stability in the valuation of investment, and it need not be the subject of the vagaries that accompany the stampede for liquidity. The hopes and fears that seize security markets and move them one way or the other in violent surges and collapses can then be sealed off from the real economy. The problem is that the financial institutions no less than the public want to stay liquid.

Of the maxims of orthodox finance none, surely, is more anti-social than the fetish of liquidity, the doctrine that it is a positive virtue on the part of investment institutions to concentrate their resources upon the holding of 'liquid' securities. It forgets that there is no such thing as liquidity of investment for the community as a whole. The social object of skilled investment should be to defeat the dark forces of time and ignorance which envelop our future. The actual, private object of the most skilled investment today is 'to beat the gun', as the Americans so well express it, to outwit the crowd, and to pass the bad, or depreciating, half-crown to the other fellow. (Keynes 1978: 155)

So whether it is the provision of money-loans that are tradeable or non-tradeable, the same phenomenon is evident: an unwillingness of the financial system to carry any burden of illiquidity. Yet the quantity adjustments that occur in the economy manifest themselves as money flows in the financial system; in particular in the structure of the assets and liabilities of the banking sector. The extent to which its liabilities are held in cash or near-cash is a barometer of the community's changing liquidity-preference function; and equally the extent and terms on which money loans are demanded is a barometer of the state of expectations and the marginal efficiency of capital. By defining themselves as far as they can as simple intermediaries – and classical economics describes this as their function – the banks disavow their influence on liquidity-preferences, interest rates, and the rate of capital accumulation: nor is any intellectual attempt made to enquire what the results of this abdication are. Instead theory works within boundaries in which interest rates are seen as the outcome of the supply and demand for credit, and the money supply as a variable which can only be pulled away from some natural tendency to equilibrium by an exogenous influence such as government financing policy. It is an extraordinary misdirection of intellectual and policy effort.

The impact on an individual investment decision-maker is

evident; the illiquidity involved in financing projects will be shouldered largely by himself, and consequently he must invest less, and in projects with higher pay-offs. By pushing the risk of illiquidity away from the financial system and towards the individual, the risk perception of any particular project must be higher, and fewer are likely to be undertaken. Nor is this just a question of the rate at which investment projects are launched over a business cycle, and the attempt which must then be made to equalise them; it is also about the absolute rate of investment. The tension between liquidity-preferences and illiquidity needs is at the heart of the instability and performance of the market economy.

As Keynes suggested, one answer would be to make financial investment 'permanent and indissoluble like marriage', so that it would be impossible to try and unscramble it at the first sign of trouble. The difficulty is that as soon as financial investment became immutable the volume would dry up; it is the very liquidity of financial investment that allows it to happen at all. Only in organising different behaviour on the part of financiers is there hope of salvation.

The British financial system

The pace of accumulation of fixed assets in a market economy therefore hangs on the attitude of the financial institutions towards liquidity; and fifty years on the liquidity fetish that Keynes complained of is just as evident. The most recent investigation into the workings of the City – the Review by the Wilson Committee – is redolent with this obsession.

The banks, for example, in their evidence admit that their deposit base is stable, but because deposits can be theoretically withdrawn on demand, they say they are reluctant to go beyond certain limits in the length of the loans they advance. 'The first obligation of any deposit-taking institution is to ensure its ability at all times to meet any withdrawal by its depositors under any circumstances which may reasonably be envisaged.' (BIS 1977: para 5.3: 60)[5] But how unstable are those deposits? In fact the banks admit their deposit base remains 'reasonably stable' and quote with approval the Radcliffe Report's aphorism, 'individual balances go up and down, depositors come and depositors go, but the total on current account goes on for ever' (BIS, para. 4.17: 50)[6]. The obstacle to advancing medium- and long-term money loans is not the liquidity-preference of the public, which seems to be fairly consistent, but the liquidity-preference of the banks. They see themselves simply as intermediaries; if there were more long-term deposits, then they could lend more long-term money. If the job of the financial system is to match *liquid financial liabilities* with *illiquid physical assets*, then that is not a role that the banks have any plans to fulfil. Instead they define their function as meeting industry's demands as best they can, given that the cost and quantity of finance is outside their control (BIS, para. 7.43: 97). There is satisfaction expressed in their evidence that the volume of bank lending 'does move in the way required to *accommodate* the need of industrial and commercial companies to borrow to finance any shortfall of internally generated funds when investing in fixed capital and stocks'. (BIS, para. 7.17: 84) In other words, the banks' role is to *accommodate* industry's needs, and to supplement its internally generated funds. There is no recognition that the valuation of financial assets by the banks in terms of the conditions of their money loans might influence industry's demand for funds. As a result the risk in financing an illiquid capital stock is passed on to those who actually acquire it: the banks want as little part in the process as possible.

This liquidity-preference on the part of the banks is reflected in the length of term of loan they provide; in 1980 less than 13 per cent of banks loans in Britain were for more than five years' duration, while some 67 per cent were for one year or less, and the figures have not materially changed since then (Vittas & Brown 1982: 82). The degree companies borrow from banks to finance medium and long-term investment is correspondingly low, as might be expected; the shorter the term of the loan, the heavier the burden of repayment and the greater the deterrent to borrow. In Keynesian theory it is the valuation of financial assets that sets the terms of the valuation of physical assets and as argued earlier, that valuation is now done entirely by financial institutions on behalf of their depositors and savers. If banks in their loan policy set short-term horizons with heavy repayment schedules, then the investment projects that industrialists appraise will also have short-term horizons and high cash-flow returns (Carrington & Edwards 1981). As there can be expected to be relatively few of such projects, the capacity to service such bank debt will be low. At the end of 1984 only 25 per cent of the capital employed of the 100 top British companies was financed by bank borrowings (Phillips & Drew 1984: 21).

To put these figures in perspective it is worth comparing them with the company debt levels attained in France and Germany. Although in any one year it seems that the split between internal and external finance is broadly similar in all three countries (Bayliss & Butt 1980),' the cash flow that services the external finance seems to be able to support a higher overall volume of company debt in France and Germany: the level of capital gearing in Germany is nearly twice as high as that in Britain, and it is three times as high in France (Wilson Rep., Table 39: 152). The missing link is the terms on which the external finance is provided. In Germany nearly 50 per cent of loans are for four years or more, while in France nearly 30 per cent of loans are for seven years or more (Vittas & Brown 1982).[8] In other words, the hypothesis seems to stand: if banks are more willing to hold less liquid financial assets through having a loan portfolio with longer repayment terms, then the company sector can service more debt, and concomitantly can finance a higher level of investment in an illiquid capital stock.

A persistent bias by the banks in this direction could be expected to produce a higher level of fixed capital accumulation, and a tendency to a high overall growth rate – although this cannot be taken for granted given the problems in ensuring that the final use of investment is efficient. However, the figures do seem to support the general hypothesis (see Table 2).

Table 2 Percentage change in volume of gross domestic capital formation and growth rates, 1970–80

	Capital formation	*Growth rate*
France	2.8	3.6
Germany	2.0	2.8
UK	0.6	1.9

Source: OECD, *Growth Triangles. National Accounts, 1951–80*.

In fact the figures disguise a more serious trend as far as the UK is concerned. Net domestic capital formation (gross domestic capital formation less capital consumption) has fallen calamitously: in 1981 it was running at a third of the peak 1973 level, a degree of fall unparalleled in any other industrialised country. Although there has been some subsequent improvement, by 1984 the rate of net new investment was only 1 per cent of the total capital stock. Moreover, in manufacturing, net investment has been negative for the four consecutive years 1981–84, that is, there has not been enough taking place to renew the existing capital stock, let alone add to it. Net investment in the distribution, services, and financial

160

sector has been rising strongly so that it now accounts for half of total investment: without this the overall figure would have been still worse (CSO 1984).[9]

There is no disputing the worrying implications of these figures: it is, after all, manufacturing which still directly and indirectly provides the most employment pound for pound of invested capital, and that substantial disinvestment should be taking place after a significant recovery in profitability and some four or five years of economic recovery is alarming. Yet even allowing for some secular decline in manufacturing, the overall pace of capital accumulation in the economy is tiny. Until the early 1980s banking authorities were able to argue that the root cause was not their financing behaviour, but a sharp fall in post-tax real rates of return. The Bank of England, in its evidence to the Wilson Committee, drew attention to the fall in this measure of profitability from 5.9 per cent in 1973 to 3.2 per cent in 1979, and argued that profitability is as much a constraint on investment as the cost of finance. Indeed the Wilson Report (para 1406: 371) concluded that 'It is the price of finance in relation to profitability which is the major financial constraint on real investment at present', and could reach no agreement on whether the financial system's liquidity-preference had any impact on the rate of interest or supply of finance.

This argument was taken one step further by the Banking Information Service when, writing on behalf of the London Clearing Banks, it was contested that not only was finance not a constraint on the performance of the UK economy, but that (over the 1970s) 'the differences between the investment record of the United Kingdom and those of France and Germany were very limited': (Vittas & Brown 1982: 10) By implication the fault for the UK's economic performance lay not with the financial sector but in obstacles to the effective use of finance and investment once it was made available.

However, real post-tax rates of return have risen strongly since the early 1980s and are now higher – at around 8 per cent – than at any time since the early 1970s.[10] Profitability is thus much less of a constraint, but the level of investment, while rising from a very depressed base, is still running at a fraction of the rates of even the mid-1970s, and not nearly fast enough to lift the trend rate of growth in the economy. The important influence of banking policy on both the pace and structure of capital formation is now much more apparent.

The feature of the four years 1981–84 has been the growth of investment in distribution and allied services and the substantial disinvestment in manufacturing. In this period outstanding bank loans to manufacturing have risen by less than 10 per cent in real terms; to the service sector they have jumped by half in real terms, so that outstanding loans to the service sector are twice those of manufacturing (a trend that appears to have continued in 1985)[11]. This sharp growth in lending far outstrips the relative performance of the service sector in the real economy, yet this is just what might be expected given the known terms on which banks lend. Investment in distribution is less subject to the vagaries of changes in future expectations, and distribution networks are versatile and consistant earners of income streams. Manufacturing, on the other hand, suffers from frequent reassessments of the marginal efficiency of capital and financiers have to be more sympathetic to the resulting changes in the valuation of manufacturing capital assets. It is only if they stretch their liquidity that the pace of accumulation of this class of physical assets can be maintained. It is just this policy that British bankers are reluctant to pursue.

The great advantage to the banks of this attitude is an extremely high level of profitability. Loans are short-term and highly secured, and as a result the bad-debt record is comparatively good because few companies are permitted to 'gear up' with a high level of bank borrowing. Concentration on high-margin consumer lending, 'free' deposits as current accounts pay no interest, few bad debts, and favourable terms on which to do corporate business combine to produce one of the most profitable banking sectors in the world.

It is this profitability that allows the UK banks to bid for international deposits, and expand their international lending activities: unsurprisingly their international loan book has exactly the same characteristics as the domestic loan book.[12] The fact that the UK has a weak economy and a strong financial sector is often interpreted as evidence of greater entrepreneurial skill on the part of the bankers, but it is only the high UK profits that permits the international expansion: those high profits originate in the structure of liquidity that makes it so difficult for the non-banking sector to acquire physical assets. In other words, the counterpart of a strong financial sector is a weak real economy.

But if it were the case that opportunities existed to exploit a market for industrial and commercial loans, surely, argue the 'counter-revolutionaries', an enterprising banker would have stepped in and offered longer-term loans in response to unrequited market demand? The market for money loans is like any other, responsive to the forces of supply and demand. The Keynesian reply should be familiar. The price mechanism does not co-ordinate the plans of future-guessing investors and savers except as *ex post* identities. *Ex ante* bankers have a preference for liquidity and a risk-averse approach to holding illiquid assets, and the price mechanism works within their preference set, with the only lever it has, the rate of interest, unable to clear the market except in the sense of producing accounting identities. The rate of interest cannot broker between disparate demands for liquidity and illiquidity.

But it is not just the banks who have a pronounced tendency to hold liquid (in the sense of short-term) assets; the whole of the British financial system is characterised by a zeal for liquidity which makes the accumulation of illiquid physical assets generally difficult. Institutions such as pension funds and insurance companies, who have *long-term* contractual liabilities and who are assured of a steady flow of saving over time will concentrate investment in assets that are quickly realisable in cash. Whereas the banks' liquidity-preference and unwillingness to accept risk exhibits itself in the term structure of their advances, the same phenomenon in the investing financial institutions exhibits itself as a readiness to hold chiefly those long-term assets that are marketable, that is, realisable as cash in the securities markets.

In 1978, 81 per cent of insurance company 'general investment' funds, 76 per cent of pension fund investment, and 71 per cent of long-term insurance company investment was held in marketable assets such as cash, company equity, or public-sector securities – and in 1985, the figures were broadly the same (Wilson Rep.)[13]. In 1985 nearly 5 per cent of GDP was channelled through the pension funds and insurance companies as contractual saving; a proportion that has been growing consistently over the last three decades – but nearly all the money was used to buy pre-existing assets on the Stock Exchange whose main merit in the eyes of the investment managers was their apparent liquidity.

Although stockbrokers, investment analysts, and fund managers make very considerable sums of money from the exchange of these assets, their economic function in terms of enlarging the possibilities of the system carrying a greater illiquid capital stock is negligible. The heart of the problem is that the very liquidity that the investing institutions crave, and which the security markets have come into existence to solve, make the markets work for the financial institutions rather than for the borrower. So that even while the securities that the investing institutions hold may be long term in the sense that the ultimate date of redemption may be very far in the future (in the case of equity never), that does not mean the issue of new securities is an especially attractive proposition for the borrower – and the reason for this lies in the preoccupation of the financial investor, not with the long-term prospects of the company, but with its short-term performance.

The concern to protect liquidity at all costs simply means that the entire intellectual effort of the investment community is expended in profiting, or at least avoiding losses, from short-term variations in the price of company equity, debt, and government securities. It is 'to beat the gun'.

This continual trading of shares is excused by Stock Market apologists as the inevitable outcome of the Market's permanently reassessing company prospects and market prospects in the light of always changing information, and is the nearest thing yet to a perfect market. But as Keynes wrote (1978: 151), 'It is as though the farmer, having tapped his barometer after breakfast, could decide to remove his capital from the farming business between 10.00 and 11.00 in the morning and reconsider whether he should return to it later in the week.' It is surely not the role of financial institutions managing large sums of savings, the contributors of which have already expressed a willingness to be relatively illiquid, to play musical chairs with company equity. Yet the turnover in the markets suggests that this is exactly what they are doing.

None the less it is true that company equity and debt need to be tradeable if investing institutions are to hold it. After all, the investing institution will need to sell its share in the ownership of a company at some time in the future: its liabilities, however long term, will still be finite, while the life of equity investment is infinite; and company debt may only be repaid after the institution has to meet its liabilities. But there is no liquidity for the investing institutions in aggregate. They cannot all sell at the same time. By concentrating constantly on the *marketability* of their assets, they imagine they are achieving *liquidity*. This attempt to achieve a bogus liquidity leads in turn to a concentration on the current selling value of their portfolio. They try to avoid those shares which might fall in value, even though that fall in value might be a result of factors that ensure the long-term health of the company. A firm that cuts its dividend to protect the level of real investment is shunned, and rights issues, which raise new money, are highly unpopular because they dilute the interest of existing shareholders and tend to lower the share price. The amount of new equity issued is tiny. In 1983, the best year during the period 1980–84, equity issues only amounted to around 10 per cent of industry and commerce's total capital spending, while debentures and preference shares were insignificant as sources of finance.[14]

Equity is supposed to have a variable return and to represent risk, but the probable reaction of the institutions to a capital issue deters potential issuers. Companies know that the valuation of their shares affects their general credit-worthiness not only with their bankers but with their trade creditors. They know their investors are in the business of pass the parcel, and will not support them if the going gets tough. As a result they are careful about diluting the share price through the issue of new equity; apart from anything else a low share price makes them vulnerable to takeover, and with a few notable exceptions, the institutions can be relied upon to sell to the highest bidder whatever the long-term consequences for the company concerned. This constrains not only the amount of physical capital in which they can invest, but the whole company strategy.

The prime object of a company with a Stock Exchange quotation becomes the maintenance and growth of short-term profits in order to maintain the share price, even though an increasing number of investment projects have a long-term pay off, and may require lower profits in the short term. Similarly, pricing to enlarge market share, which costs profits in the short term, is a strategy denied to all but the strongest of British companies. As a result it is very difficult to get the market share that justifies long production runs that get down the 'learning curve', and lower unit costs in sharp contrast to the operation of the Japanese financial system in supporting 'market-expanding' corporate strategies. Production tends to be focused into batches that can meet a predictable market niche, and can be quickly stopped if market conditions deteriorate. British companies have adopted a multi-product, multi-market strategy because they have not the financial muscle to push for market dominance. As a result they always suffer from a comparatively high cost structure, but as any remedial action requires long-term investment they are locked into a position of structural weakness. Any investment must be short term, and have a high pay-off, which is why British companies frequently find themselves unable to develop innovations which comparable overseas companies operating in a different financial environment might be able to develop and so achieve market leadership[15]. Neither the banks, with their liquidity-preference and general short-term lending strategy, nor the investing institutions, with their concern for short-term profit performance arising from their liquidity preoccupation, are prepared to back them.

One borrower, however, does enjoy the confidence of the investing institutions: Her Majesty's Government. Government securities are gilt edged; they are not subject to the vagaries of changes in the marginal efficiency of capital and business expectations, something with which the City is fundamentally unsympathetic. It is a straight game of liquidity-preference played on the institutions' own terms. The Government has to persuade them to part with their liquidity, and will pay them a rate of interest commensurate with the institutions' judgement about how solidly the Government's IOUs will hold their value. If the Government's spending, taxation, and borrowing plans meet with the institutions' disapproval then they can simply hold cash until the price of Government securities reflects their inceased unhappiness, that is, until the price of 'gilts' has fallen and interest rates have risen.

As a result the selling of Government securities is a game of cat and mouse, with the institutions wary of the size of the Government's borrowing, its interest rate plans, and its willingness to finance its needs in the short-term markets. On the other hand, the Government has become persuaded that short-term financing inevitably has inflationary consequences (one of the by-products of the classical 'counter-revolution') and is much keener to sell longer-term debt to the financial institutions. The balance of power has shifted even further towards the institutions, and interest rates more fully reflect their liquidity-preferences than they have for years; with the Government anxious to meet their wishes there has been a sharp rise in real interest rates, notwithstanding a fall in real Government borrowing and a deep recession.

Unsurprisingly the volume of net new investment for any given level of economic activity has been sharply depressed by this rise in real interest rates, but this has been blamed on excessive real wages. The problem, it is argued, is not the portfolio and liquidity-preferences of the financial institutions, nor the financing idiosyncracies of the Government: rather it is 'uncompetitiveness' – and that is perceived essentially as a problem of real wages. Neither the financial system, which sees itself as an honest broker, nor the Government, which sees itself as determinedly anti-inflationary, accept any responsibility for the fall in output and investment and the subsequent disappointing recovery. The perspective is one of the market being capable of producing the 'right' results, and only prevented from doing so by 'obstacles'. Monopoly and price inflexibility inhibit profit signals and the process of adjustment across too many markets of the economy; but undoubtedly the chief problem is seen as the functioning of the labour market – an echo of the thinking of the 1930s.

One financial institution in Britain has been outstandingly

successful, and has broken all the rules of liquidity. In 1948 bank deposits were six times the size of building society deposits; the building societies had a mere 7 per cent of the total savings market. (Boddy 1980, Fig. 2.1) By 1984 the situation had been transformed. Building society deposits actually exceeded bank retail deposits and their share of the personal savings market was around 40 per cent. This astounding rise was due in the main to one factor; savers knew that only through saving with a building society could they get the long-term loan they required in order to buy a house. It is true that governments of both parties were keen to encourage home ownership, and that the cause of home ownership was served by a number of tax advantages. The building societies, for example, enjoyed a concession on income tax – the composite rate – which permitted them to calculate the income tax that savers should pay at a lower rate than the standard rate (some savers are non-tax payers, but still have tax deducted, hence the concession): this was worth up to $1\frac{1}{2}$ per cent interest extra on building society savings. The societies are also accorded charitable status under the Friendly Societies Act, and enjoy a number of tax advantages; equally home owners pay no tax on any profits they make if they sell their home.

This 'inside track' created by the State has undoubtedly favoured home ownership, and helped the building society movement, giving them a competitive advantage over the banks: but it is jejune to describe the growth of the societies as largely attributable to tax advantages – as the clearing banks did in their evidence to the Wilson Committee. Right up until 1979, when the banks finally realised that they could lend long term on private houses as well, the building societies were the only financial institutions prepared to take the risk on liquidity, matching effectively what are demand deposits with 25-year mortgages. Not only has home ownership more than doubled from around 26 per cent of the population in 1945 to over 55 per cent in 1982; but the standard of the housing stock compares favourably with that of other countries. West Germany, Japan, France, and the USA all experienced higher economic growth rates in the post-war years and have higher absolute per capita incomes, but their housing stock, judged by percentage of one-room dwellings, average rooms per house, persons per room, etc., is not of any higher standard than the British, and in some areas is inferior (see Table 3).

The building societies have been ready to do what the rest of the financial system has been either unwilling or unable to do; they have offered liquidity to their savers and depositors while permitting the system to build up illiquid physical assets. As a result they

Table 3 Home ownership and housing quality in five countries

Country (and year)	Per cent owner-occupied	Per cent of one-room dwellings	Average rooms per dwelling house	persons per room	Per cent dwellings with flush toilets
France (1973)	45.5	11.6	3.3	0.9	54.8
Japan (1978)	59.5	5.0	4.0 (1973)	1.1 (1973)	45.9
West Germany (1972)	33.5	2.1	4.2	1.5	94.2
USA (1978)	64.8 (1977)	1.8 (1977)	5.1	0.6	96.0
UK–England and Wales (1971)	55.0 (1982)	2.1	4.9	0.6 (1982)	98.9

Source: *Compendium of Housing Statistics*. UN Department of International Statistics, New York 1980; Japanese and USA figures revised in *UN Statistical Year Book* 1979/80 and 1981 respectively; UK figures from: *General Household Survey 1982*. Office of Population Censuses and Surveys.

have acquired a large share of the savings market, and have sponsored a vast improvement in the using stock, which contrasts sharply with capital assets in the hands of the industrial and commercial sector, whose financing needs have been met by liquidity-conscious financial institutions unready to take the same kind of 'risk'.

The overall structure of debt is represented in Table 4. No more eloquent testimony is required to the liquidity-preferences of the British financial system. Building societies and the National Loans Fund are shown to have outstanding long-term loans to house buyers and public corporations equal to £84 billion. The clearing banks' outstanding long-term debt is less than an eighth of this total, and not all that will be to commercial and industrial customers. The British financial system is nothing less than a conduit for the transformation of liquid savings into house mortgages and public-sector debt; not only does it fail to 'lean' against the liquidity-preferences of the public when there is a general deterioration in expectations so that the pace of capital accumulation in the economy can be maintained, it also is heavily biased against capital accumulation as a rule. It is here that we should seek both an overlooked cause and perhaps an important remedy for Britain's habitually weak industrial performance.

The promise of change?

This, though, argue the 'counter-revolutionaries' is yesterday's story. London stands on the threshold of a revolution in its financial structure that will resolve all these problems – in so far it is conceded that any such problems exist. The structural revolution marries with the intellectual revolution: London's financial institutions and markets, under the need to respond to market pressures, are transforming themselves into the kind of financial system that not only conform more closely to the constitution of a textbook classical market, but in so doing they are spontaneously producing the solutions to uncertainty and risk.

Perhaps the most important innovation is the spread of instruments that allow market transactors to protect themselves against the change of values in the future – the markets in future contingencies and prices whose non-existence Keynes identified as a prime source of market instability (p 137–9). There are options markets, futures markets and 'swap' markets: dealers in foreign exchange, stocks and shares, the money markets, commodities – even freight rates – can all use one or more of these instruments to 'lock in' today's prices in the future. Even bankers can sell each other their loan portfolios. The market has come to the rescue: uncertainty need no longer, at least in the financial markets, constrain the actions of market transactors. Tomorrow's fears can be guarded against today. The preference for liquidity that had dogged the financial markets is in the process of being dissolved away, and Keynesians must be much more cautious, it is implied, about insisting that the market economy is bedevilled by the infamous two sets of guesses. Even an entrepreneur's marginal efficiency of capital computation is made more secure, because there are now the means to guard against uncertain movements in exchange rates and interest rates, which are as important for him as·for his financiers.

However it is not obvious that the new markets will work in this way, or that the liquidity proclivities that characterize the system will be significantly reduced. Financial institutions are the sources of two broad classes of illiquid finance: equity and debt. The chief 'risk limitation' tool available to equity holders is the option market: by dealing in options it is possible to generate capital profits (or losses) that can be offset against the losses (or profits) produced by short term price movements in the equity holder's base or 'core' portfolio. By making short term price movements potentially irrelevant, it is contended, equity holders can regard a larger part of their share portfolio as a 'core' holding – so ensuring a more plentiful supply of equity finance.

But the great attraction of the option market is not the protection against uncertainty it offers, but the opportunity of making highly leveraged short-term capital gains. For an outlay that is only a fraction of the value of the underlying asset, an option dealer buys the chance of capturing all the gain represented by that underlying asset's price changes; and as the required price movement can be expected to take place in the very near future in today's volatile conditions, the exposure can be quickly closed. Option turnover has ballooned, especially in the USA, but all that has happened is that short term time horizons have been foreshortened even further, resulting in near feverish trading. Indeed there is some evidence (Bianco, 1985) that options and futures trading can create even more price instability in share prices generally as option traders unwind option positions by dealing in the main markets. Far from making financial institutions less liquidity conscious, they are now more heedful of short-term price movements and the need for marketability in their equity portfolios, without which profitable position-taking in the option market is impossible.

Nor is the 'securitisation' of bank debt, the new market in hitherto untraded bank loans and mortgages, likely to change liquidity preferences. It might be supposed, that by offering banks a market in their loans they need be less liquidity conscious, because they now have the option of selling their loans. However identifying the marketability of debt as liquidity is an illusion, for the same reason that marketability of shares does not provide liquidity for the system: not all banks can sell at once. Indeed, as in the share and options markets, the very marketability and daily price fluctuations of assets encourages a short-term view. The market should be viewed more as a means of asset swapping within a given preference for liquidity, rather than greatly transforming the willingness of banks to run a more long-term loan portfolio.

As for the much vaunted protections that are now available to the entrepreneur, these seem overstated. Exchange rate volatility, perhaps the single most important source of uncertainty, can be guarded against by dealing in the 'swap'[16] and futures markets. So while the system is unstable, it is argued, the individual transactor is able to secure much more stability.

But from the 'swap' and futures market-maker's perspective, however, the markets offer parallel possibilities of highly leveraged speculative position-taking to the options markets. By keeping exposures open for hours or even minutes, tiny price changes can produce very large capital gains, given the vast currency sums in which the institutions habitually deal. The object of the exercise is not to bet against the market trend, but to establish a direction of price movement and to keep a position 'open', in anticipation that the trend will continue (page 181). Taking a position contrary to the prevailing market trend may take very much longer to prove profitable, and the preference for liquidity is much less attractive than betting that an existing trend will continue. In this way the potential for the system of floating rates to get locked into fundamental misalignments, where market values do not correspond to any estimate of 'real' values, is greatly magnified (p 193–4). The markets may allow the individual transactor to diminish one level of uncertainty, but by enlarging the possibilities of a systemic tendency to non-equilibrium only create a much more serious level of uncertainty – the chance that over the life of an investment project overseas earnings may be substantially reduced by a persistently overvalued currency.

At the same time the volume of turnover in the financial markets has exploded, even though there has been little or no accompanying rise in the free capital underwriting this extra business. Given the close inter-relationships that exist between the various markets and institutions there is now much more risk of problems in one area being transmitted to another; and more risk that such problems could occur. The 'Big Bang' has if anything enhanced the system's fragility; the creation of new financial 'supermarkets' to take advantage of the decartelisation of stock exchange commissions, and the merging of investment and commercial banking activities into these new operations means that the capital, formerly underwriting the generation of illiquid money loans, is now supporting the added burden of major market-making and position-taking in the old and new financial markets. Given the extra claims and risks, it is improbable that financial institutions will run more illiquid loan portfolios – if anything the pressures will be to make them yet more short-term.

Indeed the competitive forces that the banks are confronting will push them even further in this direction. Their ability to attract cheap high street deposits has been weakened by the building societies, and to stabilise their market share they have been compelled to match the societies in the rates that are paid for deposits. The lost high street savings have been replaced by bidding for money in the more expensive wholesale London money markets, and with their margins compensatingly narrowed the short term profitability of their lending has become an even more over-riding requirement. Mortgage lending to the consumer sector has exploded in the search for risk-free volume business, and there has been a sharp increase in the level of short-term consumer advances.

The deregulation of the building societies, with their new ability to move into all forms of consumer lending, will intensify the tempo. In the competition for high street retail deposits and consumer business, more and more of a blind eye is being turned to long term mortgage lending not being used for house purchase, but for all forms of consumer spending; and it is likely that, to win consumer deposits, even orthodox consumer credit will become longer term so as to make its servicing easier. Paradoxically the result of deregulation and the mushrooming of the new financial markets will be to provide more illiquid finance for the personal sector, and less for the corporate sector – thus further entrenching the system's already problematic liquidity preferences.

The change in the financial structure has also brought severe difficulties for monetary control. The 'monetarist' presumption is that the inflationary chain of causation runs from the growth of the banks' liabilities, to the growth of their assets, to prices. The policy objective, therefore, has been to control banks' *liabilities*, rather than the Keynesian concern with the growth of their *assets*. Yet the change in the financial structure makes the case against concentration on liability control even more pressing.

The banks' heightened concern to generate volume lending, and the illiquid advances they are providing to the personal sector to achieve that objective, makes it much more difficult for high interest rates to reduce the demand for their loans. By stretching the repayment terms into the future, current payments of principal are reduced so making it easier to pay high current rates of interest. The lax policing of the final uses of mortgage finance reinforces the trend, allowing the personal sector in effect to borrow long-term to pay current high interest rates.

But if the demand for a certain pattern of finance is not reduced by high interest rates, nor is the banks' ability to bid for deposits. Banks in a volatile environment increasingly do not pay a fixed rate for their funds; they negotiate to pay a fluctuating or floating rate as interest rates change, so avoiding the risk of being saddled with a potentially costly mismatch between inflows and outflows. With their customers paying a floating rate in turn, the key determinant of profitability is the margin. As long as there is a demand for their loans, therefore, the banks are able to bid for more funds relatively indifferent to changes in the rate of interest. The absolute level of interest rates needed to make the banks' liabilities grow within some predetermined range has risen, giving another twist in the system's bias to deter investment.

Nor are these trends only discernable in the UK: the internationalisation of the world's financial markets has led to a twentieth century version of Gresham's Law – liquidity preference always drives out illiquidity preference. The system of floating exchange rates has become a major source of instability for all currencies, whilst international lending has been characterised by its short term nature, placing an impossible level of debt service obligation upon third world debtor countries. The industrialised countries, in particular the USA and the UK, have been forced to take notice: default on what are perceived as usurious loan repayment terms by a leading debtor or group of debtor countries would lead, if there were no countervailing measures, to the write-off of the banking system's free capital and a collapse in the creditor countries' bank generated credit and finance. To avoid this calamity the banks have had to accept, through a series of 'rescheduling agreements', much longer terms over which their loans are repaid: terms which had they been accepted originally would have prevented the problem from becoming so acute.

Yet it should not be at moments of crisis that it is made apparent to all how crucially important the structure of the banking systems' assets is to the effective functioning of both the domestic and international economy, and how inequitable the basis of any intervention. Government must stand watchful and ready to intervene when the banks are in trouble – but at all other times the banks are permitted great freedom in how they choose to lend. The Keynesian prognosis is clear: how the financial system distributes its assets is important at all times – and not on the terms that suit the financiers.

Table 4 United Kingdom estimated maturity of lending to non-Bank residents, 1980

	£ billion			
	A*	*B**	*C**	*Total*
Banking sector	55.3	16.5	10.7	82.5
Trustee savings banks	0.3	—	0.1	0.4
Finance houses	—	3.8	1.5	5.3
Building societies	—	—	42.7	42.7
Insurance companies	—	—	3.7	3.7
Pension funds	—	—	0.7	0.7
National loans funds	—	—	41.3	41.3
Other public sector	—	—	4.4	4.4
Retailers	1.7	—	—	1.7
Total	57.3	20.3	105.1	182.7

* A: Short-term loans – up to one year.   B: Medium-term loans – between 1 and 5 years.   C: Long-term loans – 5 years and over.
Source: Vittas & Brown (1982), Table UK5, p. 82

Notes

1. After two centuries of attempts to prove this thesis the authors now claim to have discovered 'economic research' that finally settles the issue. They list: I. & F. Adelman (1959), 'The dynamic properties of the Klein–Goldberger Model', *Econometrica*, (Oct.); A. Goldberger (1959), *Impact Multipliers and Dynamic Properties of the Klein–Goldberger Model*, North Holland; B. G. Hickman (ed.) (1971), *Econometric Models of Cyclical Behaviour*, National Bureau of Economic Research. Unsurprisingly each model has the constitutional properties that ensures its success.

2. 'The depression also produced a far-reaching change in professional economic opinion. The economic collapse shattered the long held belief . . . that monetary policy was a potent instrument for promoting economic stability. Opinion shifted to the opposite extreme, that "money does not matter". John Maynard Keynes . . . offered an alternative theory . . . provided an appealing justification and a prescription for extensive government intervention.'

3. Calculated from Tables 13 and 15.

4. Quoted in Leijonhufvud (1968: 309, 310).

5. Evidence by the Committee of London Clearing Banks to the Committee to Review the Functioning of financial Institutions (Wilson Committee), November 1977.

6. Evidence by Committee of London Clearing Banks.

7. In this 1980 study Bayliss and Butt Philip show that German and French companies rely substantially on internally generated funds. In Germany the share fluctuates around 50 per cent (see their Tables 2.3 and 2.4, pp. 16 and 17 respectively) and in France the share had fallen from around 65 per cent in 1966–70 to 41 per cent in 1976, and may be even lower today (Table 5.6, p. 119). The key difference, as argued in the text, is the *terms* on which the external finance, is available.

8. Tables F5(p. 61) and G5(p. 68).

9. Figures from Tables 11.4 and 11.7, UK National Accounts. Little improvement has taken place in 1985 but at the time of writing no complete figures are available.

10. See *Bank of England Quarterly Bulletin*, July 1985.

11. Figures from *Financial Statistics*, Nov. 1984, adjusted by the RPI and July 1985.

12. The short-term structure of Euro-dollar assets has been a major reason why all international banks have been keen to expand in this area, and profits have been high. On the other hand, the short-term debt poses major problems for developing countries – witness Mexico's loan renegotiation and debt moratorium of August 1982, and the continued debt 'rescheduling' agreements over the last few years.

13. See Table 10 in the Report and *Financial Statistics*, July 1985.

14. See *Financial Statistics*, July 1985, Table 8.2.

15. See Magaziner, I. & Hout, T. (1981). *Japanese Industrial Policy*, Institute of International Studies, Univ. of California for an assessment of how the Japanese financial system enables Japanese corporations to adopt market-expanding strategies.
16. The 'swap' market is a technique by which foreign exchange dealers can swap future liabilities, thus squaring their position. Banks have developed the market so that the interest rates and currencies in which loans have been made can also be swapped.

References

Bayliss, B. T. & Butt Philip, A. A. S. (1980) *Capital Markets and Industrial Investment in Germany and France*. Saxon House.

Biano, A. (1985) 'Playing with Fire', *Business Week*, Sep 16th 1985.

BIS (Banking Information Service). (Nov. 1977) *Evidence by the Committee of London Clearing Banks to the Committee to Review the Functioning of Financial Institutions*.

Boddy, M. (1980) *The Building Societies*. Macmillan.

Brittan, S. (1981) *How to end the 'Monetarist' Controversy*. IEA Hobart Ppr 90.

Buchanan, J. M., Burton, J. & Wagner, R.E. (1978) *The Consequences of Mr Keynes*. IEA Hobart Paper 78:1.

Carrington, J. & Edwards, G. E. (1981) *Reversing Economic Decline*. Macmillan.

CSO (Central Statistical Office) (1984) *Blue Book*. HMSO.

Friedman, M. (1976) *Inflation and Unemployment*. IEA Occasional Ppr 51.

Friedman, M. & Friedman, R. (1980) *Free to Choose*. Secker and Warburg.

Hahn, F. (1973) 'The winter of our discontent', *Economica* (new series) vol. XL:34.

Hayek, F. (1973) *Economic Freedom and Representative Government*. IEA Occasional Paper 39.

Hayek, F. (1975) *Full Employment at Any Price?* IEA Occasional Paper 45.

Keynes, J. M (1937) 'The ex-aute theory of the rate of interest', *Economic Journal*.

Keynes, J. M. (1971) *The Treatise on Money* (vol. 1 & 2). Macmillan/Royal Economic Society.

Keynes, J. M. (1978) *General Theory of Employment, Interest and Money*. Macmillan.

Lange, O. (1964) *On the Economic Theory of Socialism*. McGraw-Hill.

Leijonhufvud, A (1968) *On Keynesian Economics and the Economics of Keynes*. Oxford U.P.

Phillips & Drew, (1984) *Equity Market Indicators* (Dec.)

Plender, J. (1982) *That's the Way the Money Goes*. Andre Deutsch.

Vittas, D. & Brown, R. (1982) *Bank Lending and Industrial Development: A response to recent criticism*. Banking Information Service.

Wilson Report: Committee to Review the Functioning of Financial Institutions, June 1980. HMSO.

Chapter 8

The role of the State

Summary

This chapter is split into two parts: the first is a review of Keynesianism as an economic philosophy, together with some notes on policy; the second is a review of the structures and weaknesses of the British State – weaknesses that severely constrain the chances of success of any Keynesian programme.

Part I

This section reviews the Keynesian view of the market system, and suggests that it should be interpreted as a fundamental critique of the potential of prices to co-ordinate the plans and actions of economic agents. Expectations are uncertainly held, the market is quantity-adjusting and the financial sector is the fulcrum on which all turns, representing as it does the financial counterpart of the quantity adjustments and the area where changes in expectations can be most quickly felt. Policy should thus be centred on the management of expectations and this means that an essential precondition of successful policy-making is that economic agents allow state action to have an impact on their expectations: in short, policy has to be seen as credible and agents have to believe in its continuity.

The principal focus of policy is a twin-track approach to influencing the 'two sets of guesses' that beset the market economy: the decision over liquidity in the financial markets, and the marginal efficiency of capital decision in the business sector as a whole. The financial system has to be levered into the provision of more investment credit, both as a contra-cyclical influence and as an effort to maximise the rate of capital accumulation. Monetary policy has to be subordinated to this aim, with the object of producing that term structure of interest rates which reinforces government policy on liquidity and portfolio preference.

The other prong of policy is fiscal action to produce the expectations, and consequently more generous valuations of illiquid physical assets, that match the increased flow of illiquid financial assets. Fiscal policy has two objects: to counteract quantity adjustments in the current period, and to produce expectations that similar action will take place in the following time periods – thus lifting the pace of investment. Credibility can be gained through making clear that fiscal action can be contractionary as well as expansionary, through signalling the responses to developments ahead of those same developments (contingency of borrowing, spending, and taxation), and through focusing changes around public-sector capital spending.

There is an international dimension to policy; the system of floating exchange rates can be expected to exaggerate cyclical movements in the exchange rate, given the nature of adjustment in the economy. It will require active management to prevent over- and undervaluation of the currency. Moreover, calculations about real investment are international, so the State may have to influence the marginal efficiency of capital computations that are taken on a global basis, and which have the potential to be self-feedingly adverse, and insist on access to markets (and the flows of income therefrom) being conditional on compensating national investment. And lastly, policy towards monopoly may need to be more accepting of the tendency towards monopolisation, while developing better ways of controlling monopoly power than ineffective attempts at imposing competition.

The unifying principle of policy is that the markets, unable to protect themselves from uncertainty, exhibit behaviour patterns that require contra-cyclical management, active superintendance, regulation, and arbitration by the State. In the absence of a *deus ex machina* – or markets in future contingencies – the State perforce has to play a role in shaping, maintaining, and counteracting both quantity adjustments and the formulation of expectations.

Part II

There is considerable unease at the apparently growing in-ability of the British State to think creatively and act strategically – and this would be a major disability in the implementation of a Keynesian economic programme. Two difficulties are singled out. The first is the lack of any British 'State' tradition, a tradition that argues that the common interest can and should be asserted. Instead, British liberalism takes the view that the public good is the sum of private interests; and Marxism takes the view that the State can only represent a class interest. As a result, no serious enquiry has been undertaken into how the State could possess in its Constitution some (however imperfect) institutional embodiment of the common interest. The second difficulty is the particular operation of British parliamentary democracy. The constitutional model supposes there to be a separate executive branch of government – the Queen and her ministers – which performs the creative and strategic thinking in the State; no such function is actually undertaken, and instead the legislative and executive are merged. Herein lie the problems of co-ordination, secrecy, and lack of strategic and coherent action. A solution is required, and it is improbable that it will be effected without some kind of separation between the executive and legislative.

Part I The Keynesian framework

Keynesianism as an economic philosophy

The idea that the market economy, if only it were left to regulate itself, would produce the 'best' outcome has not stood up to examination. The market is certainly an effective mechanism for allowing many individuals and organisations to freely express their wishes, and for transmitting those wishes to producers and traders. However effectively it is considered that the market can and does play this role, the proposition has proved too thin a reed on which to build a whole theory of economics. The stumbling block is that markets are not atemporal phenomena: the action of buying and selling takes time; the act of production takes time; and saving and investment hinge on expectations about what will happen at a future time.

In short, every economic transaction involves time or a calculation about time, and the problem is that the future is by definition unknowable. Thus to say that the market is not atemporal is equivalent to saying that it is riven by uncertainty about the future – and markets behave differently under conditions of uncertainty than under certainty. Yet the whole imposing edifice of classical and neo-classical theory is built on the assumption that time is not a problem; demand and supply analysis assumes that all transactions

178

take place in circumstances where the possibility that the future may be different from the present does not intrude into traders' deliberations.

The problem has two aspects. How are markets expected to co-ordinate their activities in the present in the face of uncertainty over the future, and how can the system ensure that plans for the future still take place notwithstanding the fact that nobody knows what the future holds? The first aspect of this dilemma can be thought of as essentially an information problem. In classical theory, prices are supposed to provide not only the *information* that traders require to form their plans so as to produce an equilibrium, but also the *incentive* for traders to adjust their plans if an equilibrium does not result. Prices perform the job of providing an incentive well enough, but their supposed job of disseminating all the information that is required to produce an equilibrium is wrecked by the intrusion of time. Traders need to know all possible combinations of price and quantity not only now, but in the future – but this information is unobtainable, and the only message given by current prices and quantities is that these are the current prices and quantities now obtaining. Traders have to guess what the parameters that will influence their conduct in the future are likely to be, and then base their decisions today on those expectations.

Once this Rubicon has been crossed it is no longer possible to hypothesise a world of perfectly 'clearing' markets. The prices and quantities that rule in a particular market in the present also represent a series of hunches and guesses by different market operators about the future course of prices. Current transactions and current production demand a view on the future, and this upsets the co-ordination of today's activities. The smoothly intersecting curves of the economists' atemporal imagination are chimera: the existence of the forces of supply and demand in a market guarantees nothing; there may not even be a point of intersection. Confident claims that the market has the potential to perfectly satisfy consumer preferences or organise some optimal distribution of resources dissolve away. The whole idea that the prices and quantities set in markets will lead to perfect co-ordination of buyers' and sellers' activities becomes very dubious indeed.

The second aspect – how the system manages to plan for the future notwithstanding the presence of uncertainty – presents classical economic theory with even more of a conundrum. Prices and profits are supposed to propel the economy in the same way as they keep it constantly co-ordinated, and savings are always made equal to investment by the rate of interest. Once again the 'dark forces of time and uncertainty' intrude, only with even more impact. Savers are abstaining from consumption because they anticipate some need for money in the future, and investors in physical assets recognise that the asset will only yield a return in the future. Calculations about the future dominate both sets of decisions, and they are taken by different sets of people. As argued in the previous chapter, the problem is one of liquidity: savers require liquidity, access to their savings, while investors acquire investment goods whose very character is their illiquidity. The apparently irreconcilable needs are only fulfilled by the mediation of the financial system, and the rate of interest becomes the rate paid to persuade savers to forego their desire for liquidity – not the rate to make savings equal investment.

The market economy is thus beset by a struggle for liquidity and a struggle for information; and both have their origins in the fact of time. If a *deus ex machina* were to intervene and inform all the participants in the economy not only of the prices that would produce an equilibrium given their present intentions, but of the prices that would produce an equilibrium in the future, then the market could cease to be beleaguered by uncertainty. Classical and neo-classical economists have spilled a lot of ink in trying to devise price-determination mechanisms that obviate the need for such an *intellectus angelicus*, but as described earlier in the book all founder on the central problem of how to deal with uncertainty. The continuing theme is that it is impossible theoretically to preserve the idea of a competitive market and equilibrium while at the same time incorporating the notion that prices are set by the independent interaction of supply and demand. Transactors do not behave in the way that theory requires when confronted by uncertainty, that is, their actions cannot be reduced to a response to current prices that can be systematically relied upon to converge.

However, the identification of liquidity and information as two key problem areas does offer a ray of theoretical hope. Classical theory has a black hole over the question of 'finance', and its function in reconciling savers' and investors' liquidity needs. Liquidity is not even recognised as a difficulty by classical theory – indeed theorists such as Modigliani & Miller (1958) and Meiselman (1962) conceive a world where the financial markets themselves spontaneously match the needs of savers and investors, with arbitrageurs and speculators acting to counteract the tendency of the public and the financial system to hold short-term financial assets.

The writers seem oblivious of the real experience of risk-averse and liquidity-conscious financial institutions; in order for speculators to counteract the system's liquidity proclivities they would have to take the medium-term risks that the system is unwilling to do – but it is not by taking risks on liquidity that arbitrageurs and speculators make money. They make a profit by being even more liquid than the institutions themselves; only holding financial assets for a very short time and generally being in cash. The general liquidity-preference of the system is unchanged by their operations, and even increased. Their desire, for example, to hold cash and sell financial assets into any rise in their price (or the converse) actually prevents (in the Keynesian system) the quick interest-rate adjustments that the real economy needs to compensate the downward quantity-adjusting impact of a pessimistic revision of expectations, and the consequent fall in the marginal efficiency of capital.

This failure of counteracting speculation is nowhere more apparent than in the international markets for foreign exchange. During the era of floating rates, exchange-rate movements have actually been exacerbated by the actions of speculators. What has been needed to balance out the upward and downward movements of the currencies, typically following cyclical movements in countries' current-account balances, is speculative activity in the contrary direction; that speculators take a medium-term contra-cyclical view of the course of exchange rates. Such a development was confidently expected by the classical economists who were in the forefront of advocating freely floating exchange rates; any instability would be short-lived, a feature of the 'infancy of floating' (Minford 1978) around fundamental economic relationships. Taking a medium-term view is not the way to make money speculating in financial markets, however. What operators in the foreign exchange markets have been doing is keeping very liquid and betting on an established upward and downward trend in the market continuing – they have gone with the trend, not bet against it. Because governments have been persuaded by the conventional orthodoxy that they cannot beat the markets and that the market is 'right', they have refused to take over the role. In the absence of any contra-cyclical influence the markets have been wildly unstable and have substantially contributed to the decline in the rate of growth of international trade. Making short-term money in markets for exchange rates and securities requires nerve and flair, but these heroes of the market economy do not save it from its information and liquidity dilemmas; there really is no *deus ex machina*, however fervently classical economists may wish it.

The importance of the behaviour of the financial system in

181

allowing the economy to resolve these matters is overwhelming. It is the financial system that is the custodian of the money flows in the economy, and whether these are current money flows arising from current production and consumption, or flows that arise out of actions the results of which will occur in the future – savings and investment – the response and behaviour of the financial institutions and markets is pivotal.

The quantity adjustments that occur in the economy, whether they arise from a mismatch of transactions in the present or in the future, manifest themselves as money flows in the banks' balance sheets. Above all others the banks have a bird's-eye view of the economy; the extent to which their liabilities are held in cash or near-cash is a barometer of the public's liquidity-preference, and the extent and terms on which money loans – their assets – are demanded is equally a barometer of the state of expectations and the marginal efficiency of capital. If they define themselves as simple intermediaries they can excuse away their responsibility, but that does not mean they do not have the power to substantially influence liquidity-preference, interest rates, and the type and speed with which illiquid physical assets are accumulated by the industrial and commercial sector. The financial institutions in general and the banks in particular play a pivotal role in the functioning of the market economy: but about this role, classical theory is silent.

This lacuna results from the first conclusion of classical theory – that inexorably market forces drive a competitive market economy to equilibrium and no obstacle to this process is possible. The institutions of an economy – its enterprises, its labour organisations, its financial structure – are nothing but creatures of these ineluctable forces. They are instruments for bringing about the equilibrium outcome, and their own preferences and behaviour can delay, perhaps obstruct the process for a period, but ultimately market forces will out. The possibility that there is no inexorable logic about market forces whatsoever, that the economy could be 'driven' almost anywhere and that the system has no means of containing the problems posed by time and uncertainty and so attempts to protect itself, is inadmissible. Hence there is no room to discuss the role of finance, despite the evidence that its behaviour and attitudes are critical factors in allowing the market to function effectively.

Notes on policy

The object of policy, then, is to tease the goose into laying the golden egg: to find some way of leveraging the two sets of guesses that bedevil the market economy – over the classes of financial and physical assets that market participants choose to hold – so that the market economy grows and prospers as painlessly as possible. The most effective pressure point, therefore, is that part of the economy where these decisions are taken: the financial system. But the policy-maker is confronted by a dilemma: while it is true that the financial system is the fulcrum on which the economy turns, and that its generation of certain classes of financial asset over others has substantial and widespread effects on the classes of physical assets that are created, its role in this regard arises from time, and the uncertainty with which expectations of future market behaviour are held. Meddling with the liability and asset structure of the financial system is thus a high-risk strategy: it promises the best and most effective results if successful, but if it fails then the fall-out in terms of depressed expectations and heightened uncertainty may have a worse impact on economic activity than the original problem which policy was designed to solve.

This highlights a more general problem about policy making in a market economy. At the heart of the difficulty is the formulation of expectations which produces the quantity-adjusting bias in the economy and which the State has to ensure it does not make worse. Some economists in the classical tradition have argued that all policy initiatives are effectively barred, because the chances of the State not actively destabilising the formation of expectations are zero. Either the State's action is anticipated – in which case its initiative will have no impact – or its action will be unanticipated – in which case it will upset the progress of the market towards equilibrium (Barro, 1977). In the Keynesian lexicon, neither position is admissible because both presuppose a world of clearing markets and atemporal, certainly held expectations. Yet this does not solve the problem that market transactors must be persuaded that the Government's intervention is likely to be efficacious: without credibility, any attempt to influence the behaviour and expectations of market agents will be stillborn.

It is this growing lack of credibility that market agents have attached to Government attempts to manage the economy that makes any current policy initiative so difficult to implement; but that does not make the intellectual case any less compelling. Rather, it means that any Keynesian programme is going to have to be better worked out, better grounded in theory, and better implemented than those since the War if it is to stand any chance of success.

The relative failure of post-war Keynesianism (and it is only in the 1970s that the charge of failure is really fair) from this perspective has three principal causes. Firstly, there was little or no attempt to influence the financial system. Secondly, fiscal policy came to have an inbuilt expansionary bias. And thirdly, and perhaps most importantly, market agents came to recognise this bias and *built it into their expectations*. Thus any reduction in Government borrowing was perceived as a short-term phenomenon, forced upon the State, but which would be succeeded as quickly as possible by a return to expansion. As a result fiscal policy became progessively less credible as an instrument of managing expectations; and as it became less credible, so it became less effective. Market agents began to set prices in the expectation that fiscal policy in the next time period would accommodate the current period's pricing policy, so that the environment became more inflationary – and this eroded the credibility with which market agents regarded Government attempts at economic management. By the mid 1980s, the transformation is nearly complete, and expectations can be viewed as 'monetarist', so that any attempt to revive Keynesian tools of economic management is likely to be judged as counterproductive, especially in the financial markets.

So, Keynesian policy-making is an uphill task. The State has to take into its hands the weapons for influencing the sets of guesses that beset the market economy, and it has to ensure that market agents judge those weapons to be credible. But at the same time the very act of assuming this kind of responsibility is likely to be judged, in the current climate, as an action which is foredoomed to fail and which will therefore upset the very expectations that the State is trying to influence. Interestingly, Japan and France, two states that have been most prepared to influence behaviour in the financial markets through state initiatives, and expectations generally through fiscal and planning policy, have done so under the direction of political parties ideologically sympathetic to free enterprise. It may be that a successful Keynesian programme can only be implemented by a government which market agents judge to be friendly and to which they are prepared to grant some influence over their expectations.

What, then, are the range of options open to the Government in trying to manage the market economy? First and foremost there is the financial system. Leveraging the financial institutions into maximising the flow of investment credit is likely to pay the highest rewards both in raising the absolute level of investment and in producing the strongest contra-cyclical influences. However, it is not only the flow of long-term investment credit that the policy-maker needs to police, but the rate at which it is priced.

Monetary policy should be designed to support – when needed – long-term bond prices, and to supplement the mixture of compulsion, interest-rate subsidy, direct controls, and open market operations that will be required to coerce the financial sector into accepting more illiquidity.

An essential counterpart to any active financial policy is an aggressive fiscal stance. The object of fiscal policy is not only to counteract quantity adjustments by direct management of demand, but *to create the expectation that the State will act* in this manner. Thus at the same time as the financial sector is encouraged to value illiquid financial assets more favourably, the production economy is encouraged to expect a continuity of market buoyancy which, when built into marginal efficiency of capital computations, throws up a higher estimation of the value of investment.

The key to expectation management of this type is, as argued above, the credibility which market agents attach to the likelihood of successful fiscal and financial policies actually being prosecuted. The credibility of fiscal policy will be reinforced if it is perceived to be contingent on events, that is, it may be managed purposefully in either a contractionary or expansionary fashion as circumstances change, and it may be useful to indicate *in advance* the degree to which this will be done. Credibility will also be served if spending and borrowing are focused on additions to the State's capital stock, rather than current spending. Clearly the public sector's physical assets require replacement and addition; and the State should expect to borrow from the financial sector as part of that sector's share in shouldering the burden of the illiquidity involved. Changes around some normal level of borrowing are thus an important element in any contra-cyclical programme of economic management.

The economy, however, is now internationalised. Marginal efficiency of capital computations involves assessments of sales and profits in many different countries, as well as inter-country comparisons of the relative costs of capital. The acceleration of the international division of labour means that very few corporations do not take investment decisions in this way; and these are even less likely to be co-ordinated by interest rates and the price mechanism than wholly national decisions. Not only is the penalty for poor economic management more quickly felt in terms of lost investment; but the State may have to use other tools apart from leverage on the financial system and fiscal policy to produce its target levels of capital accumulation. Marginal efficiency of capital calculations can be changed by making access to the national market conditional (say) on a quid pro quo in accompanying investment; if many decisions are taken to locate overseas, this can make the preconditions of underperformance in the national economy self-fulfilling. It is the parallel of quantity adjustment arising from the failure of the price mechanism; therefore the State may have to act to lean against the markets' trend.

A principal determinant of investment in an internationalised economy is the exchange rate, and again the *expectation* of the degree to which it will be managed and the guidelines invoked. Paradoxically, in a world of floating rates, given the quantity-adjusting bias in a market economy, the exchange rate must necessarily over- and undershoot its cyclical highs and lows. There is no tendency to an 'equilibrium rate'; and the actual rate may enforce the direction of already strong quantity adjustments in the economy. If the rate is left to find its own level there are two consequences; firstly there is a reinforcement of the cyclical tendencies in the economy, but secondly and more importantly the *expectation* that this will occur will lead to more investment being located in areas where the exchange rate may be managed to produce less intense cyclical behaviour. Moreover, an expectation of overvaluation will bias marginal efficiency of capital calculations away from investment in the home country. An active and interventionist exchange-rate policy is thus a key adjunct to any economic policy.

And lastly there are some interesting insights into the foundations of monopoly policy. The model of competition is used to judge that monopoly implies higher prices and lower output than a competitive environment; but if a competitive market is a logical impossibility then such a judgement is inadmissible. It may be that some accommodation to monopoly may be required in the sense of acknowledging it as an inevitable market development rather than imposing an unviable standard to which market structures should conform. This would imply that the control of monopoly may have to be rooted in legal and regulatory devices: refereeing the market behaviour of large organisations (or groups) rather than attempting to introduce more 'competition' (Arnold, 1937).

The following details of the individual areas are not meant to be definitive, nor to add up to a programme. They are simply tentative suggestions in the light of the conclusions of the preceding pages.

Financial policy

The proper object of economic policy towards the financial system is the exact opposite of that now practised: the focus on controlling the growth of the banking system's *liabilities* needs to be redirected towards stimulating the growth of certain categories of financial *asset*, not only via the banking institutions but throughout the financial system. Instead of leaving the markets and institutions to 'compete' and so regulate themselves, policy should be directed to acting on the financial institutions' liquidity-preference so that it is not only as contra-cyclical as possible but also that it results in a general willingness to hold relatively illiquid financial assets by way of money loans, bonds, and so on. The idea that competition alone will produce the desired result denies the capricious and pivotal role of liquidity.

The authorities have to use every tool at their disposal to achieve this end: they must create mechanisms that reassure financial institutions that while they may appear to hold less liquid assets they are none the less no less 'liquid' than before; they must themselves undertake operations in the money market that produce the required valuations of the various maturities of financial assets; they must introduce an element of compulsion in the kinds of asset holding the financial institutions are permitted; and they must offer to subsidise, either directly or indirectly, interest rates on certain classes of financial asset. The 'fetish of liquidity' is so deep-seated that only a vigorous combination of compulsion, subsidy, and direct market intervention will succeed.

The illusion of liquidity can be achieved quite easily through a 'rediscounting' mechanism, by which the Bank of England agrees to terms by which it will monetise, or discount, the classes of long-term financial assets that the system needs in abundance if it is to function properly. Any bank can thus be assured that its longer-term loan book is not imprudent. The authorities can give an additional support to the long end of the financial securities markets by supporting long-term money-loan values when they are traded as bonds: in other words, open-market operations *à outrance*. In this context it is worth noting that restricting money supply growth, the kind of policy the Bank has been pursuing over the past five or six years, by sole reliance on the financing of budget deficits at *the long end of the Government security market*, is a policy calculated to produce exactly the wrong results. It raises the rate of interest on long-dated stock, and given the liquidity-preferences of the financial institutions, mops up the already restricted flow of funds that might have been advanced as long-term money loans to industry. It thus raises the long-term interest rate and restricts the availability of long-term debt just at the moment when they need to be moved in the contrary direction to offset the decline in the marginal efficiency of capital.

And finally, the banks must be statutorily obliged to lengthen their loan books, and other long-term investing institutions must be similarly obliged to invest in financial assets that correspond to the creation of new physical capital assets; despite price signals and a Central Bank discounting mechanism, the institutions will still want to preserve their liquidity. They must be compelled to take risks in the common interest, and not be allowed to shelter behind the fiction that the composition of their loan books and investment portfolios is the result of a competitive market and is the 'best' outcome. The detailed policy measures are well developed elsewhere, (Carrington & Edwards 1980: 167–78) but the general argument stands: a mixture of monetary policy, institutional change, incentives, and, in the extreme, straight compulsion, must be deployed by the State in order to change the function and modus operandi of the financial system.

One model, for example, is the French 'mobilisable' medium-term credit – a mechanism to remove the banks' liquidity fears by offering refinancing facilities (Yao-Su Hu 1975). Broadly speaking, a credit is 'mobilisable' after prior agreement with the Bank of France, although the Central Bank deals at arm's length with the leading institutions through the special umbrella group responsible for particular sectors, for example the Credit National in the case of equipment loans. Usually mobilisation will be checked with the Commissariat du Plan, so that the central authorities can, if they choose, support industrial policy objectives through the credit mechanism rather than disbursements from the Treasury. In the case of a credit squeeze, this category of loan has been excluded in an attempt to protect industrial investment, that is, the authorities have acted to maintain the flow of investment credit through the business cycle, the exact Keynesian policy prescription, and levels and rates of investment have reflected this priority. Similar mechanisms for both the stimulation, and protection, of the flow of investment credit exist in Japan and Germany and were experimented with in the 'New Deal' by the USA in the 1930s. A first policy move in Britain could be to extend the guarantees that already exist for export loans under the Export Credit Guarantee Scheme to investment loans, and to vastly expand the operations of the Industrial and Commercial Finance Corporation so that it matches the scale of the Industrial Bank of Japan, the German Kreditanstalt für Wiederaufbau, and the French Credit National. An expansion of at least 10 times is needed in order to match these institutions in their ability to mobilise investment credit, as much as 25 times in the Japanese case. (Yao-Su Hu 1984).

Fiscal policy

There have been a number of references in the text to a need to organise fiscal policy on a contra-cyclical basis; for the State to stand as a 'spender of last resort' in a quantity-adjusting world. Financial policy without a supporting fiscal policy is unlikely to be successful; investment decisions are determined both by the valuation of financial assets and physical assets; and in the latter, case expectations of future demand are as significant as the current fiscal stance.

The starting point for fiscal policy is that the State itself is responsible for the maintenance of a substantial part of the nation's capital stock (roads, hospitals, etc.) and it is patently financially unsound for expenditure on these assets to be financed entirely out of revenue. The State will itself be a legitimate borrower of financial assets for illiquid investment: but it is also a borrower of last resort; its borrowing can be regarded as strategic in the sense of balancing any cyclical movements in the economy. Because the Government's assets have long lives there is comparatively little damage in bringing forward or deferring the pace of annual investment, and it is this expenditure upon which the instrument of fiscal policy should be targeted. Although changes in taxes on incomes and consumption are also important variables in the management of demand, capital expenditure is much more easily variable *politically*, and its impact much more controllable.

The size of the State's claims on the capital markets will depend on the size of the public sector, but it would not be unreasonable to suppose that there is a calculable proportion of national income that represents the investment required to maintain the capital stock – the analogy is with a corporate annual depreciation charge. A proportion of this will properly be borrowed, and this could be regarded as the 'normal' proportion of national income that the State could expect to borrow.

The impact of fiscal policy is felt, therefore, not through the absolute level of borrowing, but by the rate of change – and this change would be assessed in the light of market conditions, in particular the liquidity-preferences of the financial markets and their developing portfolio choices.

The key, however, to the successful implementation of fiscal policy is its credibility: the importance of fiscal action is as much the actual corrective impact on 'uncleared' quantities in the product, labour, and capital markets as the *expectation* that the State will prosecute an active fiscal policy, and more importantly still, will

189

continue to do so. However, the expectation that the circumstances of the market will be managed as favourably as possible depends on the credibility attached to the State's actions, and although a certain amount can be done by focusing spending on capital investment and pre-announcing what the reaction would be to unfavourable developments (contingency planning), it may be important during the initial stages of the new policy to proceed cautiously, within the bounds of what market transactors judge to be 'reasonable'.

At the time of writing, for example (December 1984), expectations in the financial markets are 'monetarist', and an aggressive fiscal stance would be regarded as unsustainable. While these expectations alone need not upset borrowing plans, they constrain fiscal options because their very existence is likely to produce a higher level of interest rates for any given increase in Government borrowing. If a 'new Keynesian' approach relied entirely on generating financial flows within the current structure of ownership and control of the financial institutions, then early fiscal policy measures would have to be smaller than they otherwise might be, if *expectations of continuity of action were to be maintained*. And it is only through the assurance that fiscal policy will be continually and progressively applied that the rewards in an upward revision of the valuations of real physical assets, and thus investment, can be secured. There is therefore a delicate trade-off between the need for extra demand in the current period, the need to win credibility by not boosting demand in the current period, and the temptation to forgo persuasion in the financial markets and opt for compulsion so as to give greater room for manoeuvre. But any immediate gains from this last course of action have to be offset against the decline in expectations that would be associated with such a move.

Monopoly and competition

For classical theory, any kind of action by an enterprise to control its environment is *a priori* a disturbance of the competitive forces in the market, and in so far as competitive markets produce the best outcome, is against the public interest. Prices tend to be higher, and production tends to be lower than they would be if more 'competition' were evident, so while in the long run market forces will out, in the short run there will be 'welfare' costs. Moreover, monopoly tends to stifle the general advance of the economy, which depends on free competition as the main motor of initiative and innovation.

However, as argued in an earlier chapter, the theoretical problem for a competitive market is not how 'competitive' it is in the sense of freely permitting the interaction of supply and demand, but how to organise a process of price determination at the same time as preserving that element of independent and exactly equivalent interaction that must define a competitive market. This can only be done if we assume either that there is instantaneous price and quantity adjustment, or that one of the parties to the price-determination process is a price-maker, able to manipulate the price and quantity at which he will sell.

Because the assumption of instantaneous adjustment is improbable in the context of an actual market system, we must suppose that the other assumption holds: that in every market there is a 'price-maker', and so a degree of imperfect competition or monopoly. This is not surprising. Not only is it theoretically impossible to hypothesise a price-determination process in any other circumstances, but given the facts of time, uncertainty, and imperfect knowledge, the first reaction of any trader or producer will be to attempt some control of the environment in which he operates – otherwise the business of production collapses into a nightmarish struggle against continually changing expectations of the future. The stock market operator has the option of selling his shares if he loses his nerve or the enterprise in which he is invested appears to go wrong – this is not an option open to the controller of an enterprise investing in physical assets. He only has one life and there is no escape hatch if his judgement proves wanting.

Monopoly, therefore, can be seen as a rational and logical attempt to manage uncertainty, and it arises inevitably from the conditions of price and quantity determination associated with private production in a money exchange economy. Clearly, monopoly means that the market no longer produces the 'best' outcome; but does that mean that it deserves the opprobrium heaped upon it? If time and uncertainty upset the neat world of harmony produced by competitive markets, they also upset the ability of any monopolistic producer, however significant his control of the market, to sustain that control over time. There are always new products and techniques pressing upon any market and threatening to upset any temporarily gained stability. The opening up of new markets, and the release of new technologies, are incessantly destroying one kind of economic structure and resurrecting another; rather than the classicist view of the invisible hand wondrously co-ordinating the interests of buyers and sellers into a harmonious whole, the capitalist economy, in Schumpeter's words, is a process of 'creative destruction'. It is by its very nature 'a form of economic change and not only never is, but never can be stationary' (Schumpeter 1970: 82). Monopoly may arise because of the existence of time, and is an important mechanism—in allowing the market economy to function in the sense that it reduces uncertainty; but its lifespan is limited by just the same phenomenon. Firms do not compete with each other in a competitive market: they compete against time in a monopolistic market.

Thus although monopolists may objectively appear to be in a position of market dominance, that is not how the world appears through their eyes. The rise of new technologies and techniques always threatens to make the existing technology and associated products obsolete; the monopolistic firm perceives itself to be in constant danger of losing its position, of the ground slipping from beneath its feet as firms incorporating new ideas rise to challenge it – often from totally unexpected quarters. Planning for the future remains hazardous, whatever market control there may be. Schumpeter (1970: 88) wrote 'Long range investment under rapidly changing conditions is like shooting at a target that is not only indistinct but moving – and moving jerkily at that.' It is only when the firm's position is underwritten by some extra market power like the State – as in the British nationalised industries – that a corporation can be truly said to be a monopoly. The State ensures that it is never 'creatively destroyed' and effectively guarantees its existence in perpetuity, although the recent policy over privatisation (the selling of nationalised industries to private shareholders) has changed even that assumption.

With the exception of the nationalised industries, whose source of monopoly power is evident, classical theory finds itself in the position of concluding that the commonest feature of the market economy – some form of monopoly control or market dominance – is an aberration. It is a departure from a norm. The view that it is a response to time and uncertainty, and will, in its own turn, be 'creatively destroyed' is outside the framework of reference. Markets are atemporal phenomena; therefore the classicist must explain monopoly – if he is to preserve his system – by factors other than time. So it is that monopoly is interpreted as resulting from technological necessity (some industries have a monopolistic structure because the 'economic' size of productive plant permits but several producers, e.g. electricity generation, oil refining) or lack of preventative Government action. It is not the market itself that produces monopoly, but the Government, technology and the self-interest of market transactors, who will as soon manipulate the market as honestly buy and sell in it.

In this view of the world the aim is to see as much 'competition' promoted as possible, and to obstruct the development of monopoly. The thrust of policy is to inhibit mergers, to break up potential monopolies, to outlaw 'restrictive practices'. But let us suppose that monopoly is not an aberration or obstruction to some paradigm of a (theoretically impossible) competitive market, but a protective mechanism set up by industry to limit the devastating consequences of time and uncertainty on production and investment. Then insisting on their abandonment without any replacement mechanisms will either be unsuccessful – in which case the market continues with its own imperfect response to the problem – or successful – in which case the rate of accumulation will be slowed down and the cyclical influences in the economy magnified.[1] It is noteworthy that both Japan and Germany have been willing to tolerate the widespread use of cartels to allocate and control production: the performance of neither economy appears to have suffered indeed they may actually have been improved by such anti-competitive devices (Zysman, 1983).

The task is therefore to manage and regulate monopoly rather than to impose an unrealistic model of the market upon market agents. A variety of mechanisms are possible: one would be a change in company law, so that corporate articles of association acknowledged other responsibilities than to shareholders, thus giving the right of prosecution by private interests if the abuse of monopoly power was proven. Equally the idea of licences might be developed, so that any holder of a substantial amount (to be defined) of market power could only trade if there was an accompanying agreement to submit to the regulation of some supervisory or regulatory agency – for example, OFTEL (Office for Telecommunications) and the licence under which the telecommunications companies operate.

All of this, necessarily, is tentative: but the object is to open other lines of policy than that informed solely by the need to make the market economy conform to the model of competitive markets. The reorientation holds rich possibilities, even though it might imply a major challenge to the basis of company law – itself organised around the idea of individual interest – and the much more intensive development of the notion of the regulatory agency as the custodian of the public interest.

International policy

This discussion of international policy falls into two categories: the exchange rate, and the approach towards the growing internationalisation of the economy. The quantity-adjusting nature of the market economy, and the accompanying financial flows, are certain to mean that the exchange rate in a system of floating rates is likely to depart from some notional equilibrium level. The paradox is that this rate above all others in the economy more perfectly reflects both planned and actual supply and demand; but as these flows are very unlikely to correspond to any equilibrium quantities, the exchange rate is 'perfectly' reflecting non-equilibrium values. As such it is reinforcing the processes that cause quantity adjustment, and magnifying the difficulties of the price mechanism in being able to co-ordinate economic agents' intentions. Thus an active exchange-rate policy aimed at leaning against the overcompensation of the exchange rate is essential if the tail is not to wag the dog; if the economy is not to adjust to the overexaggerated movements of the exchange rate.

The volatility of the exchange rate and the expectations of its management have become a critical element in the location of investment by an increasingly internationally mobile corporate sector. Marginal efficiency of capital computations are now made globally, both in terms of markets and estimates of costs of capital. An expectation that the exchange rate will be volatile in relation to another country's, or that nothing would be done to correct a persistent overvaluation, would clearly affect the anticipated return on capital, and lead to investment being located in markets other than the domestic market – a trend that has become very marked in the UK.

The global division of labour has another implication. Corporations judge investment decisions on a global basis; in the context of their own global production and investment plans. These decisions are no longer co-ordinated within one national savings and investment market, so that the possibilities of these national markets 'clearing' becomes even more remote, as indeed does the possibility of the price mechanism in any one country being able to compensate for quantity adjustments that may be global in their origin. In this context a series of decisions to invest in other countries because of individual marginal efficiency of capital calculations may have a multiplier effect; for example, corporation A leaves, changing corporation B's marginal efficiency of capital, who then also decides to relocate abroad. The process, like hoarding of money, may become self-fulfilling and irreversible within the rules of the price system. This has two key policy implications:

(a) The State must ensure that the exchange rate is not volatile nor overvalued, and its policy must be widely understood. Equally it must guarantee a supply of investment credit. Failure to do so will be more quickly felt in terms of lost investment than in the period when the economy was less internationalised. The penalty for mismanagement of the market economy is now more acute.

(b) The State must influence investment decisions where they threaten to become self-feedingly averse. Viability of most projects will depend on access to the widest market, which places an important bargaining counter in the hands of the State: market access in exchange for investment.

So the State has to add another dimension to its policy objectives: what share and what kind of economic activity does it expect to obtain, or is it prepared to obtain, in a world where the international division of labour is accelerating? Not taking a view in these circumstances is tantamount to a decision by default, namely, that investment will be low in value added and production will be located abroad. The State is on its mettle as never before; competition depends as much on the effectiveness of economic management as on any concept of comparative advantage.

In conclusion, the State has to act as the *deus ex machina* that the markets lack; but that is precisely the action that economic orthodoxy forbids. Equally, the State must not forebear from acting as an economic agent to stabilise the quantities produced in a quantity-adjusting market economy; it must organise its taxation, spending, and borrowing decisions so that their effect is contra-cyclical, and in the financial markets (for securities, money, foreign currency) it must not hesitate to stand as the buyer against a majority of sellers, or seller against a majority of buyers. Only in this way can the market be expected to produce the benefits that its own spontaneous processes fail to produce; and in thus failing to place the whole institution in jeopardy.

Part II The British State

If the State wishes to protect the market, then it must intervene to protect it from itself. The problem is that economics does not concede that the market requires this action: but even if the argument were to be accepted, then is the British State capable of responding to the need? The network of state institutions organised around the constitutional formula of Crown-in-Parliament as fountainhead of executive, legislative, and judicial power is not built to survey and manage a complex market economy. Its current structure has more to do with the exigencies of British history and the success of economic and political liberalism in the nineteenth century than with any attempt to devise constitutional procedures and processes that could allow better surveillance of the economy; and while this is unremarkable in a historical sense, it becomes of immense importance in terms of the current situation. The British State is so embued with the liberal philosophy and so institutionally structured that sustained, coherent, and disinterested arbitration and sponsorship of the economy is extremely difficult, if not impossible. And herein lies the British conundrum: neither the financial system, which is unwilling, nor the state institutions, which are incapable, relieve the economy of the endemic problems of liquidity and uncertainty that beset it.

The weakness of British state institutions has been evident for most of this century; and British Prime Ministers as disparate as Lloyd George, Winston Churchill, and Edward Heath have all recognised the desperate inability of the State to think creatively and act in a co-ordinated and strategic manner. Churchill with his ministerial 'overlords' and Heath with the CPRS (the so-called 'Think Tank') both initiated reforms that have not survived; but that does not mean the problem is not still pressing. The most recent criticism suggests that it is as acute as ever. Sir John Hoskyns, former head of the Prime Minister's Downing Street Policy Unit, has said (1983)[2] that: 'The reason why the thinking and planning is not done is that Whitehall is not organised to do it . . . In organisational terms government is a creature without a brain', and Norman Strauss (1984), a former member of the same Policy Unit, talks of an 'overmighty, underthinking Executive', an 'ossified Civil Service', and concludes that 'The time has come for a radical change in our system of government.'

The extent of the growing unease was underlined by the 1983 Reith Lectures; no less an authority than Sir Douglas Wass, former Permanent Secretary to the Treasury and Joint Head of the Civil Service, came forward to deliver his views under the rubric 'Government and the Governed'. The underlying theme of the lectures was a need to promote more efficient and responsive government – a need presumably that would be less necessary if the current arrangements were functioning well. He conceded that the Cabinet 'can too easily be railroaded', and he, alongside the rest, cast about for ways to 'promote strategic decision-taking'. (Wass 1983b)

This structural weakness at the heart of the British State is a major liability if something akin to a successful Keynesian programme is to be implemented. The sketch of policy options at the end of Part 1 of this chapter presumes that the State has an intelligent organising ability to act strategically and disinterestedly in the interests of the market economy as a whole, to follow Zysman (1983), to be a 'player state'. Plainly, some reform is required as a prerequisite to any pursuit of policy; and arguably at least part of the failure of post-war Keynesianism can be laid at the door of a clumsy system of governance.

In this last part of the book we will attempt to challenge the usual basis for discussion of this issue. The problem is typically understood as an organisational one: lack of skilled outsiders and too many claims on ministerial time (Hoskyns); the need for more raw intelligent data (Strauss); the need to beef-up the supply of skilled and disinterested advice to the Cabinet, individual Ministers, and the Opposition (Wass). The difficulty is actually more profound. The lack of co-ordination and strategic thinking lies in the Constitution.

In the constitutional model, strategic thinking in the executive branch of government would take place where it is *de jure* located; with the Queen and her Council of Ministers. But this is not how the model works. Strategy passes to the Cabinet, whose origins are in the legislature. *De jure* there is separation of the executive and legislative, so strategic problems should not arise; *de facto* there is none. Herein lie the organisational problems of co-ordination and strategy.

But to pitch the debate at the level of the Constitution means a prior acceptance that Constitutions of states matter; that it is a matter of importance that the collective and commonly held institutions of society are so structured that they can reflect some conception of a 'public' or 'common' interest. Here is a major and particularly British problem. The principal intellectual traditions in British life refuse to admit this is a potential or even desirable attribute of the State. British liberalism regards the power of the State as one that should be constrained, and considers that its scope for autonomous and independent action be prevented; the model is one of individualism, of public good emerging from the interaction of private interests rather than the assertion of a common interest. The Marxist tradition, on the other hand, views the State as the prisoner of class interests and thus unable, even if it chose, to represent some common interest. Indeed, common interest is definitionally an absurdity in a class society. As a result Britain's non-written Constitution has gone unchallenged. There is no thinking about the State, about the assertion of the common interest, about what structure and shape of government might embody such interest. It is a political and philosophical 'black hole'; but one a Keynesian cannot ignore.

The State and the common interest

The Keynesian insistence that in economic terms the public interest can be guaranteed *not* to be produced by the free interplay of markets, and that the State must act purposively in the economy if the public good is to be ensured, is in effect a challenge to the entire panoply of classical liberalism – political as well as economic. In the first place the idea of the 'public interest' can no longer be simply defined as the outcome of private interest. Economic liberalism, with its suggestion that the free interplay of private interest will be combined by the 'invisible hand' of the market to yield a harmonious public good, goes hand in glove with political liberalism. In this world-view the State is legitimate only to the extent that it protects private interest (the Civil Contract) and it is with that objective that individuals agree to submit to the State's power. As a result the State must confine its economic activities to the minimum: to providing a framework of law in which private interest can operate, to policing the markets and in no circumstances acting as an economic agent itself. The state, wrote Herbert Spencer, is a 'joint stock protection company for mutual assurance'. (Dyson 1980: 17)

The entire philosophy rests on a presumption about the relation between public and private interest that does not exist. Markets which permit the free expression of private interest have been shown not to produce the best economic out-turn; but if the community wishes to retain the market as the principal means of exercising economic choice then the State perforce finds itself playing a role: not as guardian of the markets, but as their manager. This is not a shading of meaning, but a transformation – and the first casualty is the definition of public interest.

In the liberal model the public good emerges from the interplay of private interest, and is defined in terms of the private interest. The building block is the individual, who acting autonomously and rationally in pursuit of self-interest produces the paradoxical result of the collective best interest. The contrasting position is that the public interest has to be asserted and cannot be relied upon to be created spontaneously from the interaction of market forces. There are two statements bound up in this position: that there is such a thing as the public interest which is more than the sum total of private interest; and that it falls to the institution that embodies the common will, the State, to embody that public interest.

But reinterpreting the idea of the 'public' so that it contains the idea of commonality, of generality, is virtually impossible without simultaneously understanding that the State is the institution which will give life to the notion. Words, culture, and concepts are all 'things held in common', and it is clear that the general interest lies in sustaining their function. Economics requires the same understanding. If there is decentralised decision-making in a market which uses money as the medium of exchange, then time and uncertainty unhinge the simple classical nostrums; there is a common interest in the impact of time and uncertainty being reduced and it falls to the State as the 'commonly held' institution *par excellence* to discharge this obligation. But this in turn requires an ability to act autonomously, and the power and authority to ensure that its will is obeyed. Without autonomy and independence the State is the prisoner of the interests it seeks to regulate and manage; without power and authority its wishes are worthless. The State must thus have autonomy and power: but it must also be controlled by, and accountable to those whose general will it seeks to represent. For the liberal, however, the issue is not how to reconcile the necessity of State power with making that power accountable: rather it is to 'limit' the State in the belief that unimpeded individual interaction will produce the public good. However it is dressed up, though, the idea that the State somehow loses its power through not exercising that power is bogus. As Karl Popper wrote (1966:179)

Which freedom should the state protect? The freedom of (say) the labour market, or the freedom of the poor to unite? Whichever decision is taken, it leads to state intervention, to the use of organised political power, of the state as well as the unions, in the field of economic conditions. It leads, under all circumstances, to an extension of the economic responsibility of the state, whether or not this responsibility is consciously accepted.

The potential of a public power to act independently in the economy is ever present; it is implicit in the very notion of the State. The choice not to use that power in no way detracts from the fact that it exists, and orthodox economics, in imagining that it has constructed a world in which not only is the State minimally necessary but also its power requires to be sparingly used, is committing a self-delusion. The road to hell is paved with good intentions.

It is whether the concept of commonality can exist as an abstract concept apart from the world of private interest that is the heart of the problem. And that is inseparable from the idea that if the public interest is to be expressed, then it must be expressed autonomously. Instead of rationality and independence of action being the sole province of the individual, it becomes a necessary quality of the State. The collective outcome of the world of individual choice proves irrational; the State takes on the responsibility of making it rational.

This is very tricky country we are now crossing, because the whole landscape of political debate is being shifted about by immense degrees. The classical liberal concern is to bind the institutions of State to Society so that the potential for autonomous action by the State is small; the State is an object of suspicion rather than a vehicle for the public interest. The expression of 'democracy' in a liberal society is understood as the representation of interests *within* the institutions of government so that electorally accountable representatives can ensure that the State is severely circumscribed in its freedom for manoeuvre. The public interest is ensured by private interest being protected from autonomous action by the State, because private interest is represented within the State; public interest arises from bargaining between private interests. The State is a process of arbitration; it has no independence of action apart from that process. This, of course, is a grave simplification; but it serves the purpose of dramatising a clear difference of philosophic view.

Instead of the public interest being defined as that interest which a disinterested and benevolent institution has reason to believe is general, or held in common (peace, education, health, etc.), the public interest emerges as the result of a process of sectional interaction. Instead of the State as a creative intelligence attempting to resolve and manage the problems of the community, the State is cast as the cockpit in which private interests compete.

In fact, the more extreme economic liberals deny that the State has any potential for rational, disinterested, and autonomous action. Using the same model in the political arena as in the economic, they assert that state agencies will be 'captured' by sectional interests (Posner 1974) and put to work for those same interests. The extent of the penetration will depend on the potential economic value of the 'capture'; State power is a resource which like any other, can be acquired at a cost but none the less yields a return so that if the return is high enough, the asset yielding that return will inevitably be bought. It is possible, declares Posner, to think of State regulation as supplied in response to the demands of interest groups 'struggling among themselves to maximise the incomes of their members'. (Posner 1974:335)

While it is true that this is a fertile framework in which to interpret the behaviour of state agencies and interest groups – especially in the USA – what is not possible is to draw Posner's conclusions. Together with Stigler (1975) the argument is that regulation in the name of a public or common interest is a dead letter; that the attempt is still-born because of the power of interest groups to suborn state agencies. But this is evidence of liberal reasoning at its most circular: of course state agencies in a Constitution like that of the USA are likely to be susceptible to the influence of private interests – that is their function. In a liberal society the State does not assert a common interest; it has to arbitrate between those interests, and its constitutional agencies will reflect that priority. Indeed, that can by constructed on no other basis. Stigler and Posner are analysing a liberal polity, blaming it for its liberality and using its shortcomings to argue for more liberality. There is a case for a liberal economy and polity; but it is not this one.

Paradoxically, the closest intellectual allies of this kind of reasoning are the Marxists. For them the idea of commonality, of a public interest, in a capitalist society is a definitional impossibility. The State is not the embodiment of the public interest, insisted Marx and Engels, but as quoted by Freedman (1968:216)[3]:

the form of organisation which the bourgeois necessarily adopt both for internal and external purposes, for the mutual guarantee of their property and interest . . . the State is the form in which the individuals of a ruling class assert their common interests.

And again (Freedman 1968:309)[4],

Society, based upon class antagonisms, had need of the State. That is . . . an organisation . . . for the purpose of forcibly keeping the exploited classes in the condition of oppression corresponding with the given mode of production (slavery, serfdom, wage-labour).

In this world of private property and class conflict it is impossible to define the public interest independently; of necessity a class must control the State, a class of property owners. The interest that is proclaimed as the public interest is in fact their private interest, and far from autonomous and disinterested action, the State is their creature. Law, the military, the police – the fabric of state power is nothing but an agency of economic exploitation of one class by another, and is as pervasive in the 1980s as it was in the 1880s. (Miliband 1980).

The difficulty with this position is, as Crouch (1979) argues, that the capitalist state has proved remarkably insensitive to the needs of capital and, at the same time, demonstrably responsive to the demands of labour. 'Two of the most remarkable facts about liberal democratic capitalist societies are, first, the extent to which their ruling class mistrust the state and try to limit its activities, and second, the relative responsiveness of the polity (in contrast with the situation in virtually all other known large-scale societies) to working class demands.' (Crouch 1979:27) Not only this, finance capital has been allowed to dominate state policy to the detriment of the interests of capital as a whole – a view with which any Keynesian would concur – and important sections of industry have been brought into public ownership in the face of outspoken opposition from the capitalist interests concerned. To categorise the State as the simple instrument of capital and the bourgeois class does not fit with the facts, nor does it help our understanding; it is clear that it is an altogether more subtle institution than Marx and Engels portrayed it.

In trying to grasp this subtlety, contemporary Marxists are obliged to redefined the State's structural role. It may be true that the State can display an autonomy of action independent of the capitalist class, but to do so effectively requires that the State maximises its revenues. In a capitalist society this means that the State finds itself on the side of capital whatever its interest in welfare, reducing poverty and the like; the prime concern must be to stimulate capital accumulation and economic growth – which means protecting profits, subsidising capital, and generally attempting to make the private owners of capital maintain the momentum of capital accumulation. (Offe 1972; Habermas 1976). The State is not directly the agent of economic exploitation, but indirectly; capital is in a position of structural privilege because the State's prosperity relies on capital's prosperity.

Poulantzas (1973, 1975) has given the argument an extra twist. Late capitalist society has a tendency to fragment into its constituent parts – finance, monopoly and non-monopoly capital – and this fragmentation means that the system functions less effectively. If the State were not autonomous then it would inevitably be taken over by one of these interests and state policy would be organised around that faction's particular interests rather than of capital as a whole. The State's relative autonomy is therefore a *necessity* for the effective arbitration of late capitalist society, and the State is truly 'an unifying social formation', even if its autonomy is required to save capitalism from itself.

So whereas the classical liberal effort is engaged in attempting to show how the State is ineffective and disruptive in its intervention in the economy, the Marxist effort is paradoxically engaged in proving just the opposite. Both schools deny of course that there is such a thing as the public interest. There can be no commonality of purpose in a capitalist society, declares the Marxist, even though the State may insist that there is; there is only private interest masquerading as public interest. For the classical liberal the idea of the public interest as assertable over and above the private interest is equally an anathema. It is this misguided belief that has led government to take on more and more responsibilities and so overburdened it and the economy that neither function as they should.

The Constitution of the British State

The issue is this: is it possible for a community to create a system of governance that can claim to act in the name of the community as a whole? Put another way, can the State embody a public interest apart from the private interests that constitute society? The liberal and Marxist positions are clear: it cannot. But if the economic theory that lies behind both sets of conclusions is faulty, this is not a very satisfactory manner in which to leave our understanding of the State.

The question of how the State can be organised so that it reflects the wishes of its citizens and is accountable to them, at the same time as exercising a wide measure of authority in the name of the public interest, has been ignored. The liberal bends his efforts to claiming that any such effort is valueless given the essential self-regulating nature of economy and society; while for the Marxist the problem is not to develop a theory of what the State should do, but to explain how the State actually behaves in a class society – although presumably some form of state organisation is hypothesised after the Revolution. What Constitution it would have is left begging.

For it is the institutional form the State takes that determines its ability to attain a measure of disinterestedness and autonomy in regulating the affairs of economy and polity. In other words, the Constitution, setting out the relationships between the constituent elements of the community in the State, is the touchstone of any attempt to express the public interest. The ability of the political parties or party to assume control of the levers of state power, the accountability of the Government to the people, and the ability of the Government to use State power in an autonomous and benevolent manner, are all shaped by the Constitution. This is true whatever principles lie behind the organisation of production, distribution, and consumption.

The vehicle for any expression of communal wishes may be the State, but the actual expression of those wishes is in the law. By defining the institutional procedures for the making of law, the Constitution also delineates the kind of political process that will be undergone in the making of law. Herein lies the opportunity for the formalisation of the public interest; as the law has universal applicability and demands universal compliance it is the quintessential means of expressing commonality of purpose, but the degree to which the law expresses that commonality will depend on the constraints on the law-makers to act in the public interest. The constitutional structure is thus vital in driving political processes in the direction of overriding sectional and party interest rather than simply providing a forum for their free exercise.

It is this concern that is exhibited in continental European countries' interest in legal codes and constitutional courts; the object is to institutionalise the moral idea of community in a rational, depersonalised, and disinterested system of public order and public authority. The law is critical: if it is to be universal in scope then the basis for law-making had better be as universalistic and above party as possible: thus the concern to 'codify' and systematise the law and to provide a Constitutional Court to adjudge the rights of the individual citizen against the all-powerful State – 'the home of all citizens without respect of persons' (Dyson 1980).

Judged in this light, Britain is 'stateless'. The basis of the Constitution is the Bill of Rights of 1689, the culmination of a fifty-year struggle between Parliament and the Crown over exactly what constituted the British State, where the monarch consented to govern 'according to the Statutes in Parliament agreed on'. In other words, the British Constitution, as Vernon Bogdanor (1981) writes, can be summarised in eight words: what the Queen in Parliament enacts is law. The institutional procedure for law-making – the control of which represents control of the State – is a combination of monarchical and parliamentary approval. The idea of the State as a self-consciously designed set of procedures to permit both the exercise of public interest in a rational and autonomous way and the participation and protection of the citizen in that process, is simply nonexistent.

The unwritten nature of the British Constitution, bringing with it a happy malleability, has permitted the British State to go through a series of transmutations without the upheavals that state-conscious European societies have experienced when there is a change in the political order. The basic institution, Crown-in-Parliament, has been used, successively, as a basis for feudal, aristocratic, and now party government in an age of universal suffrage, and has survived into the late part of the twentieth century fundamentally intact. However, whether this is as healthy a development as is often claimed is debatable. The British State has certainly built up an impressive legitimacy among its public that probably no other state on earth enjoys, and the element of absolute monarchical power that is wielded by the majority party in Parliament makes it enormously powerful. The constitutional tool of the 'Order-in-Council', for example, by which the Government can take a wide measure of discretionary action if it so chooses, is a relic of a feudal past, the Order being an order that the monarch makes in Council and which commands instant obedience. In other words, a democratically elected government, once in control of the House of Commons, has at its command an instrument of government whose legitimacy is rooted in the Royal Prerogative. But although the *de jure* position of the majority party in the House of Commons appears strong, with control of the legislative and thus the executive guaranteed so long as it can ensure a majority of votes in the Commons and with the additional leavening of monarchical power, the *de facto* position is very much weaker; paradoxically as a direct result of the State's continued seventeeth-century structure.

The explanation of this paradox lies in the integration of the executive and legislative branches of government in the House of Commons, which obliges an already overburdened Cabinet to discharge incompatible functions. This combination of the *political process* and *system of government* into just one body results from the now amomalous position of the Crown as head of the executive; the role may be nominal but that makes it no less important. The Crown remains the *de jure* head of the executive, but the *de facto* exercise of executive power has become the monopoly of the other wing of the law-making process: Parliament, and in particular the House of Commons. The Constitution admits no other authority in the State but the Crown and Parliament and given that the executive role of the monarch is now defunct, there is no other constitutional possibility but for the House of Commons to monopolise *not only legislative, but also executive power*.

The means of this monopolisation is the Cabinet; in the words of Bagehot (Harvey & Bather 1977:261) it is 'a combining committee – a hyphen which joins, a buckle which fastens the legislative part of the state to the executive part of the state. In its origins it belongs to one, in its functions it belongs to the other.' Bagehot could proclaim this as the key to effective and democratic government in a world in which the Commons was not organised into mutually exclusive political parties and in which the executive branch of government remained comparatively small. The hardening of the political parties into disciplined and partisan forces, and the multiplication of the responsibilities of the State in an increasingly complex society have transformed the effectiveness of the Cabinet. The Constitution may confer the majority party in the House of Commons with control of both the executive and legislative, and the means of that control in the Cabinet, but the fact that authority is exercised through, and has its legitimacy in, institutions that retain their seventeenth-century form gravely weakens the process of decision-making, and thus the effectiveness of the British State.

The difficulty is that in constitutional terms the Cabinet is a monarchical commission, whose ministers hold power by leave of the Crown, and who receive advice from an executive *who are servants of the Crown* (Dyson 1980). Constitutionally the Civil Service is not the instrument of an elected Cabinet, but the Cabinet in lieu of the monarch; and the Civil Service offers advice not to a minister as the Prime Minister's appointee in the Cabinet, but to the minister as the Crown's appointee as head of the department of state. It is this constitutional fiction that gives Whitehall its special flavour, and presents the Cabinet with all kinds of problems of administrative co-ordination and political control of the executive that other democratic states do not experience.

It was a former Head of the Civil Service, Sir William Armstrong, who said that Whitehall was a 'federation of departments' (Heclo & Wildavsky 1974:xiv–xv) and this character of the British executive originates in the strong identification of each department with its ministerial head; the chain of command runs hierarchically right up to the Cabinet, where the co-ordination of policy is supposedly performed. Herein lies the British Constitution's 'Catch 22'. If the Cabinet really were a monarchical commission carrying out monarchical policy then the co-ordination of the executive would be unnecessary; policy would be co-ordinated inside the head of the monarch and his Cabinet, and officials would do his bidding. But while the Cabinet retains its role as the supreme committee of departmental heads in Whitehall, it is no longer in the business of channelling advice up to the monarch and instructions back down to the officials. It channels advice up to itself, it counsels itself, then it instructs the executive; the systematic integration and direction of policy as a whole now lies with the same department heads whose job is to be responsible for and represent the particular policy of their department in Cabinet.

It is this which makes political decision-making in Britain more a question of broking and horsetrading between ministerial heads of department than the clear pursuit of publically articulated policy. The fusing of executive and legislative power in the House of Commons is what gives the Cabinet its unique position as a Council of State with monarchical power; but because of that unique position all decisions rise to Cabinet level for their resolution, and no institutional mechanism exists to ensure that the Cabinet's strategic objectives are contained in the advice flowing up from the departments, or that the actions of the departments will be pulling in the same direction when policy is implemented. The only mechanism is the collective will of the ministers themselves, but the decision-making process that the structure of the executive obliges them to undergo forces that collective will into a process of compromise between competing departments – a system of cabinet government so tellingly described by Sir Douglas Wass in the second of his 1983 Reith Lectures.

There is not a government in the twentieth century that has not confronted this conundrum, but all attempts at reform – like Mr Heath's creation of the CPRS or the last Labour Government's WIPs (Wider Implications of Policy) – founder on the constitutional Catch 22. To co-ordinate the system better requires that the Cabinet itself delegates its power, but the Constitution cannot permit this; decisions keep floating back to the highest level for their resolution, and then the Cabinet as a committee of department heads compromises over the decision or is 'rail-roaded' into accepting a decision that has already been taken. The position is further complicated by the double role of the Cabinet as the supreme council of state and the ruling council of the majority party in the House of Commons. The process of formulating public policy will inevitably oblige the Cabinet to define its policy in the context of an array of interests and ideas wider than those embraced by the party, so that there is constantly a gulf between the policy as espoused by the party leadership in government and policy as wanted by those MPs whose continued support is necessary to maintain control of the Commons. This gulf cannot be allowed to grow too large, and it imposes clear limits on the ability of the Cabinet to free itself from its base in the legislature as it attempts to cast policy in a more 'public' manner.

This has led to a series of parliamentary conventions in an attempt to minimise the danger of overtly sectional government, probably

207

the most important of which is the doctrine of collective responsibility. By insisting that all members of the Government are collectively responsible for policy, the party leadership in government can protect itself against criticism from its own supporters, or the canvassing of that criticism by dissenters inside the Government. Even today, with well 'whipped' party machines enjoying substantial powers of patronage, collective responsibility remains an important means of maintaining party unity and continued control of the House of Commons; by closing down the scope for criticism and dissent it allows the Government to pursue policies that although unpopular with the party membership it none the less judges to be in the public interest. But whatever conventions are deployed to limit the damage, the twinning of the legislative and executive branches of government puts the Cabinet in an invidious position; it is constantly wrestling with its party conscience and its public duty; its leadership of the party with its leadership of the State; its role of supreme council of state with its position as committee of department heads.

This is a problem encountered by every democracy, because the very concept of 'party' implies only part of the whole (Sartori 1977) and the common problem is to make the party system, which seems the most effective way of representing and expressing opinion in a political democracy with regular elections and universal suffrage, work to the benefit of the polity as a whole. How are the parties to be persuaded to serve the public interest when they exercise executive or legislative authority – or both, as in the case of Britain?

One of the most common mechanisms in other democracies is to keep the executive and legislative branches of government separate, to have separate elections to both, perhaps even spaced apart in time, and to make voting strength inside each chamber proportional to the votes cast. As a result the kind of dilemma faced by the British Cabinet is avoided; one party can only enjoy complete hegemony if it wins both a majority of votes cast and control of both chambers – and if it manages that, the presumption is that it has managed to identify its policies very closely with those the public consider to be in the public interest. For the main part such complete control will not occur and the parties will be forced into a dialogue with each other – and it is out of their dialogue that public policy will be formulated.

Constitutions that shape political behaviour in this way are typically those in polities which have a strong 'state tradition', attempting to organise the State so it can play an autonomous and beneficial role in the collective life of the nation. Procedures for the taking of public decisions are consciously designed so that those decisions are not only rational but responsive to the wants of the citizenry, who are deemed to have clearly articulated rights, among which the most important is the right to participate continuously in the process of government.

But there is no perfect constitution, and all attempts at building one inevitably fail. Even the French Constitution, which is designed to permit strong executive authority through the office of the Presidency, to be responsive to local and national interest through the National Assembly, and to protect citizens' rights through its constitutional court and legal code, is unable to protect public policy from vested interests like the agricultural lobby or from the executive developing a culture and organisational momentum all of its own.

It is all a matter of degree, and while the French State may be better able to articulate a 'public' policy and to insist on coherent and sustained action across all government departments, it is weaker in accommodating and representing interest groups within the decision-making process. A planning decision in France, concerning say the construction of a new highway, is not subject to the interminable delays that accompany such a decision in Britain: but those interminable delays arise from a concern with the proper representation and consultation with local interests that the French system is able to ignore. The state society with its panoply of constitutional courts, legal codes, carefully calibrated electoral procedures, and institutional checks and balances is inherently a more legalistic and inflexible system than a 'stateless' society like the British. A change in the social or political structure which the Constitution has not foreseen usually demands nothing less than the complete rewriting of the Constitution – in other words, a form of revolution. The British State is a great deal more supple; it is able to accommodate political change with great ease, and as it does so it acquires a further legitimacy which entrenches its position all the more.

But however legitimate and representative the British State, however great its reservoir of power, its inability to act systematically in the pursuit of a wider interest than purely party interest or the compromise between vested interest is a grave weakness. The problem is that the integration of executive and legislative into one body makes the structure of the system inherently open to particular interest groups, and the continued participation of the Crown in the Constitution has obviated the need to define what could be meant by the idea 'public'.

Because the Crown has so successfully come to personify the State – and because it is so desirable for this function to be prosecuted in this way – no necessity has been felt to carry the parallel conception of commonality into the actual institutions of government: executive, judiciary and legislature. Instead, the idea of the public interest has become muddied in ideas like parliamentary accountability and scrutiny. Dyson writes (1980:211) 'the concept of the Crown has not generated any theory about the relationships among institutions in an extensive sense or about the relations between government and the individual'. In this the Crown has been the innocent accomplice of the great political parties who have not wished to challenge the operation of the system; the electoral process which prevents smaller parties from national representation, the minority party's status in the House of Commons as an official Opposition with associated privileges and the wide measure of patronage that accrues to party leaderships are all handsome windfalls which no political party would wish to endanger. The great prize is that the winning of one election every five years by a simple first-past-the-post method of voting gives complete control of not only the legislative, but also the executive; and that considerable prerogative power accompanies this control, all neatly validated by the fact that power was won through a democratic process. This juicy plum has been too tempting for all parties to resist, whatever lip service they pay to concepts like accountability, public scrutiny, and democracy, and attempts to create an independent check to the system, like the Parliamentary Ombudsman, are always invalidated by the concept of parliamentary sovereignty. The citizens of the United Kingdom, alone among western democracies, have no *guaranteed* legal redress through either the Ombudsman or through law, against the actions of Parliament. The protection against abuse rests solely on convention, public opinion, and the good behaviour of the political parties when in government. It is a thin reed on which to rest individual liberty.

The supremacy of Parliament together with the *de jure* role of the Crown combine to give British public life its unique flavour. Although the system permits more than adequate expression of private and sectional interest, it only does so for those who 'know the ropes'; in other words, the lack of a formal structure and any rationality in political procedures require an immense knowledge of the many quirks and peculiarities that exist if an interest is to be successfully prosecuted or defined. This personalisation of the system, with its emphasis on who you know rather that what you know, is a considerable constraint on the development of rational government. Indeed, the whole thrust of the executive's organisation is to personalise relations: a minister is *personally* responsible for the policy of his department, so the whole focus of the department is on him; moreover, advice is offered on a confidential and secret basis, as befits a personal relationship in which the object is to serve the minister rather than the community. Official skills are learnt 'on the job', and the esteem of fellow administrators in the Whitehall village becomes more important than the exercise of good judgement in the prosecution of public policy (Heclo & Wildavsky 1974). Departments exist in competition, linked only through the deliberation of the Cabinet – itself adjudicating between their claims rather than enforcing a public policy. It is a private, chaotic world of compromise, bargaining, and continual reaction to events. If Keynesian economics suggests that rational surveillance by the State of the market is a prerequisite for the effective functioning of the market, then the British machinery of government and the ideas that pervade it are inadequate for the task.

The clearest example of this vacuum in British political thought and its impact on the economy is the definition of a public corporation. Because there is no definition of the idea 'public' or the embodiment of this concept in the institutions of state, no possibility exists for the clear elaborating of the role and responsibilities of a publicly owned body.

Clearly the only institution to which a public corporation can be made accountable is Parliament, but this only means that the unanswered questions in Parliament about what constitutes the public interest become transferred to the public corporation – as exemplified by the continual problems of the nationalised industries. A nationalised industry must be responsible to its owners, the State; but the supreme authority in the State is Parliament. Thus a nationalised industry is accountable to Parliament; but what concept of the public interest does Parliament represent? And what instrument does Parliament have for the implementation of its view? The answers are thin. Despite efforts by successive governments to 'take the nationalised industries out of politics' by establishing consistent 'commercial criteria' for their operations, the objectives of the nationalised industries are continually changing. Thus every attempt by a nationalised industry to build an organisational structure and internal system of control that sets out to achieve a particular goal is immediately upset by a redefinition of the goal. Unsurprisingly, the performance of the industries is poor.

But even if a consistent definition of the nationalised industries role could be formulated, and then protected from the whimsy of

211

party ideology, the Constitution has no place in its structure for these anomalous bodies. They are not departments of state, and the executive, organised as it is on a hierarchical and unco-ordinated basis, can find no way of integrating the industries into its chain of command, nor institutional devices for their control. Autonomous public organisations acting on a widely understood definition of the public interest and with a brief to structure themselves in the way they think best so as to better implement that interest are simply impossible in the British context. As a result the nationalised industries have developed as privileged but chronically inefficient entities; privileged because as public bodies the only limit to their expenditure is that which an executive, wholly ill-equipped to control or monitor them, is able to construct, and inefficient because they are provided with no consistent objective or goal around which they can elaborate an organisational structure and strategy.

The attempt by Herbert Morrison to overcome these problems by giving the board of directors of a nationalised industry as much scope for action as possible while simultaneously being held accountable to Parliament was the only possible solution in constitutional terms, but equally the only possible development has been for increasing ministerial involvement. The lack of any concept of the public interest or any ability to embody that interest has simply meant that ministers have been obliged to define the public interest as the party's policy, and although each minister has doubtless been sincere in presenting the party line as the public interest, nationalised industries have found themselves as one of the main instruments of government policy. Over the 1970s they have, under successive governments, frozen their prices and run up large deficits as part of a counter-inflation strategy; undertaken large foreign borrowing as part of an exchange-rate support policy; raised their prices and cut back their capital expenditure programmes as part of a strategy of limiting public expenditure and public borrowing. Over this period major capital projects have been deferred, cancelled, or changed in order to support government in its macro-economic or regional policy. As long as the public interest is that defined by the majority party in the House of Commons, the nationalised industries will continue to have their responsibilities continually redefined.

This continual changing of the industries' targets is seen by all – the industries themselves, the political parties, and leading commentators – as a major cause of their indifferent performance (Redwood 1980). They must have a consistent target around which they can organise themselves. The next stage in the argument, at least among conservative politicians and some economists, is to argue that the industries should be denationalised ('privatised') because it is clear that the only rational target is some measure of commercial viability and the best means of assessing this is the market rather than the State. In a sense they are right. Because it is impossible in the British context to decide on a public role for the nationalised industries, the next best course is to change their status as publicly owned bodies so that the problem is removed. But this strikes at the symptom, not the cause. It is a measure of the seriousness of the position that Britain's ability to develop (say) a cheap subsidised public transport system or indeed any other enterprise in the public sector has to be shelved or abandoned in the face of the weakness of the Constitution in expressing the public interest. This failure is typically explained as a failure of 'collectivism' or socialism, but the nationalised industries are no more socialist than the Crown, either in their organisation or in their function. Their inefficiency is the inevitable result of a constitutional structure whose chief beneficiaries, the political parties, will make no attempt to reform.

The same weakness is evident in the planning and allocation of public expenditure. The departments of state are organised as hierarchical and self-contained entities, whose chain of authority runs up to the minister: the apex of the pyramid of command. His is the responsibility for policy and the department is his territory. Officials' attention is not focused on the implementation of public policy in the public interest, but on the representation of policy options to the minister, who the Constitution judges will be acting in the public interest when he decides on a particular policy. Because the department's responsibility is to the minister and not the State, the department becomes a ministerial preserve rather than an agency of the State. In turn, the minister's ability to run his department and his status within the department depend on the strength with which he fights the department battles in Cabinet. Baroness Sharpe wrote (Heclo & Wildavsky 1974:133) 'The thing you ask of your minister is that he should be able to get his way in Cabinet.' 'He must know what he wants. He must be decisive. And he must have weight in the councils of government.'[4]

Each department of state is thus permanently engaged in a process of bargaining for resources so that it can prosecute its own objectives rather than locating its objectives within the larger totality of public policy. The idea is that the Cabinet should arbitrate between these bids by exercising its own judgement about the overall direction of policy; but then ministers are simultaneously bidding for resources and adjudicating between the various bids. They are judges of their own cases. The result is what Wass describes as the 'inertial' feature of public spending, governed by two great principles. Number one, 'as things have been, so broadly they will remain'; and number two, 'he who has the muscle gets the money'. (Wass 1983a) So public expenditure has an inbuilt tendency to increase, and the best that can be expected is that for a period the rate of increase can be arrested. For a Keynesian administration intent on using fiscal policy, in part by adjusting public expenditure upwards and downwards in a contra-cyclical fashion, control over public expenditure is of crucial importance.

Ministers are obliged by their constitutional position to defend their departments' interest, which means their budgets: so cutbacks in public expenditure can only be achieved if the immediate budgetary plans and staffing levels of the departments are unaffected. Only a very weak minister will accept a major diminution in his department's standing. Consequently any cutbacks in public expenditure almost inevitably are focused on planned capital expenditures around which the department's *raison d'être* is not threatened. The transfer of responsibilities between departments will be stoutly resisted, whatever their intrinsic merit, as will any major redirection of funds from one spending programme to another. The main characteristic is one of institutional resistance to almost any change, unless there is a concession granted elsewhere to compensate; spending programmes acquire a tremendous momentum all of their own, and the best any government can do is to change spending and departmental responsibilities at the margin.

This hierarchical structure of the executive together with the self-contained nature of departments is highlighted by the Public Expenditure Survey Committee (PESC), whose annual review of departmental spending plans is the heart of the British system for the regulation and scrutiny of public expenditure. The Committee is made up of senior officials from each department – the Principal Finance Officers – whose responsibility is the formulation of their respective departments' spending plans. The Committee is chaired by a Treasury official, and its job is to hammer out a consistent plan for the following year's public spending. This may appear as a perfectly rational means of going about the allocation of spending, but it too suffers from the constitutional structure. The hierarchical nature of departments and the fact that the chain of responsibility runs up to the minister means that the Treasury has no constitutional authority in checking each individual department's assessment of its needs or its efficiency. The Treasury supply officers who have to monitor expenditure of many millions of pounds have to do so at arm's length and on trust. The PESC is not a system for the allocation of resources, the scrutiny of spending, or the implementation of priorities: it is a clearing house for the various self-contained departments to compete with each other for money. And if the battle gets tough, it rises straight to the Cabinet for resolution (Pliatsky 1982) – a resolution which will be based in its turn on compromise rather than on the clear articulation of public policy.

British public expenditure is thus a battleground over which the great departments of state fight their causes and fiercely resist any change. It is a system where although the contours of public expenditure are set by publicly expressed wishes in elections, these can be reformulated or even overturned by the skill and adroitness with which ministers and officials fight their case. They are not malicious or especially ill-willed, although the results of their endeavours may appear in this light: rather the constitutional structure drives them in this direction. The three services in the Ministry of Defence, who above all could be expected to formulate an overall defence strategy and to set priorities among themselves for ships, tanks, planes, etc., are perhaps the worst offenders (Johnson 1980). Internecine rivalry between the services has meant that overall defence strategy has been subordinated to the need of successive Ministers of Defence to find some basis of compromise, so that Britain's military capacity is not the result of careful and rational military planning within publicly determined expenditure limits, but the result of intense in-fighting in the Whitehall village. If the services cannot agree on priorities, what chance the rest of the Government's departments?

The British structure of government and the lack of any state tradition is a grave disadvantage in the prosecution of public policy. This is a serious enough handicap in itself, but it is doubly so as the market economy demonstrably demands sensible and coherent superintendance by the State if it is to function successfully. The price mechanism does not communicate all the information that actors in the market-place need in order to co-ordinate their activities; the financial system's preference for liquidity upsets the necessary investment in illiquid assets that the economy must make if it is to grow. In both these areas the State must intervene, but it is not apparent that the British State could intervene successfully even if it chose to do so nor is it evident that market agents *believe* that the State has any capacity for credible economic management, and without credibility any Keynesian project is unlikely to succeed. In a world in which state action and initiatives are imperative, the medieval foundations and Victorian ideology of British political institutions and economic practice are a major obstacle not only to properly understanding the economics of Keynes; but also to implementing it.

Notes

1. A parallel argument is advanced by Keynes (1926:48).
2. Quoted in the *Daily Telegraph*, 29 September 1983.
3. From K. Marx and F. Engels, *The German Ideology*, pp. 58–62.
4. From F. Engels, *Socialism: Utopian and Scientific*, pp. 149–53.

References

Arnold, T. (1937) *The Folklore of Capitalism*. New Haven: Yale University Press.

Bano, R. (1977), 'Unanticipated Money Growth and Unemployment in the United States' *American Economic Review*, March.

Bogdanor, V. (1981) *The People and the Party System*. Cambridge U.P.

Carrington, J. & Edwards, G. (1980) *Reversing Economic Decline*. Macmillan.

Chapman, L. (1979) *Your Disobedient Servant*. Penguin.

Crouch, C. (1979) 'The state, capital and liberal democracy', in C. Crouch (ed.) *State and Economy in Contemporary Capitalism*. Croom Helm.

Dyson, K (1980) *The State Tradition in Western Europe*. Martin Roberts.

Freedman, R. (ed.) (1968) *Marxist Social Thought*. Harcourt Brace and World, Inc: New York.

Habermas, J. (1976) *Legitimation Crisis*. Heinemann.

Harvey, J. & Bather, L. (1977) *The British Constitution* (4th edn). Macmillan Education.

Heclo, H. & Wildavsky, A. (1974) *The Private Government of Public Money*. Macmillan.

Hoskyns, Sir John (1983) Lecture to the Institute of Directors, 28 September 1983.

Yao-Su Hu (1975) *National Attitudes and the Financing of Industry*, PEP Broadsheet no. 559.

Yao-Su Hu (1984) *Industrial Banking and Special Credit Institutions*. Policy Studies Institute

Johnson, Franklyn, A. (1980) *Defence by Ministry*. Duckworth.

Keynes, J. M. (1926) *The End of Laissez-Faire*. Hogarth Press.

Meiselman, D. (1962) *The Term Structure of Interest Rate*. Prentice Hall: Englewood Cliffs N. J.

Miliband, R. (1980) *The State in Capitalist Societies*. Quarterly.

Modigliani, F. & Miller, M. H. (1958) 'The cost of capital corporations:

finance and the theory of investment', *American Economic Review*, June 1958.

Minford, P. (1978) *Substitution Effects, Speculation and Exchange Rate Stability*. North Holland: Amsterdam.

Offe, C. (1972) *Strukturprobleme des Kapilisticnen Staates*. Suhrkamy: Frankfurt.

Pempel, T. J. (1978) 'Japanese Foreign Economic Policy', in Katzerstein (ed.) *Between Power & Plenty*. Madison, Univ. of Wisconsin Press.

Pliatsky, L. (1982) *Getting and Spending*. Blackwell.

Popper, K. (1966) *The Open Society and Its Enemies*. Routledge & Kegan Paul.

Posner, M. (1974) 'Theories of economic regulation', *Bell Journal of Economics and Management Science*, 5(2) Autumn

Poulantzas, N. (1973) *Political Power and Social Classes*. New Left Books: London.

Poulantzas, N. (1975) *Classes in Contemporary Capitalism*: Veno.

Redwood, J. (1980) *Public Enterprise in Crisis*. Blackwell.

Sartori, G. (1977) *Parties and Party Systems*. Cambridge U.P.

Schumpeter, J. A. (1970) *Capitalism, Socialism and Democracy*. Unwin U.P.

Stigler (1975) *The Citizen and the State: Essays on Regulation*. University of Chicago Press: Chicago.

Strauss, N. (1984) 'The case for more live wires in Whitehall', *Guardian*, 8 January 1984.

Wass, Sir Douglas (1983a) The Reith Lectures: 'Government and the Governed': Lecture 1 – 'Limited thoughts and counsels'. BBC Radio 4 broadcast, 9 November 1983.

Wass, Sir Douglas (1983b) Op. cit; Lecture 2 – 'Cabinet: directorate or directory?' BBC Radio 4 broadcast, 16 November 1983.

Zysman, J. (1983) *Governments, Markets, and Growth*. Cornell University Press.

Conclusion

The discourse of economics remains that of the classical tradition. The nucleus is rational economic man; the process voluntary exchange; the outcome balance. Although the perspective is economic, there is an inescapable political and philosophic context. The State is limited; the liberty of the individual is paramount. The whole is the sum of the parts.

Keynesianism may begin as an economic doctrine, but it must conclude as a challenge to this entire intellectual tradition. The outcome of voluntary exchange is not balance. The State, therefore, must assert a commonality of interest. Liberty may have to be redefined by the response to the unpredictable motion of the market system. The whole is greater than the sum of the parts.

Keynes's assault on the citadel was foredoomed. The clash between two ways of looking at the world cannot be settled by compromise, and as Keynesianism became retranslated into the language of economic orthodoxy, so the message was lost. The discourse of economics was not recast by Keynes's efforts: it quivered momentarily before swallowing him whole. Uncertainty, expectations, involuntary unemployment, and liquidity-preference have been denuded of their meaning and robbed of their theoretical significance. The half-truths of classical political economy are abroad once more, but the case for their qualification is just as pressing.

To this theory and practice, Keynes was resolutely opposed; and in this respect he belongs more to European than to British thought. The theme that the common interest cannot be guaranteed by the felicitous interaction of private interests, but must rather be asserted in the collectivity of individuals in the form of the State is European. Classical economists and the new 'counter-revolutionaries' are often scornful about the (alleged) need for Keynesian economic policy to be operated by a mandarin élite setting themselves up against the market. However, to an observer not schooled in the presumptions of Anglo-Saxon individualism, such a jibe would be seen as undeserved and incomprehensible.

The unspoken assumption behind this liberal British tradition is that it is not only *rational* for an association of individuals to attempt to make the basis of their association one of individual interaction, but that it is *the only means of maximising any gains that there are from association*. Action by the State is objectionable because it cannot be better than individual action; indeed, it will intrude upon and upset processes that must needs be left to their own unfettered operation. Thus, while an individual's association in a liberal community may seem to be irrational if he ends up disadvantaged, that is only a surface appearance. The steel worker who is made redundant, the car worker who forgoes a wage increase, or a pool of unemployed labour, are all only *apparently* losing out: the system is actually rational, and the invisible hand of the market is behind what appears to be an irrational position. The price mechanism is actually working, and its fundamental tendency is benevolent: moreover, it is the sole means of producing a rational economic order for the individual and community alike.

By challenging this view of how the price mechanism can be expected to work, Keynes is assaulting both a conception of economic rationality and how an individual should view the gains or losses from associating in a liberally ordered community. His insistence that in the absence of some motion of the economy towards equilibrium the State has an obligation to manage the economy, is a *de facto* assertion of some kind of notional original contract as the basis for intervention – and by so doing he stands in the mainstream of European (as opposed to Anglo-Saxon) thought (Rawls 1980).

An individual accepts membership of an association of individuals in a community because that opens up possibilities of benefits through collaboration that do not exist for him as an individual. If *a priori* we were to ask: of what would a collection of individuals want to be assured if they were pondering the principles upon which they should construct their community (if, say, they were shipwrecked on a desert island), and no one knew beforehand who would be gainers or losers, it would surely be the assurance that losses and gains from their collaboration would be justly distributed. Nobody could know in the new circumstances who would succeed or fail, and to permit liberty above societal obligation might be a matter of life or death. A notional 'contract' assuring a mutual interest in the just distribution of any associational gains would therefore be essential. Such a situation may be hypothetical, but it underlines the nature of association: it is irrational for an individual to join a community if he as an individual is to suffer, even if the community as a whole could be shown to benefit by that sacrifice, unless he can be assured of some compensation from the community.

Herein lies the problem. If there was a 'contract' assuring such corrective action, then the individual's association would be rational even if he proved to be one of the 'losers'. But the economic liberal denies the need for such a contract; the only contract that is required is between individuals, not between individuals and society. It is in individual interaction that the benefits of association are to be gained. If, however, that interaction is shown to be unsuccessful as a mechanism for ensuring a community of interest – as Keynes showed the market *as a system* to be – then the end result could be that neither an individual member of the system, nor the system itself, need be better off for the individual's sacrifice. There is no contract by which to judge compensation for loss; and as loss for someone is certain, the omission is doubly damnable. In these terms classic liberal philosophy is not only morally indefensible; it is irrational.

In the European intellectual tradition the necessity of a 'contract' between individuals asserting their community and denying that interaction alone will produce that community is commonplace. Rousseau's general will is an assertion of the generality of interest, while Kant insists that the *a priori* precondition of human association is an institution capable of reflecting the general will. Not only is there an interest over and above the result of individual interaction, but its assertion may be necessary to protect individuals from being disadvantaged in the community in which they live. In the same way, Keynes must be interpreted as arguing that the State has to assert the common interest because no other device is moral given the basis of association. The State is the guardian of individuals associating in a community, and as the markets require regulation because of the preference for liquidity and the fact of the future, it is legitimate and necessary for the State to act in the community's interest.

Action by the State in a market economy is in this sense a contractual necessity: the markets cannot themselves spontaneously organise the means to prevent adjustment to changes in expectations causing changes in the quantities of goods traded, and the involuntary unemployment that results is no fault of those who are made unemployed. It is not merely an economic necessity for this action to be taken, but a moral imperative; membership of a market economy does not mean that individuals should suffer undeserved hardships, and it is in the name of the original 'contract of association' that the State should act. Indeed, if the rest of the community is to enjoy the benefits that accrue to a market economy, the freedom of individual decision-making, the freedom to make profits, to own property, etc., then what begins as a moral imperative rapidly becomes a self-interested political imperative. Unless the principles by which the economy and polity are run are just, and seen to be just, then the whole enterprise is in peril.

But what action and form should the State take? An important theme of this book is that whatever the conclusions drawn by economic theory for economic policy, any attempt to manage the economy in a purposive and disinterested way is stillborn if the political process and instruments of state power are not substantially reformed. The State cannot act as a credible economic agent or transform the behaviour of the financial institutions if it is overtly influenced by the markets and institutions which it attempts to regulate and change. Any mechanisms the State constructs to minimise the problems of uncertainty and unco-ordinated economic activity will be inoperable if the State is perceived as incapable of acting intelligently and consistently, or if it is perceived as being more frequently at the behest of expedient and vested interests than in command of them in the process of ordering the economy: yet this is substantially the position under the present political and governmental arrangements. If the State is to prosecute successfully an active fiscal and monetary policy, to influence the liquidity and portfolio preferences of the financial institutions, to arbitrate and regulate monopolistic economic behaviour, and above all, to attempt some management of expectations, then the current political and institutional structure demands root-and-branch reform.

The presumption behind Keynesian theory (and policy) is that in the main individuals wish for choice and the freedom to make their own decisions, and that the market has the important property of enabling such freedoms. But the case for the market is not just that it is a forum where decisions are taken by many people in the light of their own interests and circumstances, but that over the years and across cultures it has shown more ability to promote economic efficiency and prosperity than any other economic model. Yet the market economy does *not* have the self-regulatory powers or inherent capacity to produce a 'best' result ascribed to it by economic theory; and Keynes shows that the attempt to prove that it does has inadequate theoretical foundations. The paradox is that for the market to do its work its constituents require constant superintendance and its trends constant correction.

Yet what kind of state could perform such a role without sliding towards either bureaucracy on the one hand or the possession of too much arbitrary power on the other? The need is for a political process which can embody some notion of justice, of commonality of interest and purpose, of equity in relationships. Here there is some hope, for although the British State at present is gravely deficient in these respects, the principles around which it purports to be organised are the very ones that it needs to embody. The idea that the political system should be fair and representative is deep-seated; and in the Crown there is an important conception of commonality. The values exist which could cast the political system more in the image of a societal contract. The first step will surely be some separation of the executive and legislative, some strengthening of local decentralised power against a necessarily stronger central power, and the prising of the judiciary from the jealous hands of the legal establishment. In questions of constitutional reform a good starting point is the idea of checks and balances; and Britain's Constitution has become a salutary warning of the dangers of merging and dissolving the distinctions between the branches of government. Good governance is a precondition for any successful collective action.

Economic recovery is thus a political, not to say moral and philosophical issue. The question of how we as individuals wish to associate, and the responsibilities that we are prepared to insist that economic agents have one to another, are central to any economic programme. The myth that all that is required is to 'let the market go free' is the siren call of our age, and great and unnecessary risks are being run with the stability and prosperity of our society in its name. We make the world in which we live; it does not arise spontaneously from individuals' interaction in either markets or parliaments.

The simple possession of free elections, political parties and five-year parliaments is not a sufficient condition for the expression and articulation of any common interest. Unless the Constitution obliges the law-making process to be associated with the continual gathering of consent and confers possibilities of intelligent executive action then the common interest is likely to be fulfilled only haphazardly, if at all. Equally, it is not through the sole institution of the market economy that an association of individuals can organise its economic decisions most effectively; rather it is through the activities of the State in seeking to help the markets overcome the problem of the future and the preference for liquidity, that the extent to which markets can combine the prosecution of individual interest and the generation of the common economic good will be determined.

This view of the responsibility of the State and the dynamics of the market system are the essence of the economics of Keynes, and they are as unpalatable today to the British political and financial establishment as they were fifty years ago. As the hopes of the last few years dissolve into a pervasive feeling of helplessness and disillusion, there will be renewed questioning of economists and their so-called truths; but on this occasion the insights of Keynesian economics must not be traduced. Too much depends on economics for it to be left to economists.

References

Polyani, K. (1980) *The Great Transformation*. Octagon Books.
Rawls, J. (1980) *A Theory of Justice*. Oxford.

Selected Bibliography

Chapter 1

De Cecco, M. (1974) *Money and Empire*. Blackwell.

Dobb, M. (1973) *Theories of Value and Distribution since Adam Smith*, Cambridge U.P.

Hobsbawn, E. J. (1980) *Industry and Empire*. Penguin.

Manning, D. J. (1976) *Liberalism*. Dent.

Mathias, P. (1978) *The First Industrial Nation. An Economic History of Britain 1700–1914*. Methuen.

Wiener, M. (1981) *English Culture and the Decline of the Industrial Spirit*, Cambridge U.P.

Chapter 3

Arrow, K. (1974) *The Limits of Organisation*. W. W. Norton: New York.

Arrow, K. (1980) *Social Choice and Individual Values* (10th edn). Yale University Press.

Dobb, M. (1979) *Theories of Value and Distribution since Adam Smith*. Cambridge U.P.

McKay, Alfred (1980) *Arrow's Theorem. The Paradox of Social Choice*. Yale U.P.

Robbins, L. (1935) *An Essay on the Nature and Significance of Economic Science*. Macmillan.

Whynes, D. K. & Bowles, R. A. (1981) *The Economic Theory of the State*. Martin Robertson.

Chapter 4

Dorfman, R. (1978) *Prices and Markets* (3rd edn). Prentice Hall.

Lipsey, R. G. (1980) *An Introduction to Positive Economics* (5th edn). Weidenfeld and Nicholson.

MacIntyre, A. (1966) *A Short History of Ethics*. Routledge and Kegan Paul.

Moore, G. E. (1903) *Principia Ethica*.

Pareto, V. (1909) *Manuel d'Economie Politique*. V. Giard and E. Briere: Paris.

Shackle, G. L. S. (1967) *The Years of High Theory*. Cambridge U.P.

Walras, Leon (1954) *Eléments d'Economie Politique Pure*, trans. William Jaffe, Allen and Unwin: London. Irwin: Homewood, Illinois.

Warnock, Mary (1965) *Utilitarianism* (3rd edn). The Fontana Library.

Chapter 6

Friedman, M. (1977) Inflation and unemployment, *IEA Occasional Paper 51*.

Keynes, J. M. (1971) *A Treatise on Money*, vols 1 and 2. Macmillan/Royal Economic Society.

Keynes, J. M. (1978) *The General Theory of Employment, Interest and Money*. Macmillan/Royal Economic society.

Klein, Laurence R. (1980) *The Keynesian Revolution*. Macmillan.

Leijonhufvud, Axel (1979) *On Keynesian Economics and the Economics of Keynes*. Oxford U.P.

Shackle, G. L. S. (1967) *The Years of High Theory*. Cambridge U.P.

Chapter 7

Goodhart C. A. E. (1982) *Money, Information and Uncertainty*. Macmillan.

Yao-Su Hu (1975) 'National attitudes and the financing of industry', *PEP*, vol. XLI, Broadsheet no. 559.

Chapter 8

Kellner, P. & Lord Crowther Hunt (1980) The Civil Servants.

Index